The Middle East
Since Camp David

Also of Interest

The Gulf and the Search for Strategic Stability: Saudi Arabia, the Military Balance in the Gulf, and Trends in the Arab-Israeli Military Balance, Anthony H. Cordesman

†*Political Behavior in the Arab States,* edited by Tawfic E. Farah

†*The Foreign Policies of Arab States,* edited by Bahgat Korany and Ali E. Hillal Dessouki

Local Politics and Development in the Middle East, edited by Louis J. Cantori and Iliya Harik

The Problems of Arab Economic Development and Integration, edited by Adda Guecioueur

Middle East Politics: The Military Dimension, J. C. Hurewitz

†*The Middle East Military Balance, 1983,* Mark A. Heller, Dov Tamari, and Zeev Eytan

†*A Concise History of the Middle East,* Second Edition, Revised and Updated, Arthur Goldschmidt, Jr.

†*Red Flag Over Afghanistan: The Communist Coup, the Soviet Invasion, and the Consequences,* Thomas T. Hammond

The Kurds: An Unstable Element in the Gulf, Stephen C. Pelletiere

Sadat and Begin: The Domestic Politics of Peacemaking, Melvin A. Friedlander

Women and Revolution in Iran, edited by Guity Nashat

†*The Government and Politics of Israel,* Second Edition, Updated, Don Peretz

Abandonment of Illusions: Zionist Political Attitudes Toward Palestinian Arab Nationalism, 1936–1939, Yehoyada Haim

†*Islam: Continuity and Change in the Modern World,* John Obert Voll

†*Religion and Politics in the Middle East,* Michael Curtis

†*The Government and Politics of the Middle East and North Africa,* edited by David E. Long and Bernard Reich

†Available in hardcover and paperback.

Westview Special Studies on the Middle East

The Middle East Since Camp David
edited by Robert O. Freedman

Since the Camp David agreements of September 1978, the Middle East has experienced a series of major military and political developments that have affected not just the nations of the region and the two superpowers, but the rest of the world as well. The fall of the Shah of Iran, the Soviet invasion of Afghanistan, the Iraqi invasion of Iran, the assassination of Egyptian President Anwar Sadat, and the Israeli invasion of Lebanon—to name only a few events—have had a major impact.

In this volume, a group of internationally recognized scholars, many of whom are present and former U.S. government officials, analyze these Middle Eastern developments from the perspectives of the superpowers, the region in general, and the five major actors during this period (Egypt, Israel, the PLO, Syria, and Iran). Although the individual authors speak from differing perspectives and viewpoints in their analyses, the book as a whole presents a balanced examination of the key developments in the volatile Middle East since Camp David.

Dr. Robert O. Freedman is dean of the Peggy Meyerhoff Pearlstone School of Graduate Studies of the Baltimore Hebrew College.

The Middle East Since Camp David

edited by
Robert O. Freedman

Westview Press / Boulder and London

Westview Special Studies on the Middle East

Copyright © 1984 by Westview Press, Inc.

Published in 1984 in the United States of America by
  Westview Press, Inc.
  5500 Central Avenue
  Boulder, Colorado 80301
  Frederick A. Praeger, President and Publisher

Library of Congress Cataloging in Publication Data
Main entry under title:
The Middle East since Camp David.
  (Westview special studies on the Middle East)
  Bibliography: p.
  Includes index.
  Contents: Introduction / Robert O. Freedman—Superpower perspectives. Soviet policy toward the Middle East since Camp David / Robert O. Freedman—U.S. policy on the Middle East in the period since Camp David / Barry Rubin—[etc.]
  1. Near East—Politics and government—1945– . I. Freedman, Robert Owen. II. Series.
DS63.1.M545   1984   956′.05   83-19798
ISBN 0-86531-657-0
ISBN 0-86531-658-9 (pbk.)

Printed and bound in the United States of America

5   4   3   2   1

To my children, Debbie and David,
in the hope that in their lifetime
the Middle East will become a region of peace

Contents

Preface

The Middle East has long been one of the most volatile regions on the globe. Wars, coups d'etat, rapid shifts in alliances and alignments, numerous intra-Arab and regional conflicts, and constant superpower intervention have wracked the region since the first Arab-Israeli war of 1948. In an effort to increase public understanding of this complex region, the Center for the Study of Israel and the Contemporary Middle East of the Baltimore Hebrew College has held a series of conferences bringing together Middle Eastern specialists from different perspectives to analyze and discuss the region.

The first conference, held in 1978, examined the impact of the Arab-Israeli conflict on the Middle East, and the papers were later published in *World Politics and the Arab-Israeli Conflict* (Robert O. Freedman, ed., New York: Pergamon, 1979). The second conference, held in 1979, two years into the administration of Israeli Prime Minister Menahem Begin, made a preliminary analysis of the dynamics of the Begin regime. Following the Israeli election of 1981, the conference papers were updated and published in *Israel in the Begin Era* (Robert O. Freedman, ed., New York: Praeger, 1982). The third conference, from which this book emerged, dealt with Middle Eastern developments since the Camp David agreements of 1978. Those agreements were a major milestone in Middle Eastern affairs, and the papers, delivered in May 1982, almost four years after the Camp David conference, analyzed the effect of the agreements on the region as a whole as well as on the superpowers that seek influence in it. Less than a month after our conference, the Israeli army invaded Lebanon in an effort to destroy the PLO infrastructure in that country; as a result, the contributors have updated their papers to include analysis of the impact of the Israeli invasion and the subsequent PLO withdrawal from Beirut.

The third conference and the book before you were made possible through the help of a number of individuals and institutions. The conference was cosponsored by the Baltimore Jewish Community Relations Council and the Peggy Meyerhoff Pearlstone School of Graduate Studies of the Baltimore Hebrew College. Dr. Leivy Smolar, president of the Baltimore Hebrew College, has provided strong support for the Institute for the Study of Israel and the Contemporary Middle East since its founding in 1977. The Baltimore Hebrew College Library staff, and its director, Dr. Jesse Mashbaum, provided invaluable research services, and my secretary, Elise Baron, did a masterful job of typing the manuscript while also helping to manage the college's graduate program. Special thanks are due to Fabian Kolker and the Kolker Foundation for the financial support that enabled the Baltimore Hebrew College to hold the conference that served as the basis for this book.

Finally, a word about the transliteration system used in this book. Every editor dealing with a Middle East topic must decide between using the exact transliteration of Arabic names, including the initial *hamza*, and using a system that reflects the more common Western transliteration. To aid those readers who do not know Arabic, we have chosen the latter system for Arab leaders and place-names, which are more widely known to English-speaking audiences. Thus, for example, the reader will find Gamal Nasser for Abd-al-Nasir, Hafez Assad for Hafiz al-Asad, Muammar Kaddafi for al-Qadhafi, King Hussein for Husayn, and place names such as Dhofar for Dhufar and Oman for 'Uman. In addition, given the often bitter controversy over the name of the body of water lying between Iran and Saudi Arabia, known to the Iranians as the Persian Gulf and to the Arabs as the Arab Gulf, the authors have chosen to employ the neutral term "Gulf."

Robert O. Freedman

Abbreviations

ADF	Arab Deterrent Force
AID	Agency for International Development
ALF	Arab Liberation Front
AWACS	Airborne Warning and Control System
CENTO	Central Treaty Organization
CIA	Central Intelligence Agency
Comecon	Council for Mutual Economic Assistance
CPSU	Communist Party of the Soviet Union
DFLP	Democratic Front for the Liberation of Palestine
DFPE	Democratic Front for Peace and Equality
DMC	Democratic Movement for Change
EEC	European Economic Community
GCC	Gulf Cooperation Council
GNP	gross national product
IAEA	International Atomic Energy Association
NATO	North Atlantic Treaty Organization
NLP	National Liberal party
NPT	Non Proliferation Treaty
NRP	National Religious party
OAU	Organization of African Unity

OPEC	Organization of Petroleum Exporting Countries
PDRY	Peoples Democratic Republic of Yemen
PFLP	Popular Front for the Liberation of Palestine
PFLP-GC	Popular Front for the Liberation of Palestine–General Command
PLA	Palestine Liberation Army
PLO	Palestine Liberation Organization
PLO/EC	PLO Executive Committee
PNC	Palestine National Council
PSF	Popular Struggle Front
RDF	Rapid Deployment Force
SALT SALT II	Strategic Arms Limitation Talks
SAM	surface-to-air missiles
UAE	United Arab Emirates
UAR	United Arab Republic
UN	United Nations
UNEF	United Nations Emergency Force
UNRWA	United Nations Relief Works Administration

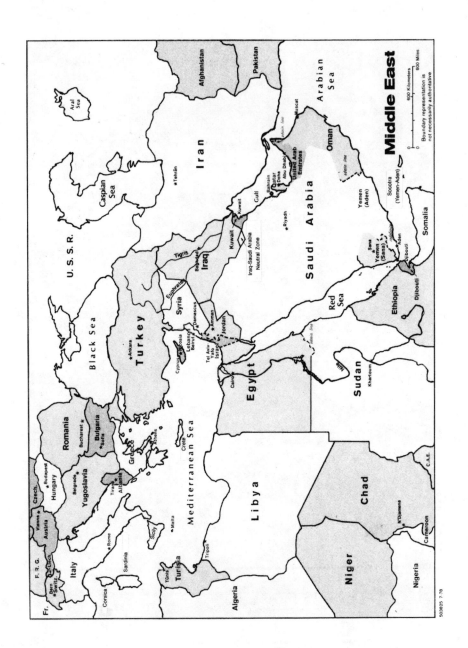

Middle East

0   600 Miles

0   600 Kilometers

Boundary representation is
not necessarily authoritative

503925 7-78

Introduction

Robert O. Freedman

In the period following the Camp David agreements, which themselves were a watershed in Middle Eastern affairs, a number of major political and military developments rocked the region. The fall of the Shah of Iran and the rise of the Ayatollah Khomeini; the Egyptian-Israeli peace treaty; renewed conflict between Iraq and Syria; the Iranian hostage crisis; the Soviet invasion of Afghanistan; the Iraqi invasion of Iran; the formation of the Gulf Cooperation Council; the assassination of Egyptian President Anwar Sadat; the Israeli invasion of Lebanon; and the exodus of the Palestine Liberation Organization (PLO) from Beirut—all had a significant impact on the course of Middle Eastern politics. In order to assess the significance of these events and their impact on the Middle East, it is necessary to analyze them at the superpower level, the level of regional politics, and the level of domestic politics, because these events have had repercussions at all three levels.

Part 1 deals with the policies of the two superpowers, and in the first chapter Robert O. Freedman analyzes the role of the Soviet Union in the Middle East during the 1978–1982 period. Freedman contends that Soviet policy in this period was essentially reactive in nature, as Moscow sought to respond to a series of developments that the USSR had not caused and found increasingly unable to shape to fit Soviet goals in the Middle East. Moscow was clearly pleased by the anti-Egyptian Arab coalition that came into being following the signing of the Camp David accords and hoped that this coalition could be transformed into the "anti-imperialist" Arab unity it had so long desired, but the renewal of the Iraq-Syria conflict, the Soviet invasion of Afghanistan, and the outbreak of the Iran-Iraq war combined to seriously divide the Arab world once again. Similarly, although Moscow warmly welcomed events like the fall of the shah and the Iranian

1

hostage crisis that weakened the U.S. position in the Middle East, the USSR found itself unable to build a close relationship with the new Iranian leaders or to prevent Iranian policies from driving the Gulf Arabs back toward the United States. Freedman concludes that Soviet influence in the Middle East is very limited and that the USSR was in a weaker regional position in 1982 following the Israeli invasion of Lebanon than it was in 1978 following Camp David.

In Chapter 2, Barry Rubin examines the course of Middle Eastern events from the perspective of the United States. He notes several major failings in U.S. policy during the 1978–1979 period, including an undue degree of optimism as to the possibility of gaining Arab approval for the Camp David accords and the inability to understand the internal developments in Iran that led to the hostage crisis. Rubin does, however, credit the Carter administration with "hanging tough" in the hostage negotiations with Iran so that the United States obtained a satisfactory settlement by the time Carter left office. Rubin also notes that much of the thrust of the Reagan administration's policy toward the Middle East was set during Carter's last year in office when, in reaction to the Soviet invasion of Afghanistan, Carter proclaimed what has come to be known as the Carter Doctrine, pledging U.S. protection of the Gulf from Soviet attack. Finally, after noting the numerous crises the Reagan administration has had to grapple with and its uncertain policy vis-à-vis Israel, Rubin concludes that although the U.S. position in the Middle East has clearly improved, the Reagan administration was lucky rather than skillful in benefitting from Middle Eastern developments such as the evolution of the Iran-Iraq war and the Arab-Israeli conflict.

Freedman and Rubin analyzed Middle Eastern developments from the perspective of the superpowers; in Part 2, Shireen Hunter and Robert Hunter lead off by assessing the Arab world in the 1978–1982 period with a focus on the close interrelationship between events in the Gulf and the Arab-Israeli conflict. They analyze the rise and fall of Iraq as the leader of the Gulf Arabs and explain the constraints on the policy of Saudi Arabia in this context. They also examine the development of the Gulf Cooperation Council and conclude that despite a number of internal frictions, its role is likely to grow in the future. The authors note, too, that while Syria continues to be the "odd man out" in the Arab world, Egypt, particularly since the assassination of Sadat, has been drawn closer to the Arab Gulf states because of the threat from Iran. They caution, however, that if the Arab-Israeli peace process runs into difficulties, the Egyptian-Arab rapprochement could slow down.

One of the major factors affecting the Arab world and the region as a whole has been the Islamic fundamentalist regime of the Ayatollah Khomeini, which took power in Iran following the fall of the shah. In Chapter 4, Robert G. Darius analyzes the rise of the Khomeini regime and the challenge it poses to the other states in the Middle East. Although Iran has been beset by a large number of serious internal problems since the ayatollah took power, Darius feels that Khomeini's regime will survive—at least as long as he lives. Khomeini has been successful in maintaining power, but Darius contends that the ayatollah's foreign policy has been far less successful. He describes the evolution of Iranian foreign policy since 1979 and concludes that Khomeini has not accomplished his objectives of toppling conservative, pro-Western regimes, boosting the Palestinian cause, or "freeing" Jerusalem; rather, Khomeini's words and actions have contributed to the outbreak of the Gulf war, a crisis Darius feels may cause enduring harm to Iranian-Arab relations.

While the policies of the superpowers and the dynamics of regional developments have played a major role in the Middle East in the 1978–1982 period, one cannot understand what has happened in the region without a knowledge of the policies of the key states within the region. Since Iraq, Iran, and Saudi Arabia are examined in detail in Part 2, Part 3 concentrates on the policies and politics of Syria, Israel, the PLO, and Egypt—the main actors in the Arab-Israeli conflict. Syria's role in inter-Arab affairs and in the Arab-Israeli conflict is a critical one, and John F. Devlin analyzes the complex factors that have shaped Syrian behavior. Devlin notes that since 1977 there has been a rising degree of antiregime activity on the part of Syria's Sunni Moslem majority against its ruling Shia minority, culminating in demonstrations in Aleppo in 1980 and in Hama in 1982, both of which were harshly suppressed by the government. The Assad regime has also faced difficulties in foreign relations. Its backing for Iran in the Iran-Iraq conflict has led to problems not only with Iraq but also with the Gulf Arabs as a whole. A relationship with Shia Moslem Iran has helped the Assad regime with its religious legitimacy and in its ties to the increasingly powerful Shia community of Lebanon, but Devlin suggests that, on balance, close Syrian-Iranian ties are not in Syria's best interests given the growing hostility between Iran and the Arab world as a whole. Devlin analyzes Syria's involvement in Lebanon and its clashes with Israel during both the 1981 missile crisis and the 1982 Israeli invasion and finds that, despite extensive efforts, Syria has failed to achieve its goals in Lebanon. In sum, given the internal and external problems facing the country, Devlin concludes that the Syrian regime's position is shaky and predicts continued internal turmoil and possibly a change of regime.

While Syria was coping with rising internal opposition and a host of foreign policy problems, Israel—where the democratic process of elections substitutes for the coups d'etat and assassinations that are the means of governmental change elsewhere in the Middle East—underwent a major election in 1981 that retained Menahem Begin and his hard-line foreign policies. In Chapter 6, Don Peretz assesses the reasons for Begin's electoral success, in particular the increasing importance of the ethnic factor in Israeli politics. He also analyzes the numerous economic difficulties facing Israel and the Begin regime's largely unsuccessful attempts to solve them, although he does credit Begin with extending free public education through the end of high school. Peretz's primary emphasis is on the Begin regime's policies on the West Bank and toward the Arab world. He discusses the debate within Israel over settlement policy on the West Bank and assesses the development of Egyptian-Israeli relations from the signing of their peace treaty in March 1979 until the Israeli invasion of Lebanon, with particular attention to the normalization process and to the difficulties caused by disagreements about Palestinian autonomy. Peretz then examines the invasion of Lebanon and concludes that although Israel's military security was assured by the operation and the PLO was severely weakened, the invasion cost Israel heavily in terms of its relations with Egypt and weakened Israel's ties to the U.S. government and to the Jewish community of the United States.

The peace treaty with Egypt was seen as a major achievement by Israeli Prime Minister Menahem Begin, but relations with Israel have proved to be, at best, difficult for Egypt and may possibly cause the existing regime to become unstable. This is the central theme of Chapter 7, in which Louis J. Cantori analyzes the nature of Egyptian foreign and domestic policy under Sadat and his successor, Husni Mubarak. Cantori emphasizes that following the Egyptian-Israeli peace agreement, which led to Egypt's ostracism in the Arab world, the Egyptian government's failure to achieve progress on the autonomy talks or to stop Israel's settlement activities on the West Bank provided ammunition for both domestic and foreign opponents of the Sadat-Mubarak regime. He also notes that although Egypt has been unjustly condemned for having abandoned the Palestinian cause, the Israeli invasion of Lebanon showed that no Arab state, including Syria, really put the Palestinian cause ahead of its own national interests. Both Sadat and Mubarak were committed to peace with Israel and to close ties to the United States, but, Cantori says, Mubarak tends to stress such themes as nonalignment and positive neutrality in his foreign policy and places more emphasis on the public sector in his domestic policy.

While Assad, Begin, and Mubarak were trying to cope with both domestic and foreign policy problems, PLO leader Yasir Arafat faced a major dilemma of his own. Although the PLO had seen its prestige abroad rise sharply, it faced an equally sharp decline in its ability to maneuver within the Arab world and vis-à-vis Israel. Aaron D. Miller traces the ups and downs in PLO policy from the Camp David agreements to the Israeli invasion of Lebanon in Chapter 8. After describing the various components of the PLO and their respective loyalties, Miller notes that the PLO's continued vulnerability lies in its inability to obtain a genuinely secure base of operations or a source of independent and reliable financial and military support, and that vulnerability is greatly exacerbated by the PLO's ouster from Lebanon. Miller asserts that the PLO is badly divided in its own ranks, is exploited by Arab states (especially Syria), and lacks reliable great power support; as a result, despite its acts of terrorism and attempts to build a conventional military force, it is at a considerable disadvantage vis-à-vis Israel. After describing Arafat's dilemma of having to enhance the PLO's respectability and moderate image abroad while maintaining his revolutionary credentials within the movement, Miller concludes that unless the PLO leader can turn the support and sympathy resulting from the Israeli invasion of Lebanon into concrete political gains, the road from Beirut will become increasingly hazardous and the PLO itself may split over such questions as "Who lost Lebanon?"

In sum, the authors of this book have presented an encompassing analysis of the major developments in Middle Eastern politics from the Camp David agreements of 1978 until the Israeli invasion of Lebanon of 1982. It is hoped that this volume will serve to aid understanding of this highly complex period, one that has proven to be perhaps the most volatile in the history of the contemporary Middle East.

Part 1

Superpower Perspectives

1
Soviet Policy Toward the Middle East Since Camp David

Robert O. Freedman

In the four-year period between the Camp David agreements and the death of Soviet Party Secretary Leonid Brezhnev, a number of major political and military developments took place in the Middle East that were to significantly affect Soviet policy in the region. The Camp David agreements themselves, the fall of the Shah of Iran, the Egyptian-Israeli peace treaty, the Iranian hostage crisis, the Soviet invasion of Afghanistan, the Iraqi invasion of Iran, and, finally, the Israeli invasion of Lebanon all had a substantial impact on Soviet policy. In order to fully understand how Soviet policy was affected, however, it is first necessary to deal with the problem of defining Soviet goals in the Middle East and to analyze the strategy and tactics Moscow uses in quest of its goals. Observers of Soviet policy in the Middle East are generally divided into two schools of thought on the question of Soviet goals in the region.[1] Both groups agree that Moscow wants to be considered a major factor in Middle Eastern affairs, if only because of the USSR's propinquity to the region, but they differ on what they see as the ultimate Soviet goal in the Middle East. One school of thought views Soviet Middle Eastern policy as primarily defensive in nature; that is, as directed toward preventing the region from being used as a base for military attack or political subversion against the USSR. The other school of thought views Soviet policy as primarily offensive in nature, aimed at the limitation and ultimate exclusion of Western influence from the oil-rich, strategically located region in favor of Soviet influence. It is my opinion that Soviet goals in the Middle East, at least since the mid-1960s, have been primarily offensive in nature, and in the Arab areas of the Middle East, the

9

Soviet Union appears to have been engaged in a zero-sum competition for influence with the United States. A brief discussion of the tactics and overall strategy employed by Moscow in its quest for Middle Eastern influence will serve as a background for the subsequent analysis of Soviet policy during 1978–1982.

In its efforts to weaken and ultimately eliminate Western influence from the Middle East, and particularly from the Arab world, while promoting its own influence, the Soviet leadership has employed a number of tactics. First and foremost has been the supply of military aid to its regional clients.[2] Next has been economic aid; the Aswan Dam in Egypt and the Euphrates Dam in Syria are prominent examples of Soviet economic assistance, although each project has had serious problems. In recent years Moscow has also sought to solidify its influence through the conclusion of long-term Friendship and Cooperation treaties such as the ones concluded with Egypt (1971), Iraq (1972), Somalia (1974), Ethiopia (1978), Afghanistan (1978), the Peoples Democratic Republic of Yemen (PDRY, 1979), and Syria (1980); the later repudiation of the treaties by Egypt (1976) and Somalia (1977) indicate that this has not been an altogether successful tactic. In addition, Moscow has attempted to exploit the lingering memories of Western colonialism and Western threats against Arab oil producers. The Soviets have also offered the Arabs diplomatic support at such international forums as the United Nations (UN) and the Geneva Conference on an Arab-Israeli peace settlement. Finally, Moscow has offered the Arabs both military and diplomatic aid against Israel, although that aid has been limited in scope because Moscow continues to support Israel's right to exist, for fear of unduly alienating the United States (with whom the Russians desire additional Strategic Arms Limitation Talks [SALT] agreements and improved trade relations) and because Israel serves as a convenient rallying point for potentially anti-Western forces in the Arab world.

Although the USSR has used all these tactics with varying degrees of success over the last two decades, it has also run into serious problems in its quest for influence in the Middle East. For one thing, the numerous inter-Arab and regional conflicts (Syria-Iraq; North Yemen–South Yemen; Ethiopia-Somalia; Algeria-Morocco; Iran-Iraq; and so on) have usually meant that favoring one party alienates the other, often driving it over to the West. Second, the existence of Arab Communist parties has proven to be a handicap for the Russians, as Communist activities have, on occasion, caused a sharp deterioration in relations between the USSR and the country in which the Arab Communist party has operated. The Communist-supported coup d'etat in the Sudan in 1971 and Communist efforts to organize cells in the

Iraqi Army in the mid- and late 1970s are recent examples of this problem.[3] Third, the wealth that has flowed into the Arab world (or at least into its major oil producers) since the quadrupling of oil prices in late 1973 has enabled the Arabs to buy quality technology from the West, weakening the economic bond between the USSR and a number of Arab states such as Iraq and Syria. Fourth, since 1967 and particularly since the 1973 Arab-Israeli war, Islam has been resurgent throughout the Arab world, and the USSR, identified in the Arab world with atheism, has been hampered as a result. Finally, the United States, and to a lesser extent France and China, have actively opposed Soviet efforts to achieve predominant influence in the region, frequently enabling Middle Eastern states to play the extraregional powers off against each other, thereby preventing any one nation from securing predominant influence.

Because of the problems that the USSR has faced, Moscow has adopted one overall strategy in an attempt to maximize its influence while weakening that of the West. The strategy has been to try to unite the Arab states (irrespective of their mutual conflicts) and Arab political organizations, such as the Arab Communist parties and the PLO, into a large "anti-imperialist" Arab front directed against what the USSR has termed the linchpin of Western imperialism—Israel—and its Western supporters. Given the heterogeneous composition of the "anti-imperialist" front that it has sought to create, however, the USSR has had only mixed results in pursuing this strategy. On the one hand, it appeared to bear fruit during the 1973 Arab-Israeli war when virtually the entire Arab world united against Israel and placed an oil embargo against the United States, at the same time reducing oil shipments to the Western European allies of the United States, an action that caused considerable disarray in the North Atlantic Treaty Organization (NATO). On the other hand, in the aftermath of the war the astute diplomacy of Henry Kissinger and policy changes by Egyptian President Anwar Sadat led to a splintering of this "anti-imperialist" Arab unity. By the time of the Lebanese civil war of 1975–1976, Moscow was in a very weak position in the Middle East; the pro-Western Saudi-Egyptian axis, increasingly tied to pro-Western Iran, was the dominant force in the Arab world, and even such erstwhile Soviet allies as the PDRY (South Yemen) and Syria were increasingly attracted to the pro-Western Arab alignment. In addition, Iraq, once Moscow's closest ally in the Arab world, was exploiting its new oil wealth, as well as the end of its confrontation with Iran through their 1975 treaty, as a means of moving away from Moscow both economically and politically. In sum, by the end of 1976 Moscow's influence in the Middle East seemed at a low ebb.

The Impact of Camp David

The Soviet Union's Middle Eastern position was, however, to revive in the 1977-1979 period. One factor in the Soviet resurgence was the diplomatic efforts of the newly-elected Carter administration, which abandoned Kissinger's step-by-step approach to an Arab-Israeli settlement in favor of a comprehensive peace agreement. In pursuing this policy in 1977, the Carter administration felt that it needed the USSR to "deliver" the PLO and Syria to the bargaining table, since Washington lacked sufficient diplomatic influence to do so. The end result was the Soviet-American joint statement of October 1, 1977, that restored Moscow to the center of Middle East diplomacy, albeit only temporarily.[4] A second factor strengthening the Soviet position during this period was the marked improvement of Syrian-Soviet ties that had deteriorated following the serious clash between the two countries during the Lebanese civil war when Syria invaded Lebanon. The improvement was partly due to a weakening of Syrian President Assad's internal position because of his actions in Lebanon that initially favored the Christian forces against the Moslems and PLO, a development that helped precipitate increasingly severe Muslim Brotherhood attacks against his regime. Syria's sense of growing isolation caused by Sadat's efforts to secure a peace treaty with Israel also contributed to the improved relations.[5] A third factor of importance strengthening the Soviet position was Moscow's successful intervention in Ethiopia on the side of the Mengistu regime against the invading Somalis. Even though Moscow's choice of Ethiopia over Somalia cost the USSR some important bases in Somalia, nonetheless the strategic position of Ethiopia in Africa, its position along the Red Sea across from Saudi Arabia, and its control over the sources of the Nile made Ethiopia the greater prize.[6] In addition, Moscow's successful airlift of military supplies to its Ethiopian client enhanced the reputation of Soviet military power in the region. Reinforcing the Soviet Union's position near the Strait of Bab el Mandab was the change of government in the PDRY in June 1978 that ended that nation's flirtation with Saudi Arabia while strengthening its ties to Moscow, a development that was to lead to the signing of a Treaty of Friendship and Cooperation between the two countries in 1979.

The improvement of Moscow's ties to Syria, South Yemen, and Ethiopia seemed to strengthen the Soviet position in the Middle East during the 1977-1978 period, and the Camp David talks and the subsequent Egyptian-Israeli peace treaty appeared to recreate the "anti-imperialist" Arab unity that Moscow had been seeking since 1973. This development, coupled with the ouster of the Shah of Iran from power, appeared initially to significantly tip the Middle East balance of power against the United States and in favor of the Soviet Union. Unfortunately for Moscow, however, the Arab unity created by Camp David was to dissipate in less than a year, while the new government in Iran was to cause the Soviet Union as many problems for its Middle East policy as the shah's regime had done.

The Sadat visit to Jerusalem in November 1977 and the subsequent Camp David agreements in September 1978 led to a major controversy in the Arab world. Virtually every Arab state (the exceptions were the Sudan and Oman), including Egypt's erstwhile allies Saudi Arabia and North Yemen, lined up with the pro-Soviet Steadfastness Front (Syria, the PDRY, the PLO, Libya, and Algeria) to condemn Egypt's actions. Meeting at Baghdad in November 1978 under the leadership of Iraq, which was thrusting itself forward as the successor to Egypt as the leader of the Arab world, the Arab states voted to withdraw their ambassadors from Cairo if Egypt went ahead with the peace treaty with Israel, to suspend Egypt from the Arab League, and to invoke economic sanctions against it. The Baghdad Conference was significant not only for the isolation and condemnation of Egypt but also for the reconciliation between such long-time enemies as Syria and Iraq, and Jordan and the PLO, along with a rapprochement between Iraq and the PLO—all of which were evident at the conference. These developments led a number of Soviet commentators to assert that the long-hoped-for "anti-imperialist" Arab unity (albeit without Egypt) had been reborn.[7]

Coming soon after the Baghdad Conference, and still further strengthening Moscow's Middle Eastern position, was the fall of the Shah of Iran and his replacement by the Ayatollah Khomeini, who pulled Iran out of the Central Treaty Organization (CENTO), ended U.S. use of the facilities in northern Iran for the monitoring of Soviet missiles and military broadcasts, and proclaimed Iran's neutrality.[8] Thus, in the space of two months, the Egyptian-Saudi-Iranian alignment on which the United States had depended (along with Israel) to block the spread of Soviet influence in the Middle East seemed to have been ripped asunder. Simultaneously the vacillating and uncertain policies pursued by the United States during the fall of the shah (including the dispatch and recall three days later of an aircraft-carrier task force from the Pacific Ocean to the Indian Ocean and the subsequent dispatch of *unarmed* F-15s to Saudi Arabia) weakened the U.S. position still further as a number of Arab states, such as Saudi Arabia—already unhappy about the lack of American action to stem the Soviet tide in Ethiopia, began to openly question U.S. resolve and reliability.

While the U.S. decision to militarily aid North Yemen after it was invaded by South Yemen in March 1979 seemed aimed at reassuring the United States' Arab allies that it would come to their defense, the subsequent lack of substantive U.S. action after the American hostages were seized in Iran (see below) seemed only to reinforce the Middle East image of the United States as a weak and irresolute power—a development from which Moscow could only gain.[9]

Meanwhile Moscow was strongly endorsing the actions of the Second Baghdad Conference, which met in April 1979 following the signing of the Egyptian-Israeli peace treaty. At this meeting, the Arab states invoked the sanctions threatened in November: suspension of Egypt's membership in the Arab League, withdrawal of all Arab ambassadors from Cairo, and the cutting off of all economic aid to Egypt. Indeed, at this point Moscow may well have entertained the hopes of a wider "Middle Eastern anti-imperialist bloc" being formed as the new government in Iran broke diplomatic relations with Egypt, proclaimed its support for the PLO, and condemned the Egyptian-Israeli treaty and the United States' role in achieving it.

Unfortunately for Moscow, however, this rather halcyon Middle Eastern situation, with the United States unable to gain any additional support for the Camp David accords and the Arab world virtually unified in an anti-Egyptian front, was soon to change. The internecine strife that had so long characterized intra-Arab relations returned with a vengeance with Iran playing a significant role in the intra-Arab conflicts.

The first major problem for Moscow was to come with the renewal of the Iraq-Syria feud at the end of July 1979. This was due in part to the accusation by Iraq's new president, Saddam Hussein, that Syria was involved in a plot to overthrow him and in part to Syria's unwillingness to subordinate itself to Iraq in the proposed union of the countries. It was not long before the old animosity returned to the Syrian-Iraqi relationship, a development that was to greatly weaken the "anti-imperialist" unity Moscow had wished for so long. Compounding this problem for Moscow were Iraq's severe crackdown on the Iraqi Communist party and a number of demonstratively anti-Communist and even anti-Soviet statements by top Iraqi leaders, actions that seemed aimed at improving Iraq's ties to the strongly anti-Communist regime of Saudi Arabia.[10]

A second problem for the USSR came in its relations with the new regime in Iran. The Khomeini regime soon came into conflict with its Arab neighbor, Iraq, thus causing a further disruption in the Arab world as Syria and Libya backed Iran, and Jordan, Saudi Arabia, and Kuwait, all of whom felt threatened by Khomeini's brand of Islamic fundamentalism, backed Iraq. Other areas of Soviet-Iranian contention included charges by Iranian leaders that Moscow was aiding Iranian separatists in Kurdistan and Baluchistan, Iranian criticism of Soviet support for the anti-Islamic policies of the Communist regime that had seized power in Afghanistan in April 1978, and Iranian charges that Moscow was behind the left-wing Mujahadeen and Fedayeen opposition in Iran.[11] As increasingly anti-Communist statements were made by the Iranian government in the spring and summer of 1979, as the offices of the pro-Moscow Tudeh party were attacked by Islamic fundamentalists, and as the central government cracked down on the leftist Kurds (several of whose leaders were sympathetic to the USSR and Marxism), along with the Mujahadeen and Fedayeen, the Soviet leadership became uneasy; it saw the possibility of Iran slipping back to the United States. These fears were reinforced in early September 1979 when the Bazargan government in Iran turned to the United States for spare parts for its weapons, after having canceled a multi-billion-dollar arms deal several months earlier. As these events progressed, Moscow gave increasing backing to the aspirations of the Kurds and the left-wing forces in Iran and stepped up its criticism of Iran's fundamentalist leaders. This process culminated in early September with an attack on the Ayatollah Khomeini himself by *Izvestia* commentator Alexander Bovin, in the weekend supplement to *Izvestia*.[12]

Fortunately for Moscow, no such rapprochement took place, as the seizure of the U.S. embassy in Teheran precipitated both the fall of the Bazargan government and a major crisis in Iranian-American relations.

The Hostage Crisis

The initial Soviet reacton to the embassy seizure was somewhat guarded, as *Pravda* printed essentially factual accounts of the actions of the students.[13] Several days later, however, as the situation became more clear, the USSR tilted toward a pro-Iranian position; a Moscow Radio Persian-language commentary on November 6 termed the student action "totally understandable and logical."[14] Soviet broadcasts continued in this vein—despite protests by Washington—until December 5, when *Pravda* itself took a strongly pro-Iranian position. An article by A. Petrov, after deploring the U.S. naval buildup near Iran as "flagrant military and political pressure against Iran," stated: "The principle of immunity of diplomatic representatives cannot serve as justification, and even less as a pretext, for violating the sovereignty of an independent state—another principle that is at the heart of all international law."[15]

Petrov's rather convoluted analysis of international law ended with a warning: "Our country, as Comrade L. Brezhnev has stressed, opposes outside interference in Iran's internal affairs by anyone, in any form and under any pretext. This position of the Soviet Union remains unchanged."

In seeking the reason behind Moscow's pro-Iranian position in the hostage crisis at a time it was seeking the passage of the SALT II agreement in the U.S. Senate, one can point to the uncertain handling of the crisis by the Carter administration. The administration's reluctance to impose economic, let alone military, sanctions at a time when the United States was being humiliated on a daily basis by street mobs parading with the sign "America can't do anything," may well have struck the Soviet leadership as a sign of weakness, particularly since President Carter emphasized so strongly that the lives of the hostages were the primary American concern.[16] Indeed, the hostage situation weakened still further the position of the United States in the Middle East, as many nations in the region began to openly wonder how likely it was that the United States would come to their aid if it could not even defend its own interests, a perception perhaps reinforced by Washington's passivity after the U.S. embassy in Pakistan was stormed and burned later in November. To be sure, when the hostage issue was initially raised in the United Nations, Moscow voted for two Security Council resolutions calling on Iran to free the hostages (after all, its own diplomats could one day find themselves in a similar situation); the second one was on December 4. Yet the *Pravda* article already cited, which appeared one day after the December 4 UN vote (and was broadcast by Tass International Service), seemed to convey the USSR's true feelings.

In sum, the hostage seizure and the subsequent rift between the United States and Iran was seen by the Soviet Union as a golden opportunity to reinforce its own ties with Iran, prevent an Iranian-American rapprochement, and weaken the overall position of the United States in the Middle East. Whether or not the Carter administration's lack of firmness in handling the Iranian crisis was a factor in Moscow's decision to proceed with its massive invasion of Afghanistan in late December 1979 is only a matter of conjecture. Nonetheless, it must have struck the Kremlin leaders that if the United States was unwilling to intervene in Iran where it had major interests, it was very unlikely to take action in Afghanistan where American interests were almost nonexistent.[17] In any case, the Soviet invasion of Afghanistan was to cause Moscow serious problems throughout the Moslem world, although the USSR was to use its championing of

Iranian interests against the United States to try to deflect Moslem criticism.

The Impact of the Soviet Invasion of Afghanistan

The Soviet invasion of Afghanistan created serious problems for Moscow both in its relations with the United States (President Carter imposed a partial grain embargo, withdrew the SALT II treaty from Senate consideration, and canceled American participation in the Moscow Olympics) and in its relations with the Moslem world. The United States seized upon the invasion to try to rally the Moslem states of the Middle East—many of whom were suspicious of the United States because of its role in Camp David—against the USSR, while at the same time stepping up its search for Middle Eastern bases and hastening the deployment of its military forces near the Gulf, which Carter pledged to protect. When a resolution condemning the Soviet intervention in Afghanistan came up for a vote in the United Nations in early January 1980, only Ethiopia and South Yemen, among Moscow's Middle Eastern allies, voted against it; Algeria, Syria, and North Yemen abstained, with Libya taking a similar position by being absent from the vote.[18] Among the 104 countries voting against Moscow (only 18 states voted with the USSR, while 30 abstained or were not present) was Iraq, whose President, Saddam Hussein, publicly condemned the invasion, thus further demonstrating Iraq's independence of Moscow.[19] Also voting against Moscow were Saudi Arabia, Jordan, and Kuwait, all of whom Moscow had hoped to wean away from the West. Iran's foreign ministry issued a statement condemning the invasion and its UN representative joined with the majority in voting for the anti-Soviet resolution.[20] As a further blow to Moscow, the Islamic Conference, meeting in late January, condemned the Soviet Union in strong terms and suspended the membership of Afghanistan, while calling for a boycott of the Moscow Olympics and the breaking of diplomatic relations with Afghanistan.[21]

In an effort to overcome this Moslem backlash, which it feared the United States would be able to exploit, Moscow made several moves. One was to utilize its most trusted Arab allies, who formed the Steadfastness and Confrontation Front, to divert Moslem attention from Afghanistan to the Arab-Israeli conflict by means of actions in the United Nations and in Islamic and Arab organizations.[22] Fortunately for Moscow, Israel was again to give the USSR ammunition for its propaganda efforts. For instance, following a terrorist attack in the West Bank city of Hebron against Jews who were returning from Sabbath services, Israel expelled the mayor and religious leader of that city and the mayor of a nearby city, accusing them of creating the atmosphere for the attack. A month later two West Bank mayors were maimed by bombs; at the same time, the Begin government began to push the bill for the formal annexation of East Jerusalem through the Israeli Parliament. Moscow seized on these events to claim that Egypt had capitulated to Israel and to demonstrate that by backing these actions, the United States was, in fact, an enemy of Islam. The USSR also proclaimed its willingness to vote sanctions in the Security Council against Israel "by virtue of its solidarity with the Arab and other Islamic countries that considered it necessary for the Security Council to take some steps in connection with the Israeli occupier's defiant action."[23] Indeed, Moscow was to use the numerous condemnations of Israel by the UN in the spring and summer of 1980—condemnations that were spearheaded by its Arab allies—to try to divert attention from Afghanistan where, despite a massive troop commitment, the USSR was facing serious difficulties in suppressing the rebels.

Another of Moscow's moves was to step up support for Iran in its confrontation with the United States in the period after the invasion of Afghanistan. Not only did the USSR veto a U.S.-sponsored UN Security Council resolution calling for economic sanctions against Iran, it also strongly reiterated its warning against U.S. military intervention in Iran. *Pravda*, on January 10, 1980, stated that Moscow would not tolerate any outside interference in Iranian internal affairs. While the USSR sought to project itself as the protector of Iran, it also sought to temper Iranian criticism of the Afghan invasion by having Babrak Karmal, the Soviet-installed leader of Afghanistan, write to Khomeini with an appeal for a common front against U.S. imperialism.[24] All these efforts, however, came to naught. The two leading candidates for the Iranian presidency, Hassan Bani Sadr and Foreign Minister Sadeq Ghotbzadeh, attacked the USSR in campaign speeches in late January 1980, with Bani Sadr accusing Moscow of wanting to divide Iran and push to the Indian Ocean. Khomeini himself publicly condemned the invasion, while also ridiculing Soviet and Iranian leftist attempts to prove the compatibility of Islam and Marxism.[25]

Following the abortive American-hostage rescue mission of April 25, 1980, Moscow again sought to act as the champion of Iran, but its efforts were not appreciated in Teheran. The Khomeini regime led the chorus of anti-Soviet criticism at the Islamic Conference meeting of May 1980, the second such meeting of 1980. Foreign Minister Ghotbzadeh, who headed the Iranian delegation, condemned the USSR's invasion of Afghanistan as a "flagrant violation of international law carried out in total disrespect for the sovereignty and territorial integrity of Afghanistan." He also stated, in an obvious effort to prevent the conference from being diverted to the Palestine-Israel conflict, "For us, the liberation of Afghanistan is not less important than the liberation of Palestine." Ghotbzadeh was successful in his quest, as the Islamic Conference, despite the efforts of the Steadfastness Front, again called for the "immediate, total and unconditional withdrawal of all Soviet troops stationed on the territory of Afghanistan." It also set up a three-man committee, composed of Ghotbzadeh, the foreign minister of Pakistan, and the Islamic Conference secretary general, to seek a solution of the Afghan problem.[26] Despite the Islamic Conference's numerous criticisms of the United States, the May meeting must be considered another diplomatic defeat for the USSR, which rejected the conference's Afghan Committee Plan and denounced the "representatives of reactionary Moslem quarters" who "succeeded in pushing through a resolution on the Afghan question couched in terms hostile to the people and government of Afghanistan."[27]

Although Soviet-Iranian relations continued to deteriorate through the spring and summer of 1980, Moscow evidently held out hope for the new Iranian prime minister, Islamic fundamentalist Ali Rajai, who took office in August, as well as for Ayatollah Mohammed Beheshti, head of the Islamic Republican party, whom *New Times* Middle East specialist Dmitry Volsky cited as saying that Soviet-Iranian relations "are of a constructive nature and have good chances of developing."[28] Apparently Moscow reasoned that whereas Bani Sadr wanted the hostages released so that Iran could get on with its economic development, the hard-line Islamic Republicans, to whom Islamic purity took priority over economic development, would continue to drag out the hostage confinement, thereby preventing any Iranian-American reconciliation. While the Soviet leaders were far from happy with the suppression of Iran's leftist groups and ethnic minorities, particularly the Kurds—who again began to receive favorable Soviet press coverage, at the very least Moscow seemed hopeful that the continued holding of the hostages would keep Iran out of the U.S. camp and on the "anti-imperialist" path. Unfortunately for the USSR, however, the outbreak of war between Iran and Iraq changed the hostage equation in Iranian politics and once again held out the possibility of a rapprochement between Iran and the United States.

The Iran-Iraq War

Tension had been building between Iran and Iraq almost from the time that Ayatollah Khomeini took power. Khomeini, who had been expelled from Iraq at the request of the shah, was seen by the Iraqi leadership as a threat to the loyalty of its Shiite population, among whom Khomeini had lived for fifteen years. At the same time, Iran saw Iraq as a cause of unrest in the Arab-populated province of Khuzistan. Behind these concerns were two very different conceptions of the future. Iraq, which was seeking to become the leader of the Arab world, emphasized Arabism as its main propaganda theme and in February 1980 issued a Pan-Arab charter in an effort to rally the Arab states behind its leadership. By contrast, the central theme for Iran was Islam; Ayatollah Khomeini and his entourage, who made no secret of their desire to export Iran's Islamic revolution, sought to rally the Moslem world, both Arab and non-Arab, behind the banner of Islam.

For its part, Moscow was very uncomfortable as the Iran-Iraq conflict heated up in April 1980, for it appeared that the USSR might have to choose sides. Indeed, when the border skirmishing erupted in a full-scale war in mid-September, the Soviet Union was in a very awkward position: a good argument could have been made in the Kremlin to aid either side. On the one hand, Moscow was linked to Baghdad by a Treaty of Friendship and Cooperation and had long been Iraq's main supplier of military weaponry. In addition, Iraq had been a leading foe of the U.S.-sponsored Camp David agreements and, as a nation with pretensions to leadership in the Arab world, could one day become the focus of the "anti-imperialist" Arab unity that Moscow had sought for so long. Indeed, by its leadership at the two Baghdad Conferences, Iraq demonstrated a potential for just such a role, and the growing relationship between Iraq and Saudi Arabia that was in evidence before the Iran-Iraq war erupted may have been seen by Moscow as a development that would further move the Saudis out of the American camp. It could also have been argued in the Kremlin that aid to Iraq would be a demonstration to the Arab world that Moscow was indeed a reliable ally (some Arab states had questioned this, despite Soviet aid to the Arab cause in the 1973 war). From the point of view of the Soviet economy, aid to Iraq would help assure the continued flow of Iraqi oil to the USSR and its East European allies.

Soviet opponents of aid to Iraq could point to the continued persecution of Iraqi Communists and Iraq's clear move away from the USSR since the treaty was signed in 1972, as typified by its condemnation of Moscow because of the invasion of Afghanistan, its February 1980 Pan-Arab charter that called for the elimination of both superpowers from the Arab world,[29] and its growing economic and even military ties with France and other West European nations.

On balance, however, since the Russians see Iraq as "objectively" a major anti-Western force, a very good argument could have been made to aid the Iraqis in the war.

On the other hand, however, a good case could also have been made for aiding Iran. First and foremost, the Khomeini revolution detached Iran from its close alignment with the United States, thereby striking a major blow to the U.S. position in the Gulf and in the Middle East as a whole. In addition, by holding on to the American hostages, the Khomeini regime carried on a daily humiliation of the United States, a factor that further lowered American prestige in the region. Consequently, any major Soviet aid effort to Iraq contained the possibility of ending the hostage impasse (indeed, as the war heated up, the Islamic fundamentalists in Iran suddenly seemed more responsive on the hostage issue and on November 2, 1980, the fundamentalist-dominated parliament voted to release the hostages, albeit conditionally) and even moving Iran back toward the U.S. camp because of Iran's dependence on U.S. military equipment. Given Iran's large population (three times that of Iraq) and its strategic position along the Gulf and at the Strait of Hormuz, such a development would clearly not be in Moscow's interest. Another strategic factor that the Soviet leadership had to take into consideration was that Iran, unlike Iraq, had a common border with the USSR, as well as with Soviet-occupied Afghanistan. While Iranian efforts on behalf of the Afghan rebels had so far been limited, one could not rule out a major increase in Iranian aid to the Afghan rebels should Moscow side with Iraq, as well as a more pronounced effort on the part of Khomeini to infect the USSR's own Moslems with his brand of Islamic fundamentalism.[30] Finally, as in the case of Iraq, there was an important economic argument. Iran had cut off gas exports to the USSR, but the signing of a major transit agreement between the two countries just before the war erupted[31] may well have seemed to Moscow the first step toward the resumption of natural gas exports. Given Iran's large available reserves of this fuel, Moscow might wish to encourage the supply relationship, particularly if—as some experts predict—the USSR might run short of oil in the mid-1980s.

Soviet opponents of aid to Iran could have pointed to the Islamic fundamentalists' treatment of the Tudeh (although it was not as brutal as Iraq's treatment of its Communists), as well as the treatment of Iranian minorities with whom the USSR hoped to cultivate a good relationship. Here again, however, Iran's treatment of its Kurds seemed no worse than Iraq's. Finally, opponents of aid to Iran could have pointed to Iran's leading anti-Soviet role in Islamic conferences, although again there may not have been too much to choose from between Iran's and Iraq's anti-Sovietism. The main factor in the Soviet evaluation of both countries was that they seemed far more anti-American than anti-Soviet, and both contributed to the weakening of the U.S. position in the Middle East. For this reason, Moscow needed a good relationship with both and could not afford to alienate either.

Given this situation, it is not surprising that Moscow remained neutral, while urging a speedy settlement of the war "lest the imperialists benefit." Indeed, the outbreak and prolongation of the war has brought with it a number of rather serious problems for Moscow. There was a major split in the anti-Sadat forces in the Arab world: Libya and Syria came out for Iran; Jordan openly backed Iraq. In addition to Iraq breaking diplomatic relations with Syria and Libya, Saudi Arabia broke diplomatic relations with Libya,[32] although the Saudis did not formally associate themselves with Iraq. The end result of the war was a further disruption of the "anti-imperialist" Arab unity that Moscow had wanted for so long, a split that was underscored when the Steadfastness Front Arab states boycotted the Arab summit in Jordan at the end of November 1980.

In addition to the split in the anti-Sadat front, Moscow feared a major U.S. gain in the conflict. The emplacement of U.S. AWACS (Airborne Warning and Control Systems) aircraft and ground radar personnel in Saudi Arabia seemed to demonstrate American willingness to help defend Saudi Arabia and other Arab states in time of need, a development that made the U.S. military buildup in the Indian Ocean more diplomatically acceptable, thereby refuting Moscow's charge that the U.S. buildup was a threat to the Arab world. Indeed, the AWACS move not only appeared to reverse the decline in Saudi-American relations precipitated by Camp David and the overthrow of the shah, but even held out the possibility of a further improvement in relations, and Moscow became concerned that Saudi Arabia might be enticed to support the Camp David process.[33]

As the war continued, Moscow appeared to be able to do little but urge its immediate end, proclaim Soviet neutrality, and warn both Iran and Iraq, along with the other countries of the Middle East, that the United States was exploiting the war for its own benefit. In addition to denouncing U.S. efforts to exploit the war, Moscow apparently tried to maintain some ties with both belligerents by allowing a limited amount of Soviet weaponry to be transshipped to both Iran and Iraq—although the USSR publicly denied any such shipments.[34] As its frustration mounted over being unable to effect an end to the conflict, which seemed to be greatly strengthening the Middle East position of the United States (and thereby weakening that of the

USSR in the zero-sum game view of the Middle East held by Moscow),[35] the Soviet leadership made two moves. The first was to utilize the signing of a Friendship and Cooperation Treaty with Syria as a demonstration of the continued importance of Moscow to the Arab world. The second was an open appeal for the neutralization of the Gulf—a rather transparent device to reverse the gains made by the United States as a result of the war—in a speech made by Brezhnev during the Soviet leader's visit to India in December.

The Friendship and Cooperation Treaty

Assad's visit to Moscow in October 1980, three weeks after the outbreak of the Iran-Iraq war, was highlighted by the signing of a Friendship and Cooperation Treaty between Syria and the Soviet Union. This document seemed to give the USSR a stronger foothold in Syria at a time when that country, as well as the entire Middle East, was wracked by the Iran-Iraq war. Given the fact that the USSR had long been pressing Assad to sign such a document, the treaty must be considered a victory for Soviet policy, although Assad's growing domestic and foreign isolation appear to be the prime cause for his willingness to sign it. The Israeli-Egyptian peace treaty and the growing normalization between those two countries left Syria in a weakened position vis-à-vis Israel, while at the same time Syria's growing conflict with Iraq had left it even more exposed. In addition, besides being bogged down in Lebanon, Assad faced a growing internal threat from the Muslim Brotherhood, which had assassinated a number of prominent Alawi figures.[36] Adding to Syria's sense of isolation was a cooling of its relationship with Jordan. Undoubtedly to the chagrin of the regime in Damascus, Jordan had become increasingly friendly with Iraq, which was granting it large amounts of economic aid.[37] These developments, which had increased Assad's dependence on the USSR, lay at the root not only of his endorsement of the Soviet invasion of Afghanistan but also of his decision to finally agree to a Friendship and Cooperation Treaty with Moscow, an action he had been resisting for almost a decade.[38]

Interestingly enough, however, despite the treaty Assad continued to seek to keep a certain amount of flexibility in his relationship with the USSR. Before signing the treaty with Moscow, he signed a unity agreement with Libya, thereby demonstrating that Syria was not as isolated as either its friends or foes may have thought. In addition, by boycotting the Arab summit in Amman and then mobilizing Syria's forces on Jordan's border at the beginning of December—at a time when a high-ranking Soviet official had come to Damascus to transmit the treaty ratification papers—Assad seems to have acted counter to

Soviet desires.[39] The Syrian-led boycott of the Arab summit was a blow to Moscow's efforts to help rebuild "anti-imperialist" unity in the Arab world, and the Syrian military threats against Jordan arrested the slow rapprochement between Moscow and Amman, while once again reinforcing American-Jordanian ties, which had been strained since Camp David. Indeed, Hussein turned to Washington with a request for arms to counter what he called a Soviet-backed threat to the security of his country.[40] Furthermore, as a result of the Syrian move, Moscow may well have felt that Jordan was more susceptible to American pressure to join the Camp David peace process.[41] Indeed, by this time the Arab world had split into three major camps: the pro-Soviet Steadfastness Front; the pro-Western Egyptian camp (Egypt, Sudan, Somalia, and Oman); and the Arab Centrists, led by Saudi Arabia and Jordan, whom Moscow feared might gravitate to the Egyptian camp and embrace Camp David. Moscow's fears were reinforced by the formation of the Gulf Cooperation Council (GCC), an organization of six conservative Arab states. Five of these were Centrist Arab states (Saudi Arabia, Kuwait, the United Arab Emirates, Bahrein, and Qatar); the sixth was Oman, which was firmly in the pro-Western Egyptian camp of Arab states and which advocated close military cooperation between the GCC and the United States.[42]

Gulf Neutralization

As the diplomatic situation in the Arab world became increasingly troublesome for Moscow, Soviet leader Leonid Brezhnev journeyed to India to try to regain some diplomatic momentum for the USSR by launching his Gulf neutralization scheme, which—like the Soviet Middle East plan launched at the height of the Lebanese civil war of 1976—seemed aimed at regaining the initiative for the Soviet Union at a time when Middle Eastern developments seemed out of Moscow's control.[43] In many ways India was an ideal place for Brezhnev's proclamation. The Indian government of Indira Gandhi was concerned about the growing military ties between the United States and China and about Chinese military aid to Pakistan. Indeed, these developments, coupled with the U.S. military deployment in the Indian Ocean and the victory of Republican presidential candidate Ronald Reagan, may have brought back memories of an earlier Republican administration's "tilt" to Pakistan in 1971. As a consequence, Indira Gandhi clearly felt the need for a close tie with Moscow, and the Russians, who had signed a major arms deal with India only a few months earlier, moved to reinforce the relationship further by agreeing to significantly increase Soviet shipments of oil and oil products to India to help compensate it for the petroleum imports lost because of the outbreak of the Iran-

Iraq war.[44] In return for Soviet military, political, and economic support, India provided an important service to Moscow. As the largest nonaligned state and as one of the founders of the movement and the host of the February 1981 Non-Aligned Conference, Indian political support for Moscow could be expected to assuage some of the nonaligned nations' unhappiness with Moscow because of its invasion of Afghanistan. Indeed, the final communique issued after the Brezhnev visit did not even mention Afghanistan and stated only that a "negotiated political solution alone can guarantee a durable settlement of the existing problems of the region," thereby echoing Moscow's call for Iran and Pakistan to begin negotiations with the pro-Soviet Afghan government. In addition, the communique also called for the dismantling of all foreign military and naval bases in the area "such as Diego Garcia" and the prevention of the creation of new bases along with the return of Diego Garcia to Mauritius—a clear anti-American position.[45]

In addition to reaching agreement with India on these issues, Brezhnev utilized his visit to offer a plan for the neutralization of the Gulf.[46] It seems clear that Brezhnev's plan had three main goals: (1) reversing the diplomatic and military gains that had accrued to the United States as a result of the war and the U.S. naval buildup in the region, by the call for the elimination of all "foreign" military bases; (2) preventing the formation of a Gulf security pact based on a U.S.-armed and U.S.-supported Saudi Arabia, by the prohibition of military groupings of Gulf states linked to nuclear powers; and (3) championing Iranian interests against the United States through the call for free use of the sea lanes and normal trade exchange (the United States had been considering a naval blockade against Iran as a step toward freeing the hostages).[47]

Although the Brezhnev plan was warmly received in India, it was rejected by the United States and received only a mixed welcome in the Middle East. If one of the goals of the Brezhnev plan was to win support from Iran for Soviet policies, it did not succeed. Indeed, as the Iranian-American negotiations toward release of the hostages moved into high gear, Soviet-Iranian relations appeared to deteriorate; Afghan refugees stormed the Soviet embassy in Teheran on the anniversary of the Soviet invasion of Afghanistan and burned the Soviet flag. Even though Moscow strongly protested the action of "the unruly mob" and called for the punishment of the attackers and their organizers,[48] the official Iranian reply, while somewhat apologetic, said the attackers were justified in their actions.[49] It is doubtful whether the Soviet leaders noted the irony inherent in the Iranian statement: only a year before the Soviet press had used similar terms in justifying the Iranian seizure of the U.S. embassy in Teheran.

Nonetheless, the USSR apparently swallowed its anger, and Soviet broadcasts to Iran continued to emphasize that the USSR wanted friendly relations with Iran.[50] One cause of the Soviet effort to continue to seek close ties to Iran despite the embassy incident was the speedup of the Iranian-American talks on freeing the hostages. As the date for the Carter administration's departure from office neared, the pace of the talks intensified, and it appeared that an agreement might well be reached before Ronald Reagan took office. In an effort to prevent such a development, the Soviet media began to print and broadcast to Iran reports of an imminent U.S. attack on that country[51] and brushed aside U.S. complaints that the Soviet broadcasts were harming the negotiations.[52] The Soviet ploy was ultimately to fail, however, and on the day President Carter left office, the hostages were finally released. Thus, as Reagan took office, Moscow had to be concerned about a number of negative trends in the Middle East: a possible reconciliation between Iran and the United States, the increasing diplomatic acceptability of the U.S. military forces in the Gulf, a very severe split in the anti-Sadat grouping of Arab states, and the possibility that Arab states like Jordan and Saudi Arabia might yet be drawn into the American-sponsored Camp David peace process. Moscow was soon to try to reverse these negative trends.

Moscow Tries To Regain the Diplomatic Initiative

By the time the Communist Party of the Soviet Union (CPSU) convened its 26th Congress on February 23, 1981, the outline of the Reagan administration's Middle East policy was already clear. The United States was seeking to build an anti-Soviet alliance of Middle East states, irrespective of their mutual conflicts, thereby pursuing a policy that was the mirror image of Soviet efforts to build an "anti-imperialist" bloc in the region. In his speech to the CPSU Congress, Brezhnev outlined the thrust of the Soviet response to the Reagan policy and to the negative trends in the Middle East that had hampered Moscow in its quest for influence in the region.[53] To counterbalance the growing military power of the United States in the Gulf and Indian Ocean region and the growing diplomatic acceptability of that presence because of both the Soviet invasion of Afghanistan and the Iran-Iraq war, Brezhnev reiterated his call, first made in India in mid-December 1980, for an international agreement to neutralize the Gulf. The Soviet leader also offered—for the first time—to combine discussion of the Afghanistan situation with that of the Gulf, although he made it clear that Afghanistan's internal situation (i.e., its Communist government) was not a matter for discussion and that the USSR would not withdraw its forces from Afghanistan until the "infiltration of counter-revolutionary bands" was completely stopped and treaties were signed between Afghanistan and its neighbors to ensure that no further infiltration would take place.

As far as the Iran-Iraq war was concerned, the Soviet leader once again called for its immediate termination, stating that the Soviet Union was taking "practical steps" to achieve that goal. In discussing the Arab-Israeli conflict Brezhnev denounced the Camp David peace process and again enumerated the tripartite Soviet solution for the conflict: (1) Israeli withdrawal from all territories captured in 1967; (2) the right of the Palestinians to create their own state; and (3) the ensuring of the security of all states in the region, including Israel. Brezhnev also repeated the Soviet call for an international conference on the Arab-Israeli conflict, with the participation of the Arabs (including the PLO), Israel, the United States, and some European states. All in all, the Soviet proposals on Afghanistan, the Gulf, and the Arab-Israeli conflict, together with the announced efforts to end the Iran-Iraq war, seemed aimed at placing Moscow at the center of the stage of Middle Eastern diplomacy, a diplomatic position not enjoyed by the Soviet Union since the 1973 Arab-Israeli war.

Interestingly enough, Brezhnev also made note in his speech of two related Middle Eastern phenomena to which the USSR was having difficulty in adjusting its policies: the Khomeini revolution in Iran and the rise of fundamentalist Islam. As far as Iran was concerned, Brezhnev noted that "despite its complex and contradictory nature, it is basically an anti-imperialist revolution, although domestic and foreign reaction is seeking to alter this character." Brezhnev also offered Soviet cooperation with Iran (no mention was made of Soviet-Iraqi relations in his speech), but only on the grounds of "reciprocity," perhaps a reference to continuing anti-Soviet speeches and activities in Iran, including the seizure of the Soviet embassy in Teheran. In discussing Islam, Brezhnev acknowledged that "the liberation struggle could develop under the banner of Islam," but also noted that "experience also indicates that reaction uses Islamic slogans to start counterrevolutionary insurrections."

In the aftermath of the 26th Party Congress, Moscow moved to cultivate two Centrist Arab states, Kuwait and Jordan, to prevent them from moving toward the United States. Fortunately for Moscow, even before Sheik Sabah al Ahmad al Sabah of Kuwait and King Hussein of Jordan visited Moscow, a number of the Centrist Arabs seemed to be pulling back from the close tie with the United States that had been precipitated by the Iran-Iraq war.[54] Thus when the new U.S. Secretary of State, Alexander Haig, toured the Middle East in early April 1981 in an effort to rally support for the U.S. plan to create an anti-Soviet alignment while putting the Arab-Israeli dispute on the diplomatic "back burner," he met with little success. Two of the Arab states he visited, Jordan and Saudi Arabia, indicated that they were more concerned with what they perceived as the threat from Israel (Saudi Arabia said this explicitly) than the threat from the Soviet Union.[55] In addition, fighting had once again escalated in Lebanon, and Haig took the opportunity to strongly condemn Syria for its "brutal" actions in that country, a move not calculated to drive a wedge between Damascus and Moscow. The lack of success of the Haig visit arrested the momentum of U.S. policy in the region and set the stage for some diplomatic successes by the Soviet Union during the visits of Sheik Sabah and King Hussein.

The USSR and Kuwait

Kuwait, whose deputy premier Sheik Sabah visited Moscow on April 23, was a key target of Soviet diplomacy. As the only state in the Gulf Cooperation Council with diplomatic relations with Moscow, it was also the most "non-aligned," and the Soviet leaders evidently hoped to use Kuwait's influence within the GCC (it is the second most important country after Saudi Arabia) to prevent that organization from committing itself too closely to the U.S. side. For its part Kuwait had been carefully cultivating a relationship with the USSR since 1975, the last time Sheik Sabah had journeyed to Moscow. Then, as in April 1981, Kuwait's regional problems made it seek protection.[56] In 1975 Kuwait was confronted with territorial demands by Iraq; in 1981, although relations had improved with Iraq, a far more serious problem lay on its border with Iran, whose warplanes were occasionaly bombing and strafing Kuwaiti territory because of Kuwaiti aid to the Iraqi war effort. Under these circumstances (and also under pressure from the powerful Palestinian community in Kuwait), the Kuwaitis evidently felt they needed support not only from the United States (whose ability to aid Kuwait was in doubt since the fall of the shah, despite the sending of AWACS to Saudi Arabia), but from the Soviet Union as well. The Kuwaiti deputy premier, who was also his country's foreign minister, went a long way toward meeting his hosts' diplomatic needs during his visit to Moscow. Not only did he denounce Camp David, he also came out in favor of an international conference on the Middle East, thereby supporting a cardinal Soviet goal. In addition he announced Kuwait's opposition to the creation of foreign military bases in the Gulf, thus supporting yet another central Soviet foreign-policy goal. Finally, he joined Moscow in calling for an international conference on the Indian Ocean aimed at turning it into a "zone of peace," thereby supporting another Soviet diplomatic ploy to eliminate the U.S. military presence from the region.[57]

To be sure, there were areas of disagreement during the talks in which *Pravda* reported a "detailed exchange of views on the situation in the . . . Gulf."[58] Probably the most important issue of disagreement was Afghanistan (Kuwait continued to oppose the Soviet presence in Afghanistan), of which no mention was made in the formal communique. Nonetheless, on balance the visit was most successful as far as Moscow was concerned, since it was able to obtain Kuwaiti support for a number of major Soviet Middle East policies.

Relations with Jordan

The visit of Jordan's King Hussein in late May 1981 could also be considered a diplomatic success for Moscow. The USSR had been seriously concerned that because of Syrian military pressure, Hussein might be pushed back into the U.S. camp and into support of Camp David (Jordan had distanced itself from the United States in 1978 because of Camp David). Perhaps heightening Soviet concern was the "Jordanian option," which was being promoted by Israeli Labor party leader Shimon Peres. Until May, Peres's Labor party was leading all the Israeli public-opinion polls for the election scheduled for June 30, and Moscow may have seen a Peres victory as yet another enticement for Jordan to become involved in Camp David. For its part, however, since the 1978 Baghdad Conference, Jordan was very much a Centrist Arab state and saw far more benefit in maintaining close ties with Iraq and Saudi Arabia (which subsidized a considerable portion of the Jordanian economy) than in joining Israel and Egypt in the highly ambiguous autonomy negotiations. By 1981, the once-isolated Jordanian monarch was now part of the general Arab consensus against Camp David, although Jordan's bitter dispute with Syria continued to simmer. Indeed, the Syrian-Jordanian conflict was undoubtedly one of the topics of discussion between Brezhnev and Hussein, and *Pravda's* reference to the talks having taken place in a "business-like atmosphere" may very well have referred to disagreements over Syria.[59] Nonetheless, Hussein did come out in agreement with a number of Soviet policies. First and foremost was the convening of an international conference on the Middle East. In both his speech at the welcoming banquet and the final communique Hussein supported this Soviet goal, thereby also demonstrating his opposition to the Camp David process.[60] In addition Hussein joined Moscow in opposing foreign bases in the Gulf, thus supporting another key Soviet goal. Given the fact that the Jordanian defense minister accompanied Hussein, the groundwork may have been laid during this visit for the subsequent Soviet-Jordanian surface-to-air missile (SAM) arms deal, as the joint communique noted that the two sides had agreed to work on further increasing trade, economic, cultural, and other (i.e., military-related) matters. All in all, Moscow was quite pleased by Hussein's visit, and *New Times* correspondent Alexander Usvatov summarized Moscow's satisfaction: "It is no secret that Tel Aviv and Washington have always regarded Jordan as a "weak link" in the Arab world, counting on drawing it by hook or by crook into the separate Camp David process and into their anti-Arab and anti-Soviet plans. . . . The results of King Hussein's talks with Leonid Brezhnev and other Soviet leaders were a disappointment for those who entertained such hopes."[61]

If the visits of Sheik Sabah and King Hussein may be considered as positive developments for the USSR, in that they seemed to arrest the pro-American swing of the Centrist Arab states that had begun as a result of the outbreak of the Iran-Iraq war, Moscow was to try to reinforce this development by capitalizing on the series of crises that rocked the Middle East during the late spring and summer of 1981.

Moscow and the Middle East Crises of 1981

The Syrian Missile Crisis

The first major crisis that Moscow sought to exploit, albeit very carefully, was the emplacement of Syrian antiaircraft missiles in Lebanon.[62] Following a Phalangist-Syrian clash near the Lebanese city of Zahle and the subsequent shooting down of two Syrian helicopters by Israeli planes flying in support of the Lebanese Christians, Syria moved surface-to-air missiles into the Bekaa Valley of Lebanon to protect its air operations. It thereby broke the tacit 1976 Syrian-Israeli agreement that Israel would not interfere in the Syrian invasion of Lebanon if Syria refrained from moving SAM missiles there. When the missiles were emplaced, Begin warned that if they were not removed, Israel would destroy them—and the crisis was on.

Once again, the USSR appeared to be caught by surprise by its Syrian ally's action, but then moved to try to extract the greatest benefit from the crisis while also playing down its severity. It did so by calling the Syrian move "defensive" and by pointedly noting that the Soviet-Syrian treaty did not extend to Lebanon.[63] The fact that a number of Centrist Arab states rallied around Syria during this crisis—though to a limited degree—helped move Syria out of its diplomatic isolation in the Arab world caused by its support of Iran. This was a plus for Moscow, as was the further weakening of the

U.S. effort to build up an anti-Soviet bloc of Arab states and the increased complication of relations between Saudi Arabia, which promised aid to Syria, and the United States, Israel's main supporter, at a time when relations had already become strained over Congressional opposition to the AWACS sale to Saudi Arabia. In sum, in the short run Moscow was to benefit from the crisis since U.S. mediator Philip Habib succeeded in preventing an Israeli attack on the missiles, thereby leaving both Syria and Moscow in an improved Middle East position; however, the fact that Habib was to successfully mediate the crisis was to set a bad precedent as far as Moscow was concerned.

The Israeli Raid on Iraq's Nuclear Reactor

If Moscow gained some benefit from the Syrian missile crisis, it proved less able to exploit the second major crisis of 1981—the Israeli destruction of the Iraqi nuclear reactor.[64] The Israeli action inflamed the Arab world far more than did the Syrian-Israeli confrontation over the Syrian missiles in Lebanon. Many Arabs felt humiliated by the fact that the Israeli aircraft, which flew over Jordanian and Saudi airspace on the way to and from Iraq, were able to come and go unscathed while eliminating the most advanced nuclear installation of any Arab country. As might be expected, Moscow moved quickly to try to exploit this situation, not only condemning the Israeli raid but also pointing to the fact that the Israeli action was carried out with U.S.-supplied aircraft and that it took place despite—or indeed because of—the U.S. AWACS radar planes operating in Saudi Arabia. Reagan's decision to postpone shipment of additional F-16 fighter bombers to Israel because of the attack was deprecated by Moscow, which sought to exploit the Israeli action by focusing Arab attention on the "Israeli threat" to the Arab world (rather than the "Soviet threat") and to undermine the U.S. position in the region as Israel's chief supporter, while at the same time improving Soviet-Iraqi relations. In addition, Moscow evidently hoped that the Israeli attack would help to rebuild the "anti-imperialist" Arab unity that had been so badly dissipated by the Iran-Iraq war.

Moscow also may have seen the Israeli raid as undercutting Egyptian efforts to reenter the Arab mainstream, since the raid took place only four days after a Begin-Sadat summit. Egypt had sold Iraq thousands of tons of Soviet ammunition and spare parts to aid it in its war with Iran—something noted with displeasure in Moscow, which was concerned about Sadat's lessening isolation. Fortunately for Moscow, the Israeli raid did serve to temporarily abort any Iraqi-Egyptian rapprochement, despite Sadat's denunciation of the Israeli action.

Moscow, however, was to be less successful in its goal of exploiting the Israeli raid to undermine the U.S. position in the Arab world and in particular to improve Soviet ties with Iraq. Although there had been calls in the Arab world to embargo oil to the United States because of the raid, the Reagan administration's decision to postpone the shipment of promised F-16 fighter bombers to Israel and to join with Iraq in a UN Security Council vote condemning Israel seemed to deflate any such Arab pressures. Indeed, the Iraqi-American cooperation at the UN seemed to set the stage for improved Iraqi-American relations in general. Iraqi President Saddam Hussein, on the ABC television program "Issues and Answers," stated his interest in expanding diplomatic contacts with the United States and announced that he would treat the head of the U.S.-interests section in the Belgian embassy in Baghdad as the head of a diplomatic mission.[65]

Israeli-PLO Hostilities in Lebanon

While the furor of the Israeli attack on the Iraqi reactor slowly died, Middle East tensions were kept alive during the summer by a number of other events that Moscow sought to exploit. In the first place, following the reelection of Menahem Begin's Likud party, Israel launched a series of attacks against Palestinian positions in Lebanon as part of its continuing effort to keep the PLO off balance and prevent it from launching terrorist attacks against Israel. The fighting quickly escalated with the PLO shelling towns in northern Israel and the Israelis bombing PLO headquarters in Beirut, causing a number of civilian casualties in the process. The United States condemned the bombing of Beirut and again delayed the shipment of F-16s to Israel—at the same time sending Habib back to the Middle East to work out a ceasefire (something that he accomplished in late July), whereas Moscow seized the opportunity to once again link the Israeli actions to the United States and called for sanctions against Israel. The bombing of Beirut served to further inflame Arab tempers against Israel and the United States (there were once again calls for an oil boycott of the United States and heavy criticism of American support of Israel not only from the Steadfastness Front but also from such Centrist states as Jordan and Kuwait). All this activity, of course, served to further divert Arab attention from the continued Soviet occupation of Afghanistan, while underlining the Soviet claim that it was U.S.-supported Israel, not the Soviet Union, that was the main threat to the Arab world.

The Gulf of Sidra

The fourth in the series of Middle East crises took place in mid-August, and for the first time it was the United States, not Israel, that was directly involved. This incident involved the shooting down of two Libyan interceptor aircraft (SU-22), which had initially fired upon two U.S. aircraft protecting U.S. maneuvers in the Gulf of Sidra. Kaddafi claimed this region as Libyan territorial waters, but the United States (and most of the international community, including the USSR) claimed the gulf was international waters.

Whether or not Libya actually planned the incident, it did not take long for Moscow to try to exploit the battle over the Gulf of Sidra for its own benefit.[66] Based on the initial Soviet reaction to the gulf battle, it appears as if Moscow was caught by surprise. Nonetheless, after a day of reporting events without commentary, once Moscow appeared certain that there would be no escalation, it sought to show the Arabs that the incident demonstrated how dangerous it was for them to have a U.S. fleet operating off their shores.

In addition to using the Gulf of Sidra to try to lessen the diplomatic acceptability of the U.S. military presence in the Gulf and noting the highly negative Arab response to the American role in the incident, Moscow also cited it as justification for the signing of the Tripartite Treaty by Ethiopia, Libya, and South Yemen. The USSR praised the treaty as "an important stage in strengthening the national liberation movement's solidarity and in stepping up their struggle against imperialism and reaction and for peace and progress."[67]

Moscow also maintained, however (in an apparent effort to reassure Saudi Arabia and North Yemen), that the treaty was "not directed against any other country or people."[68] Nonetheless, the text of the Tripartite Treaty, which noted that one of its goals was the struggle against "reaction"—a commonly used term for the conservative Arab states of the Gulf along with Egypt and the Sudan—may, in the long run, prove counterproductive to Soviet efforts to improve relations with the conservative Gulf states, given the close tie between the Tripartite Treaty nations and Moscow.[69]

The Iranian Crises

While Moscow was seeking to exploit the Libyan-American clash in the Gulf of Sidra to weaken the U.S. position in the Middle East, it was trying to follow the same policy during upheavals in Iran. These included the ouster and escape to Europe of Iranian President Bani Sadr, the assassination of his successor Mohammed Ali Rajai along with a number of key Iranian Islamic Republican party leaders such as Ayatollah Beheshti, and a series of additional bombings and other attacks directed against the fundamentalist Khomeini government by the opposition Mujahadeen.

The central Soviet concern in its policy toward Iran was a fear that after the hostage release the United States and Iran might move toward a rapprochement, particularly because of Iranian military requirements due to the Iran-Iraq war. Fortunately for Moscow, anti-Americanism remained the central foreign-policy theme of the Khomeini regime during 1981 as in the previous year, and the regime's enemies were usually branded American or Zionist agents. Given Moscow's previous displeasure with Bani Sadr, his departure was no loss, but the Soviet leadership was quite unhappy with the assassination of Beheshti, whom *Pravda* characterized on July 3 as "one of the most consistent proponents of an anti-imperialist, anti-American policy."[70] The bombings at the end of June and at the end of August, while eliminating a number of top Iranian leaders, gave Moscow the opportunity to reinforce Teheran's suspicions that the Central Intelligence Agency (CIA) was behind the incidents. Moscow also sought to link U.S. aid to the Afghan rebels (early in 1981 Reagan had announced publicly that the United States was aiding the Afghani resistance) with U.S. aid to the opposition in Iran in an effort both to discredit the Afghan resistance in Iran and to drive a further wedge between Teheran and Washington.

Yet while Iranian-American relations remained highly strained, it did not appear as if Moscow was making a great deal of headway in improving its own position in Iran. Iranian leaders continued to be suspicious of Moscow both for its centuries-long record of hostility toward Iran and because of suspected ties between Moscow and Iranian ethnic minorities fighting for independence, such as the Kurds. Indeed, Moscow may well have been placed in a difficult position when in late October 1981 the Kurdish Democratic party of Iran, led by Abdul Rahman Gassemlou, joined the opposition front headed by Bani Sadr and Mujahadeen leader Massoud Rajavi.[71] Moscow and Gassemlou had long maintained friendly ties, and the formation of the opposition front once again posed a difficult problem of choice for the USSR.

Yet another irritant in the Soviet-Iranian relationship has been Teheran's unhappiness that Moscow has taken only a neutral position on the Iran-Iraq war in the face of "flagrant Iraqi aggression," as the late Iranian Prime Minister Ali Rajai told Soviet Ambassador Vladimir Vinogradov on February 15,[72] a message repeated in October by the Iranian Ambassador Mohammed Mokri, during an Iranian delegation's visit to Moscow.[73] Disagreements have also arisen because of Iran's unhappiness with the Soviet intervention in Afghanistan, despite Soviet efforts to tie the CIA to the resistance movements in both Iran and Afghanistan. Finally, the Islamic fundamentalist regime remains suspicious of the Tudeh party and its ally, the majority faction of the Fedayeen guerrillas, as shown by Iranian Prime Minister Hussein Moussavi's declaration that members of the Tudeh and majority Fedayeen would be executed if, upon joining the revolutionary guards or other fundamentalist organizations, they failed to state their (Communist) party affiliation.[74]

Sadat's Assassination

While Moscow sought to exploit the spate of assassinations in Iran, it was the assassination of Egyptian leader Anwar Sadat, the centerpiece of the anti-Soviet Middle Eastern bloc that the United States was seeking to create, from which Moscow hoped to benefit the most. Indeed, three weeks before his assassination, the Egyptian leader had expelled 7 Soviet diplomats, including the Soviet ambassador, and about 1,000 Soviet advisers, on grounds that they were fomenting sedition in Egypt.[75] In addition, he dissolved the Egyptian-Soviet Friendship Society and arrested its president, Abd As-Salam Az-Zayyat, as part of a major crackdown on Egyptians from the Egyptian left and the fundamentalist Moslem right who were opposed to Sadat's policies.[76]

The assassination of Sadat by Moslem fundamentalists was thus greeted with considerable relief in Moscow, although there was a difference of opinion on the part of Soviet commentators on the future policies of the new regime. *Pravda* on October 14 cited the statement of the National Progressive party, which opposed the referendum for the election of Husni Mubarak to Egypt's presidency on the grounds that he intended to pursue Sadat's policies, "in particular to continue the Camp David policy and strengthen the alliance with the U.S." On the other hand *Izvestia* commentator Alexander Bovin, a senior Soviet analyst on the Middle East, said that he thought Egypt's policies might change after Israel withdrew from the Sinai in April 1982.[77] In any case, while Moscow saw the possibility of an improvement in relations with Egypt and both before and after the assassination gave propaganda support to General Shazli, the exiled leader of the Egyptian "Patriotic Front" based in Libya (Shazli was urging Egypt to return to the Arab fold and improve ties with Moscow),[78] it expressed considerable irritation with the U.S. response to Sadat's assassination. Perhaps hoping for a repeat of the uncertain U.S. reaction to the collapse of the shah's regime in Iran, Moscow seemed particularly upset by Reagan's strong response to Sadat's assassination. This response included the alerting of U.S. forces in the Mediterranean along with elements of the Rapid Deployment Force (RDF) in the United States, the movement of ships of the Sixth Fleet toward Egypt, and the dispatch of former U.S. Presidents Carter, Ford, and Nixon to Egypt for Sadat's funeral.[79] On October 12 Moscow issued a warning to the United States against what it termed a "gross interference" in the internal affairs of Egypt, stating that "what is going on around Egypt cannot help but affect the security interests of the Soviet Union," which will "keep a close watch on the development of events."[80]

Unlike the situation in Iran in 1978–1979, however, the United States did not appear deterred by the Kremlin warning. Indeed, in addition to pledging support to Mubarak, it dispatched several AWACS radar planes to patrol the border between Egypt and Libya, while announcing that it would expand the planned U.S. Middle East military exercise, Bright Star, scheduled for November 1981. In addition, the United States promised to step up arms shipments to Egypt and the Sudan, both of whom were seen as being threatened by Libya.[81]

In the face of both the U.S. pledge of support for Mubarak and the new Egyptian president's initial consolidation of power (he overwhelmingly won the referendum on October 13 and was sworn in on October 14), Moscow appeared to change course somewhat on October 15 as Brezhnev sent Mubarak a congratulatory telegram on his election, pledging that Moscow would reciprocate any Egyptian readiness to improve Soviet-Egyptian relations.[82] In making this move, Moscow may have realized that there would be no immediate change in Egyptian foreign policy despite Sadat's assassination, and the most that could be hoped for was a "change in the direction of the wind," as Bovin had stated after the Israeli withdrawal in April.

The assassination of Sadat, as a major turning point in the Middle East, also gave Moscow the opportunity to again call for an international conference to settle the Arab-Israeli conflict. This was one of the themes of the visit by PLO leader Yasir Arafat to Moscow two weeks after the Sadat assassination, when the PLO leader gave strong support to Moscow's call for the conference.[83] For its part Moscow granted the PLO mission in Moscow full diplomatic status, thus conferring increased diplomatic legitimacy on the Palestinian organization. While the Soviet move was the culmination of an increasingly close Soviet-PLO relationship, and the USSR may have wished to consolidate the relationship further in the period of uncertainty following the death of Sadat, Moscow nonetheless also may have wished to counter the possibility of the development of a formal relationship between Washington and the PLO. During his mediation of the fighting in Lebanon in July, U.S. special representative Philip Habib had conducted de facto negotiations with the PLO (albeit via intermediaries), and in August both Anwar Sadat and former U.S. National Security Adviser Zbigniew Brzezinski had advocated a U.S. dialogue with the PLO.[84] Then, followng Sadat's funeral, former Presidents Carter and Ford stated that at some point the United States would have to begin to talk to members of the PLO, if not to Arafat himself.[85]

Soviet Policy from the Assassination of Sadat to the Israeli Invasion of Lebanon

While Moscow was seeking to shore up relations with the PLO, it welcomed the election of the anti-NATO Andreas Papandreou to the premiership of Greece in late October, as well as the failure of President Reagan to convince Jordanian King Hussein to join Camp David or to reject a major surface-to-air missile deal with Moscow in favor of a U.S. system during Hussein's visit to Washington in early November. Nonetheless, a number of other Middle Eastern developments took place during the fall of 1981 that were not to Moscow's satisfaction. In the first place, after a long and bitter debate, the U.S. Senate agreed to the sale of the AWACS aircraft to Saudi Arabia in late October, a development that appeared to cement U.S.-Saudi ties. Second, in a major policy change, a number of European states agreed to provide troops for the Sinai multinational force, thereby at least tacitly supporting Camp David. Third, the United States successfully mounted a major military exercise in the Middle East (Bright Star), thus demonstrating that it was developing the capability of a quick intervention there to aid its friends.

Moscow's central fear in the AWACS debate was that congressional approval for AWACS would cement the Saudi-American relationship to the point that Saudi Arabia might be persuaded to support the Camp David agreements and also to provide facilities for the U.S. Rapid Deployment Force "in direct proximity to the extremely rich Persian Gulf oil fields"[86]—a fear that was even more openly expressed after the Senate approved (by failing to vote down) the AWACS agreement.

While the AWACS approval was a blow to the Soviet Middle East position, so too was the decision of several key European states to provide troops for the multinational force that the United States was organizing for the Sinai. The rapid evolution of the multinational force during 1981 was of clear concern to Moscow, which saw it as a cover for the American RDF.[87] Ironically, it was because of Moscow's

July 1979 veto of the United Nations Emergency Force (UNEF) to patrol the Sinai (which, most likely, would have remained composed primarily of Third World states and thus not a possible military threat against Soviet positions in the region) that the United States worked to create the multinational force.

The commitment of U.S. troops for the force, a goal long pursued by Israel (which saw the United States as a far more reliable barrier to a future Egyptian attack than the UN), was not approved by the U.S. Congress or Sadat until well into 1981, and for most of the year Western Europe held aloof from participating in the multinational force. The election of Francois Mitterand to the presidency of France, however, together with the assassination of Sadat, galvanized the Europeans to take a more active role. By the end of November the participation of France, England, Holland, and Italy in the Sinai force, despite some initial objections by Israel on the terms of their partic-ipation, was set. As might be expected, Moscow strongly opposed U.S. and especially Western European participation in the multinational force. In the case of Western Euorpe, Moscow had long seen the Middle East as an area where, because of a much greater European oil dependency, a wedge could be driven between the United States and its NATO allies.[88] Consequently, Moscow condemned what it saw as a Western European "knuckling under" to Washington's "diktat" on the multinational force.[89] Because the multinational force was tied to the Camp David agreements, Moscow saw European participation in the Sinai force as a de facto legitimatization of Camp David, a development that ended U.S. isolation as the sole Western state supporting the agreements.[90]

The Bright Star military exercise, which also involved some British and French participation, may be considered another gain for Wash-ington—and concomitantly a loss for Moscow. The exercises took place in Egypt (with the participation of units of the Egyptian army and air force), the Sudan, Somalia, and Oman. Moscow denounced Bright Star as a rehearsal for the invasion of Libya and the Middle East oil fields (the Bright Star exercise was commanded by the head of the RDF), a device for intimidating "progressive" governments in the Middle East such as Libya, Ethiopia, and South Yemen, and a technique for strengthening pro-U.S. regimes in the region.[91] It also had to be concerned about the rather impressive showing of the U.S. military, including a bombing run by B-52 bombers on a direct flight from the United States. This stood in sharp contrast to the difficulties encountered by the United States in its abortive hostage rescue mission in Iran in April 1980. Indeed, Moscow may well have been concerned that the successful U.S. Rapid Deployment Force exercise would have a positive influence on such Arab countries as Kuwait—which had turned to Moscow, in part, because it could not be sure that the United States either had the capability or will to help it in case of a conflict with an unfriendly neighbor like Iran, which had again bombed Kuwaiti territory in early October. The conclusion of a major U.S.-Pakistani military agreement, which held out the possibility of U.S. use of the Pakistani naval base at Gwandar and air base at Peshewar, seemed to further enhance U.S. capabilities for military intervention in the Gulf.[92] Finally, the Egyptian component of Bright Star, in which 4,000 U.S. and Egyptian troops participated, also served to improve relations between the U.S. and Egyptian military and between the Mubarak and Reagan governments. Egyptian Defense Minister Abdel Halim Abu Ghazala stated that the exercises were "a rehearsal for a possible joint operation" to protect the oil fields of the Gulf.[93]

While the United States continued to improve its military and political position in the Middle East, Soviet diplomacy continued to encounter difficulties. The collapse of the Arab summit at Fez, Morocco, again underlined the deep division in the Arab world and how far it was from the "anti-imperialist" Arab unity that Moscow desired.[94] Even the Israeli annexation of the Golan Heights in December 1981 did not serve to rally the Arab world around Moscow's Steadfastness Front client Syria. Interestingly enough, however, when the Syrian Foreign Minister Abdul Khaddam journeyed to Moscow in January 1982 seeking a Soviet-Syrian Strategic Cooperation Treaty similar to the one between the United States and Israel (which the United States had suspended following the Golan annexation), the Soviet leadership resisted, perhaps fearing that Syria might drag it into an unwanted adventure, and the joint communique noted that the talks had proceeded in a "spirit of understanding"—the usual Soviet code words to indicate disagreement.[95] Nonetheless in its broadcasts to the Arab world Moscow sought to capitalize on the Golan annexation, as well as U.S. pressure against Libya, to rally the Arab world around the USSR's Steadfastness Front clients, but with little success. Similarly, the Soviet leadership sought to discredit the United States by exploiting the actions of a deranged Israeli who fired into an Arab crowd in the Mosque of Omar in Jerusalem. As *Izvestia* noted: "The crime in the Moslem shrine should be viewed not as an individual terrorist act, committed by a fanatic individual, but as a logical consequence of a large scale anti-Palestinian campaign unleashed by the Zionist authorities of Israel supported by their transoceanic patrons."[96]

Nonetheless, despite these Soviet efforts, Middle East dynamics were moving in an anti-Soviet direction even before the Israeli invasion of Lebanon. Moscow's client, Libya, was discredited when the anti-Kaddafi forces of Hassan Habré consolidated their control over most of Chad. The Morocco-Algerian confrontation over the Spanish Sahara intensified as Morocco signed a major military agreement with the United States in which it provided transit facilities for the U.S. RDF in return for increased shipments of military equipment.[97] In addition, Morocco boycotted meetings of the Organization of African Unity (OAU), a pan-African organization that Moscow also hoped could unify on an "anti-imperialist" basis, because some OAU members recognized the Algerian-backed Polisario rebels. Additional problems for Moscow lay in the increasingly severe difficulties that both Syria and the PLO were encountering. In the case of Syria, there was an antiregime uprising by the Muslim Brotherhood in the city of Hama in February 1982 in which as many as 12,000 people are reported to have been killed. Two months later Syria blocked the Iraqi oil pipeline that ran through Syria, an event that, while weakening Iraq, exacerbated the Syrian-Iraqi conflict, and made Moscow's hopes for an "anti-imperialist" Arab unity dim further. Meanwhile the Lebanese-based PLO, already under heavy Syrian pressure, found itself fighting in southern Lebanon against Shiite forces who were protesting PLO activities in their section of the country.[98] Perhaps the greatest problem for Moscow, however, was the gradual rapprochement between Egypt and the Centrist Arabs. Induced in part by the Israeli withdrawal from the last part of the Sinai on April 25, 1982, the rapprochement was accelerated by Iran's success in its war with Iraq as the Iranians took the offensive and threatened Iraqi territory in the late spring. The Iranian advance frightened the Gulf states, who turned both to the United States and to Egypt for support. Iraq had long been a recipient of Egyptian military equipment and had moderated its position toward Egypt as a result,[99] and now other Gulf states moved in the same direction. In addition, the warm official greetings by Jordan and Morocco to Egypt after the final Israeli Sinai withdrawal appeared to signal their interest in improved ties with Egypt.[100] Consequently, by the time of the Israeli invasion of Lebanon, there was a clear move toward rapprochement between Egypt and the Centrist Arabs. Indeed, a special meeting of the Steadfastness Front took place at the end of May 1982 to try to reverse this trend, as the front proclaimed its opposition to any normalization of relations with Egypt until it renounced Camp David.[101]

Thus it was a badly disunited Arab world, whose pro-Soviet members were isolated and whose Centrist states were gradually moving toward a reconciliation with Egypt, that faced Soviet policymakers on the eve of the Israeli invasion of Lebanon.

The Israeli Invasion of Lebanon and Its Aftermath

The Israeli invasion, which took place on June 6, 1982, had been predicted by both Western and Soviet commentators and clearly came as no surprise. Israel had long proclaimed its desire to rid itself of the PLO artillery that threatened its northern towns, and the SAM missiles that Syria had emplaced in the Bekaa Valley of Lebanon in April 1981 had also been cited by Israeli spokesmen as targets for destruction.

This being the case, it is surprising that there was no contingency planning among Syria, the PLO, and Moscow for the invasion. The lack of coordination between Syria and the PLO may perhaps be explained by the conflict between Assad and Arafat, who feared the Syrian leader was trying to take over the PLO, and the lack of contingency planning between Syria and the USSR may possibly be explained by Moscow's unwillingness to extend the provisions of the Soviet-Syrian Treaty to cover Syrian forces in Lebanon.[102] It is the lack of Soviet-PLO preparation that is somewhat surprising. Perhaps Moscow felt that any Israeli invasion would be a repeat of the limited 1978 Litani operation; perhaps Moscow hoped that the PLO, which had frequently proclaimed its readiness for an Israeli assault (Arafat reportedly made an inspection of PLO military positions on June 2),[103] could indeed cause so many casualties among the casualty-sensitive Israelis that the invasion would halt after only a few days; perhaps Moscow thought that U.S. pressure would force Israel to withdraw as in 1978; or perhaps Moscow simply did not wish to run the risks of too close a military involvement with such a fragmented organization.[104] In any case the lack of prior consultation became quite evident in the first three days of the invasion as Israeli forces, in a three-pronged operation, overran the PLO positions in South Lebanon, pushed the PLO back to Beirut, and then destroyed Syria's SAM missiles and drove the Syrians out of the southern part of the Bekaa Valley.[105]

While space limitations preclude an extensive examination of Soviet policy during the war, there is one central point to be made.[106] Moscow's reaction to the Israeli invasion was essentially a nonmilitary one: the USSR confined its activity to seeking condemnation of the invasion at the United Nations and issuing a series of general warnings to both Israel and the United States, as the war progressed. Needless to say, these actions were not efficacious. Moscow soon came in for a great deal of criticism from its Arab clients, such as Libya, and a number of PLO factions because of its lack of aid while Israel was soundly defeating both the PLO and Syria and mounting a two-month-long siege of Beirut.[107] In seeking to explain Soviet behavior during the war there are several factors to take into consideration. First, from a purely military standpoint there were serious obstacles to any commitment of Soviet troops to the conflict. Although in the past decade the USSR had committed its troops and/or those of surrogates, such as Cuba, to Third World conflicts no less than three times (Angola in 1976, Ethiopia in 1978, and Afghanistan in 1979), in each case the opponent was not a significant military power, and Moscow had secure bases of operations for its troops. In the case of Lebanon, however, Moscow's opponent would be Israel, a formidable military power with a first-rate airforce, a highly trained army, and the latest in military technology, some of which was supplied by the United States. Second, the Soviet leadership could not be sure that the United States would not actively intervene if Soviet troops entered the fighting.[108] Third, the destruction of Syria's SAM missiles and its most modern tank, the T-72, in battles with the Israelis, along with eighty-five Syrian planes, had to give Moscow pause. These were the same weapons on which the defense of the USSR was based, and Soviet military equipment was a prime export commodity earning the USSR billions of dollars a year in hard currency.[109] Finally, it should not be overlooked that the destruction of the SAM system in the Bekaa Valley and, by implication, Israel's ability to similarly destroy the SAMs located in Syrian territory meant that Israel had virtually complete air supremacy in the region of the fighting—a significant deterrent to any major Soviet operation.

This having been said, still there were a number of things Moscow could have done that it did not do, especially the airlifting of elements of an airborne division to Syria and the dispatch of "volunteers" via Syria to aid the PLO in areas of Lebanon, such as Tripoli, to which the Israeli army had not yet penetrated. Both moves would have been seen as major deterrents to further Israeli activity and would have demonstrated to the Arabs as a whole that Moscow was indeed aiding them and would have reinforced the position of Moscow's Steadfastness Front allies. Such moves, however, entailed serious risks of involvement in the fighting, and the possible escalation into a superpower confrontation as indeed occurred during the 1973 war. In 1973 Moscow, by actively supplying the Arabs during the fighting and openly threatening armed intervention in the later stage of the war when Israel had successfully gone on the offensive, had been willing to take such risks.[110] In 1982, even when its strategic power had increased markedly vis-à-vis the United States, Moscow was to prove unwilling to risk an escalation of the fighting. In seeking to explain Soviet behavior, one can point to one major difference between 1973 and 1982. In 1973 the Arabs were united behind Cairo and Damascus in their war effort against Israel and had placed an oil embargo against the United States, and Moscow may well have seen the possibility of a decisive blow being struck against U.S. influence in the region. In 1982, however, the Arabs were so disunited that they proved unable even to call a summit conference to take action against Israel during the war. It must have seemed to Moscow that the bulk of the Arab world, unhappy with Syria because of its backing of Iran in the Iran-Iraq war, was not going to rally behind the Syrian regime of Hafez Assad or, for that matter, behind the PLO, which many distrusted.[111] In addition, given the increasingly severe Iranian military threat against Iraq and the Arab Gulf states as a whole, Saudi Arabia and its Gulf Cooperation Council allies were not about to place an oil embargo on the United States—to whom they might have to turn for protection against Iran— especially at a time when an oil glut was forcing down prices. Under these circumsances Moscow evidently decided that if the Arabs were not going to help themselves, Moscow was not going to take any risks to help them. Nonetheless, as a superpower eager to have a hand in developments throughout the world and especially in the Middle East (a region Soviet leaders frequently remind the world is in "close proximity to the southern borders of the USSR"), Moscow had to at least give the appearance that it was taking an active role as events developed, particularly since the United States was sending its Middle East troubleshooter Philip Habib to try to peacefully end the Beirut seige. Should Habib's efforts prove successful, this would further enhance U.S. diplomatic credibility in the region, while reinforcing the view of the late Egyptian President Anwar Sadat that the United States held "99% of the cards in the Arab-Israeli dispute." Moscow, therefore, adopted a two-tiered diplomatic approach. On the one hand it issued a series of warnings to Israel about the consequences of its actions in Lebanon and sought wherever possible to link the United States to the Isracli invasion so as to discredit U.S. diplomatic efforts to end the Lebanese crisis. On the other hand it began to openly appeal to the Arabs to unite so as to confront the Israelis. Moscow also made extensive efforts to show that its weaponry did work well, albeit with only limited success. Indeed, Moscow's credibility in the Arab world, already shaken by its failure to aid its Arab clients, suffered another blow when, after Brezhnev warned the United States against sending troops to Lebanon, the United States did so anyway, and the Soviet leader was compelled to openly appeal to Reagan to save the PLO from destruction.[112]

Then, just as U.S. diplomacy had dominated the discussions leading to the PLO exodus from Beirut, so too did the U.S. move to keep the diplomatic initiative following the exodus. Thus on September 1, 1982, President Reagan announced his plan for a Middle East peace settlement. In a clear effort to gain Centrist Arab support for his plan, Reagan called for a stop to Israeli settlement activity on the West Bank and announced U.S. refusal to accept any Israeli claim to sovereignty over the West Bank. To satisfy the Israelis, Reagan emphasized U.S. concern for Israel's security, asserted that Israel's final borders should not be the pre-1967 war boundaries, called for the unity of Jerusalem and direct Arab-Israeli negotiations, and re-affirmed U.S. opposition to a Palestinian state on the West Bank. In his most controversial statement, one also aimed at obtaining Centrist Arab support, Reagan called for a fully autonomous Palestinian entity linked to Jordan. Moscow, while denouncing the Reagan plan—and denigrating Begin's rapid rejection of it, was concerned that the plan might prove attractive in the Arab world. Indeed *Izvestia* correspondent Vladimir Kudravtzev noted that "judging from press reports 'moderate' and 'pro-Western' Arab regimes find positive elements in the American initiative."[113]

Given this situation, Moscow seemed pleased by the outcome of the Arab summit at Fez, Morocco, which not only indicated that the Arab world had regained a semblance of unity[114] but also brought forth a peace plan that, except for its lack of explicit clarity as to Israel's right to exist, was quite close to the long-standing Soviet peace plan.[115] The Fez plan called for (1) Israeli withdrawal from all territories occupied in 1967, including Arab Jerusalem; (2) the dismantling of settlements established by Israel in the occupied territories; (3) guarantees for worship and the exercise of religious rites for all religions; (4) affirmation of the right of the Palestinian people to self-determination, and the exercise of their inalienable national rights under the leadership of the PLO, their sole legitimate representative, with compensation to be paid for those who do not wish to return; (5) a transition period for the West Bank and Gaza under the supervision of the UN for a period not exceeding a few months; (6) the establishment of an independent Palestinian state with Jerusalem as its capital; (7) the guarantee of the peace and security of all states in the region, including the Palestinian state, by the UN Security Council; and (8) the guarantee of the implementation of these principles by the UN Security Council.[116] Moscow also was pleased that the Sudanese proposal to formally readmit Egypt to the Arab League was rejected.[117]

Nonetheless, the Fez conference did not reject the Reagan plan, thereby leaving it, along with the Fez plan, as one of the solutions that the Arabs would consider to resolve the post-Beirut diplomatic situation in the Middle East. With both the Reagan and Fez plans now being considered, Moscow evidently felt that it too had to enter the diplomatic competition, and in a speech on September 15, during the visit of PDRY leader Ali Nasser Mohammed, one of Moscow's few remaining Arab allies, Brezhnev announced the Soviet Union's own peace plan.[118] While a number of its points were repetitions of previous Soviet proposals, others seem to have been added to emphasize the similarity between the Fez and Soviet plans. The elements of the Soviet peace plan that repeated earlier Soviet proposals were Moscow's call for the withdrawal of Israeli forces from the Golan Heights, the West Bank, the Gaza Strip, and Lebanon to the lines that existed before the June 1967 war; the establishment of a Palestinian state on the West Bank and Gaza; the right of all states in the region to a secure and independent existence; and the termination of the state of war between Israel and the Arab states. These points in many ways resembled the Fez plan, except for Moscow's more explicit call for Israel's right to exist and an end to the state of war between Israel and the Arab world; the new elements in the Brezhnev peace plan seemed to be virtually modeled on the Fez plan. Thus Moscow called for the Palestinian refugees to be given the right to return to their homes or receive compensation for their abandoned property, for the return of East Jerusalem to the Arabs and its incorporation into the Palestinian state, with freedom of access for believers to the sacred places of the three religions throughout Jerusalem, and for Security Council guarantees for the final settlement. Brezhnev also took the opportunity to repeat the long-standing Soviet call for an international conference on the Middle East, with all interested parties participating, including the PLO, again characterized by the Soviet leader as "the sole legitimate representative of the Arab people in Palestine."

In modeling the Soviet peace plan on Fez, Brezhnev evidently sought to prevent the Arabs from moving to embrace the Reagan plan. Nonetheless, with the United States clearly possessing the diplomatic initiative in the Middle East after the PLO pullout from Beirut and with both Jordanian King Hussein and PLO leader Arafat, along with other Arab leaders, expressing interest in the Reagan plan, Moscow was on the diplomatic defensive. Given this situation, it is not surprising that Brezhnev seized upon the massacres in the Sabra and Shatilla refugee camps to point out to Arafat "if anyone had any illusions that Washington was going to support the Arabs . . . these illusions have now been drowned in streams of blood in the Palestinian camps. . . ."[119]

Nonetheless, despite the massacres, Arafat evidently felt that there was value in pursuing the Reagan plan, and he began to meet regularly with his erstwhile enemy, King Hussein of Jordan, to work out a joint approach to the United States. Such maneuvering infuriated Syria, which sought to use pro-Syrian elements within the PLO to pressure Arafat into abandoning his new policy, a development that further exacerbated relations between Assad and Arafat. In addition, evidently fearing the weakening of the Steadfastness Front and the possibility of the PLO's (or at least Arafat's Fatah wing) defecting from it, Moscow continued to warn the Arabs about what it called U.S. efforts to split the PLO and to draw Jordan and Saudi Arabia into supporting the Reagan plan, which the USSR termed a cover for Camp David. Despite the Soviet warnings, however, many Arabs were clearly interested in giving the Reagan plan a chance—and getting the United States to ensure Israel's departure from Lebanon. Under these circumstances there was little overt criticism of the Reagan plan, something that Brezhnev's successor, Yuri Andropov, learned to his displeasure when an Arab delegation, headed by King Hussein, journeyed to Moscow in early December 1982 to discuss the Fez plan with the new Soviet leader. Even though *Pravda* gave page-one coverage to the talks and to the significance of the Arab delegation's visit, its report that the discussions took place in a "businesslike and friendly atmosphere" and that there was "an exchange of opinions" reflected the fact that the Soviet leader was unable to get the Arab leaders to either criticize the Reagan plan or agree to Moscow's proposal for an international conference on the Middle East.

Andropov was to receive additional evidence of Moscow's diminution of influence in the Middle East, and the rise in U.S. influence, when PLO leader Yasir Arafat journeyed to Moscow in mid-January 1983.[120] Arafat, who in the past had supported Soviet plans for an international conference to solve the Arab-Israeli conflict, now only conceded that such a conference "might open a road to the settlement."[121] Even more discouraging for Moscow must have been the PLO leader's announced agreement to the establishment of a confederation between Jordan and "an independent Palestinian state after its creation." Although Moscow was in favor of the creation of an independent Palestinian state, its linkage to Jordan, a Centrist state, not only seemed to associate the PLO at least partially with the Reagan plan but also appeared to mean its defection from the Steadfastness Front, which had already been badly weakened by the Israeli invasion. Consequently, the USSR only expressed its "understanding" of the PLO position—a diplomatic way of demonstrating its opposition.[122]

Yet another negative development, as far as Moscow was concerned, was a resumption of the momentum for a reconciliation between Egypt and the Centrist bloc, which had been temporarily interrupted by the Israeli invasion of Lebanon. Indeed, the visit of Iraqi and United Arab Emirates (UAE) military delegations to Cairo in December[123] and the calls by both Arafat and Iraqi Deputy Prime Minister Tariq Aziz for Egypt to reenter the Arab world without having to renounce Camp David seemed to signal that the end of Egypt's isolation in the Arab world might soon be at hand.[124] Under these circumstances, with its Middle East position continuing to deteriorate, it is not surprising that Moscow decided to send the highly sophisticated SAM-5 surface-to-air missile system to Syria, a move clearly aimed at reinforcing Soviet ties to Syria before the Syrians might opt for the U.S. initiative.[125]

In any case, Moscow's decision to send the SAM-5 missiles to Syria provides a useful point of departure for drawing some conclusions about the thrust of Soviet policy toward the Middle East in the period since the Camp David agreements.

Conclusions

Two main conclusions may be drawn from this study of Soviet policy toward the Middle East in the four-year period between the Camp David agreements and the Israeli invasion of Lebanon. The first is that Soviet policy toward the Middle East has been primarily a reaction to a series of regional developments that Moscow not only did not cause, but was increasingly unable to shape to fit Soviet goals in the region. The second conclusion is that Soviet influence in the Middle East is very limited indeed, and the Soviet position in the region was weaker at the end of 1982 than it was at the time of the Camp David accords in September 1978.

In examining the reactive nature of Soviet policy, one must first note that a number of Middle East developments have worked to Moscow's advantage. One example of this is the highly negative Arab reaction to the Camp David agreements, as a result of which a large anti-Egyptian coalition of Arab states was formed. Moscow clearly hoped that this coalition could be transformed into the "anti-imperialist" Arab unity it had so long desired. Another such development was the fall of the shah and the rise to power of Ayatollah Khomeini. As a result of the shah's fall, not only did the United States lose its "policeman" of the Gulf, but Moscow began to entertain the hope that the anti-American, anti-Israeli, and anti-Egyptian Khomeini might join the "anti-imperialist" grouping of Arab states formed as a result of Camp David and that a large "anti-imperialist" Middle East bloc might thereby emerge—a hope that seemed closer to realization after the seizure of the U.S. hostages. Finally, Moscow also sought to exploit the policies of Israeli Prime Minister Menahem Begin—including the major expansion of Israeli settlements on the West Bank, the annexation of Jerusalem and the Golan Heights, the strike against the Iraqi nuclear reactor, and the invasion of Lebanon—to divert Arab and Moslem wrath from the invasion of Afghanistan. This met with only limited success.

The disruption of the anti-Sadat alignment caused by the renewal of hostility between Iraq and Syria and the outbreak of the Iran-Iraq war were two major developments that clearly worked to Moscow's disadvantage, but that the USSR proved powerless to either prevent or control. As a result of these events, Moscow's hopes for the establishment of an "anti-imperialist" Middle Eastern bloc were dashed, and only the somewhat shaky Steadfastness Front remained supportive of Moscow's policies in the Middle East. The front itself was gravely weakened by the Israeli invasion of Lebanon.

It also should be pointed out that there were a number of crises that Moscow did not prove too successful in exploiting. The crisis caused by Israel's destruction of the Iraqi nuclear reactor seemed to lead to closer Iraqi-American relations, rather than enhanced ties between Moscow and Baghdad. Similarly, despite the continuing upheavals in Iran, Moscow did not appear to be able to improve its position to any great degree in that country. Finally, the assassination of Sadat, the linchpin of American strategy in the Arab world, did not bring any immediate benefit to Moscow; Sadat's successor, Husni Mubarak, pledged to continue cooperation both with the United States and Israel.

The essentially reactive nature of Soviet Middle East policy is perhaps most explicitly illustrated by the Brezhnev peace plan of September 1982. Timed to follow both the Reagan and Arab peace initiatives, it was modeled on the Arab peace plan in an obvious effort to obtain Arab support. Despite the Soviet effort, it was to be the Reagan plan and not the Brezhnev plan that was to command Arab attention.

These Middle Eastern developments demonstrate the limited nature of Soviet influence in the Middle East, and nowhere have the limits to Moscow's influence been more noticeable than in Iran. Even at its time of greatest threat from the United States, in the aftermath of the abortive hostage rescue raid, Iran did not hesitate to lead the attack on the USSR at the May 1980 Islamic Conference meeting. In addition, the Iranian leaders did not allow Soviet warnings in mid-January 1981 of an imminent U.S. military attack on Iran to prevent their reaching an agreement with the United States to free the hostages, and despite their continued anti-Americanism, they have not permitted Moscow to gain much influence in their country.

Moscow has been somewhat more succesful in its policies toward Syria, as President Assad supported the Soviet invasion of Afghanistan and signed the Treaty of Friendship and Cooperation he had long been resisting. Yet these actions seem to have been taken because of Syria's isolation in the Arab world and the weakness of Assad's domestic position. It remains to be seen whether Moscow will be able to exploit its strengthened position in Syria to improve its overall posture in the Arab world, particularly in the face of Syria's conflicts with its immediate neighbors, Jordan and Iraq. Indeed, given Syria's tendency to act independently of Soviet wishes and even to the detriment of Soviet policy interests in the Middle East, as in the boycott of the November 1980 Arab summit, Moscow may find its treaty relationship to Damascus to be a mixed blessing. Indeed, this may well have been the reason why the USSR rejected Syrian requests for a strategic cooperation agreement both after the Israeli annexation of the Golan and during the Israeli invasion of Lebanon.

It was the Israeli invasion of Lebanon that probably marked the low point of Soviet influence in the Middle East. In the first place, the USSR did not provide any meaningful political or military assistance to the PLO or Syrian fighting forces in Lebanon, and Moscow's utility as an ally to Arab world clients must have become somewhat suspect as a result. While the USSR had continually appealed to the Arabs to unite during the invasion so that the Arab world as a whole could confront Israel, the lack of Arab unity did not, in the eyes of many Arabs, absolve Moscow of the responsibility of aiding its Arab allies. Secondly, the poor performance of Soviet weaponry in Syrian hands further lowered Soviet prestige. Middle Easterners with memories of the 1973 war could only remember how Soviet commentators had drawn positive comparisons between Soviet and U.S. weaponry as operated by Arabs and Israelis in that conflict. In 1982, the only comparisons that could be drawn were negative ones, despite extensive Soviet efforts to show that Soviet weaponry had worked well. Finally, Moscow had invested a significant amount of its prestige in a series of warnings to the United States not to commit its forces to Lebanon. Washington's apparent disregard of the Soviet threats, and Moscow's unwillingness to back them up, further lowered Soviet prestige in the region. Indeed, the spectacle of Brezhnev going from a stern warning to Reagan against sending U.S. troops to Lebanon (on July 8, 1982) to a position of virtually begging Reagan to save the PLO and West Beirut (in early August) illustrated both the growing impotence of the USSR and the fact that the United States was the dominant outside power in the region.

All in all, when one examines the course of Middle Eastern events in the period since Camp David, and especially since the invasion of Afghanistan, the limited nature of Soviet influence becomes evident. Egypt's gradual rapprochement with a number of Arab states, despite its peace treaty with Israel, is an indication that the basic Soviet goal of forging an "anti-imperialist" bloc of Arab states still appears far from fruition. Indeed, splits in the anti-Egyptian Arab coalition were not long in coming following the second Baghdad Conference, and both the Soviet invasion of Afghanistan and the outbreak of war between Iran and Iraq served to weaken those elements in the Middle East opposed to Egypt, elements Moscow had hoped to turn into an active anti-Western force. At the same time these developments enabled the United States to strengthen its position in the Middle East politically, as in the case of Saudi Arabia, and militarily, with the establishment of a major military force in the region that was increasingly diplomatically acceptable to the conservative states of the Gulf, who feared both Iran and the Soviet Union.

In sum, Soviet policy has proven to be essentially reactive and its influence has proven to be very limited throughout the Middle East. Whether future Middle Eastern developments will enable Moscow to improve its position in the region remains to be seen.

Notes

1. For recent studies of Soviet policy in the Middle East, see Robert O. Freedman, *Soviet Policy Toward the Middle East Since 1970*, Third Edition (New York: Praeger, 1982); Jon D. Glassman, *Arms for the Arabs: The Soviet Union and War in the Middle East* (Baltimore: Johns Hopkins, 1975); Galia Golan, *Yom Kippur and After: The Soviet Union and the Middle East Crisis* (London: Cambridge University Press, 1977); Yaacov Ro'i, *From Encroachment to Involvement: A Documentary Study of Soviet Policy in the Middle East* (Jerusalem: Israel Universities Press, 1974); Yaacov Ro'i (ed.), *The Limits to Power: Soviet Policy in the Middle East* (London: Croom Helm, 1979); and Adeed and Karen Dawisha (eds.), *The Soviet Union in the Middle East* (New York: Holmes and Meier, 1982).

For a general study of possible Soviet objectives in the Middle East, see A. S. Becker, and A. L. Horelick, *Soviet Policy in the Middle East* (Santa Monica, Calif.: Rand Publication R-594-FF, 1970). For an Arab viewpoint, see Mohamed Heikal, *The Sphinx and the Commissar* (New York: Harper & Row, 1978). For a recent Soviet view, see E. M. Primakov, *Anatomiia Blizhnevostochnogo Konflikta* (Moscow: Mysl', 1978).

2. For studies of Soviet military aid, see Glassman, *op. cit.;* George Lenczowski, *Soviet Advances in the Middle East* (Washington, D.C.: American Enterprise Institute, 1972); and Amnon Sella, "Changes in Soviet Political-Military Policy in the Middle East after 1973," in Ro'i, *The Limits to Power*, pp. 32–64.

3. For a study of Soviet policy toward the Communist parties of the Arab world, see Robert O. Freedman, "The Soviet Union and the Communist Parties of the Arab World: An Uncertain Relationship," in Roger E. Kanet and Donna Bahry (eds.), *Soviet Economic and Political Relations with the Developing World* (New York: Praeger, 1975), pp. 100–134; and John K. Cooley, "The Shifting Sands of Arab Communism," *Problems of Communism*, vol. 24, no. 2, 1975, pp. 22–42.

4. For an analysis of these developments, see Freedman, *Soviet Policy Toward the Middle East Since 1970*, pp. 275–314.

5. For an analysis of Assad's growing internal difficulties and the nature of the opposition elements within Syria, see Stanley Reed III, "Dateline Syria: Fin De Regime?" *Foreign Policy*, no. 39 (Summer 1980), pp. 176–190. See also Nicholas Van Damm, *The Struggle for Power in Syria* (New York: St. Martin's Press, 1979); and Robert O. Freedman, "Soviet Policy Toward Syria Since Camp David," *Middle East Review*, vol. 14, nos. 1–2 (Fall 1981/Winter 1982), pp. 31–42.

6. For an analysis of the Soviet intervention in the Horn of Africa, see David Albright, "The Horn of Africa and the Arab-Israeli Conflict" in Robert O. Freedman (ed.), *World Politics and the Arab-Israeli Conflict* (New York: Pergamon, 1979), pp. 147–194. See also Richard B. Remnek, "Soviet Policy in the Horn of Africa: The Decision to Intervene," in Robert H. Donaldson (ed.), *The Soviet Union in the Third World: Successes and Failures* (Boulder, Colo.: Westview Press, 1980), pp. 125–149.

7. For an analysis of these rapprochements and the overall significance of the Baghdad Conference, see Robert O. Freedman, "Soviet Policy Toward the Middle East Since Camp David," in Raymond Duncan (ed.), *Soviet Policy in the Third World* (New York: Pergamon, 1980), pp. 172–173.

8. The best analysis of the events in Iran is found in Barry Rubin, *Paved With Good Intentions: The American Experience and Iran* (New York: Oxford University Press, 1980), chapter 8. For a discussion of Soviet policy toward Iran as the shah was falling, see Freedman, *Soviet Policy Toward the Middle East Since 1970*, pp. 349–350.

9. Soviet goals in aiding the PDRY in its attack against North Yemen are discussed in Freedman, "Soviet Policy Toward the Middle East Since Camp David." See also Nimrod Novick, *Between Two Yemens: Regional Dynamics and Superpower Conduct in Riyadh's Backyard* (Tel Aviv: Center for Strategic Studies, Paper No. 11, 1980).

10. For an analysis of these developments, see Robert O. Freedman, "Soviet Policy Toward Ba'athist Iraq," in Donaldson, *The Soviet Union in the Third World*, pp. 161–191.

11. On these early Soviet-Iranian clashes, see Freedman, "Soviet Policy Toward the Middle East Since Camp David," pp. 179–180.

12. *Nedelia,* September 3–9, 1979.

13. *Pravda,* November 5, 1979.

14. Commentary by Vera Lebedeva (*Foreign Broadcast Information Service Daily Report* [hereafter *FBIS*] *USSR,* November 7, 1979, p. H-4).

15. *Pravda,* December 5, 1979 (translated in *Current Digest of the Soviet Press* [hereafter *CDSP*], vol. 31, no. 49, pp. 4, 26).

16. For an analysis of the Soviet evaluation of Carter, see Robert O. Freedman, "The Soviet Image of the Carter Administration's Policy Toward the USSR from the Inauguration to the Invasion of Afghanistan," *Korea and World Affairs,* vol. 4, no. 2 (Summer 1980), pp. 229–267.

17. For a different view of the connection between the hostage crisis and the invasion of Afghanistan, see Jacques Levesque, "L'Intervention Sovietique en Afghanistan," *L'URSS Dans Les Relations Internationales* (Paris: Economica, 1982), pp. 385–400. See also Selig S. Harrison, "Dateline Afghanistan: Exit Through Finland," *Foreign Policy* no. 41 (Winter 1980–1981), pp. 163–187.

18. Cf. *Baltimore Sun,* January 16, 1980, for a list of the states supporting Moscow or abstaining in the UN vote.

19. Cited in report by Douglas Watson in the *Baltimore Sun,* January 21, 1980.

20. Cited in report by Michael Weisskopf, *Washington Post,* January 2, 1980. Afghanis and Iranians also stormed the Soviet Embassy in Teheran but were quickly driven off by Iranian police. One year later, however, the Iranian authorities were much slower to come to the defense of the embassy.

21. The text of the Islamic Conference declaration is found in the *New York Times,* January 30, 1980.

22. For a discussion of Soviet relations with Steadfastness Front states during this period, see Robert O. Freedman, "Soviet Policy Toward the Middle East Since the Invasion of Afghanistan," *Columbia Journal of International Affairs,* vol. 34, no. 2 (Fall/Winter 1980–1981), pp. 283–310.

23. *Pravda,* August 22, 1980.

24. Cf. report by William Branigin, *Washington Post,* January 17, 1980.

25. Freedman, *Soviet Policy Toward the Middle East Since 1970,* pp. 382–384.

26. Ibid.

27. Editorial comment, *New Times* (Moscow), no. 22, 1980, p. 15.

28. Dmitry Volsky, "Iran: Sidetracking Attention," *New Times,* no. 35, 1980, p. 21.

29. The text of the Pan-Arab charter is found in *The Middle East,* April 1980, p. 20.

30. See Alexandre Benningsen, "Soviet Muslims and the World of Islam," *Problems of Communism,* vol. 29, no. 2 (March/April 1980), pp. 38–51.

31. Cf. Tass report, September 16, 1980.

32. Libya had criticized Saudi Arabia's decision to allow the stationing of U.S. AWACS aircraft on Saudi soil where they could be used against Iran.

33. Cf. *Izvestia,* October 3, 1980.

34. Cf. report by David K. Willis, *Christian Science Monitor,* October 14, 1980, and *Middle East Intelligence Survey,* October 1–15, 1980. See also Tass report in English, October 10, 1980 and Radio Moscow, in Persian, October 10, 1980 (*FBIS:USSR,* October 14, 1980, p. H-1).

35. For Western analyses of the impact of the Iran-Iraq war, see Claudia Wright, "Implications of the Iran-Iraq War," *Foreign Affairs* vol. 59, no. 2 (Winter 1980–1981), pp. 275–303 and Adeed I. Dawisha, "Iraq: The West's Opportunity," *Foreign Policy* no. 41 (Winter 1980–1981), pp. 134–153. For Soviet analyses, see L. Medvenko, "The Persian Gulf: A Revival of Gunboat Diplomacy," *International Affairs* (Moscow) no. 12, 1980, pp. 23–29; A. K. Kislov, "Vashington i Irako-Iranskii Konflikt" ("Washington and the Iran-Iraq Conflict"), *SShA* no. 1 (1981), pp. 51–56; and N. Poliakov, "Put' K. Bezopasnosti v Indiiskom Okeane i Persidskom Zalive" ("The Path to Security in the Indian Ocean and Persian Gulf"), *Mirovaia Ekonomika i Mezhdunarodnie Otnosheniia,* no. 1 (1981), pp. 62–73.

36. Cf. Reed, "Dateline Syria: Fin De Regime?" pp. 177–185.

37. For an analysis of the changing alliances of King Hussein, see Adam M. Garfinkle, "Negotiating by Proxy: Jordanian Foreign Policy and U.S. Options in the Middle East," *Orbis* vol. 24, no. 24 (Winter 1981), pp. 847–880.

38. For the text of the treaty, see *Pravda,* October 9, 1980. Essentially it was similar in form to treaties signed by Moscow with other Middle Eastern countries. The joint communique issued after the visit stated that "appropriate decisions were taken" to provide Syria with military assistance and that Syria fully backed the Soviet position on Afghanistan. For a discussion of Soviet-Syrian relations from 1970 to 1980, see Freedman, *Soviet Policy Toward the Middle East Since 1970.*

39. Vasily Kuznetzov, the Soviet official, emphasized in his speech in Damascus that "the treaty is of particular significance for actions aimed at eliminating the hotbeds of dangerous tension in the Middle East" (*Pravda,* December 3, 1980).

40. Cited in report of an interview with King Hussein by Pranay B. Gupte, *New York Times,* December 2, 1980. Hussein also stated that he had put aside plans to explore arms purchases from Moscow.

41. Cf. Moscow Radio Arabic Broadcast, December 5, 1980 (*FBIS:USSR,* December 8, 1980, p. H-1).

42. For an analysis of these intra-Arab divisions, see Robert O. Freedman, "Moscow, Washington and the Gulf," *American-Arab Affairs,* no. 1 (Summer 1982), pp. 134–135.

43. For an analysis of the events surrounding the proclamation of the Soviet peace plan of April 1976, see Freedman, *Soviet Policy Toward the Middle East Since 1970,* pp. 242–244.

44. Press Trust of India News Agency, December 11, 1980, cited in report by Carol Honsa, *Christian Science Monitor,* December 12, 1980. Moscow increased shipments of oil by 1,000,000 metric tons.

45. For the text of the final communique, see *Pravda,* December 12, 1980.

46. The text of the plan is found in *FBIS:USSR,* December 11, 1980, p. D-7.

47. For a Soviet analysis of the significance of Brezhnev's plan, see the commentary by Igor Pavlovich, Moscow Radio Domestic Service (International Round Table), December 21, 1980 (*FBIS:USSR*, December 22, 1980, p. CC-2).

48. For the text of the note, which was broadcast by Tass in English on December 28, 1980, see *FBIS:USSR*, December 29, 1980, p. H-1.

49. See the reports of the comments of Behzad Nabavi, Iranian government spokesman, on Radio Teheran Domestic Service, December 30, 1980 in *FBIS: South Asia*, December 30, 1980, pp. I-5/I-6.

50. Cf. Tass report, January 12, 1981, in *FBIS:USSR*, January 13, 1981, p. H-1.

51. Cf. *Pravda*, January 17, 1981, and Moscow Radio Persian Language Broadcast January 17, 1981 (*FBIS:USSR*, January 19, 1981, pp. A-2/A-3). Former Secretary of State Henry Kissinger's trip to the Middle East in early January was linked by Moscow to the invasion plan.

52. Cf. Reuters report, *New York Times*, January 18, 1981.

53. For the text of Brezhnev's speech to the 26th Party Congress, see *Pravda*, February 24, 1981 (translated in *CDSP*, vol. 33, no. 8, pp. 7–13).

54. At the Islamic summit in Taif, Saudi Arabia, in late January, for example, the emphasis was on Islamic opposition to Israel, and the "Soviet threat" was played down, as was the Soviet invasion of Afghanistan. (Cf. Claudia Wright, "Islamic Summit," *The Middle East* [March 1981], pp. 6–10.) The absence of Iran, which had played a militantly anti-Soviet role in the previous Islamic conference in May 1980, however, may have been a factor, along with Saudi Arabian efforts to achieve an Islamic consensus.

55. UPI report in *Jerusalem Post*, April 9, 1981. As a gesture to the United States, however, Saudi Arabia broke diplomatic relations with Afghanistan on the eve of the Haig visit (Cf. Reuters report, *New York Times*, April 8, 1981).

56. For an analysis of the 1975 visit, see Freedman, *Soviet Policy Toward the Middle East Since 1970*, pp. 220–221.

57. *Pravda*, April 26, 1981.

58. Ibid.

59. The joint communique was printed in *Pravda*, May 30, 1981.

60. *Pravda*, May 27, 1981.

61. Alexander Usvatov, "King Hussein's Visit," *New Times*, no. 23 (1981), p. 10. One issue on which Jordan and the USSR obviously did not agree, however, was the Iran-Iraq war.

62. For an analysis of this crisis, see Freedman, *Soviet Policy Toward the Middle East Since 1970*, pp. 406–408.

63. Ibid, p. 407.

64. Ibid, pp. 408–410.

65. Cited in report by Edward Cody, *Washington Post*, June 19, 1981.

66. For an analysis of both the possible Libyan motivations in staging the crisis and Soviet efforts to exploit it, see Freedman, *Soviet Policy Toward the Middle East Since 1970*, pp. 411–413.

67. *Pravda*, August 23, 1981.

68. Cf. Moscow Radio in Turkish to Turkey, August 20, 1981 (*FBIS:USSR*, August 21, 1981, p. H-2).

69. Oman denounced the treaty in very strong terms; cf. Muscat Domestic Service, August 26, 1981, and Salalah Domestic Service, August 27, 1981 (*FBIS: Middle East and Africa*, August 27, 1981, pp. C-1/C-2).

70. For Soviet attitudes toward the Iranian leadership, see Freedman, "Soviet Policy Toward the Middle East Since the Invasion of Afghanistan," pp. 290–291 and 295–297.

71. Cited in AP report, *New York Times*, November 7, 1981.

72. Cited in report in *Washington Post*, February 16, 1981.

73. Teheran Domestic Service, October 20, 1981 (*FBIS:USSR*, October 22, 1981, p. H-7).

74. Cited in Reuters report, *New York Times*, November 23, 1981.

75. *Pravda*, September 18, 1981.

76. Moscow Radio announced, however, on October 1, 1981, that the Soviet branch of the Friendship Society would continue to operate (*FBIS:USSR*, October 1, 1981, p. H-1).

77. Bovin's comments came on Moscow television on October 25 (*FBIS:USSR*, October 26, 1981, p. H-1).

78. Cf. Moscow Radio Peace and Progress, in Arabic, September 7, 1981 (*FBIS:USSR*, September 10, 1981, p. H-1); Tass, in English, October 8, 1981 (*FBIS:USSR*, October 9, 1981, p. H-1); and Moscow Radio, in Arabic, October 26, 1981 (*FBIS:USSR*, October 27, 1981, p. H-6).

79. For an analysis of Soviet and U.S. policy during the fall of the shah, see Freedman, *Soviet Policy Toward the Middle East Since 1970*, pp. 349–350.

80. *Pravda*, October 12, 1981.

81. Cf. report by Don Oberdorfer, *Washington Post*, October 15, 1981.

82. *Pravda*, October 16, 1981.

83. Moscow Radio Domestic Service, October 20, 1981 (*FBIS:USSR*, October 21, 1981, p. H-1). Arafat was quoted as saying at a press conference, "We fully endorse the Soviet proposals advanced at the 26th CPSU Congress and we view them as the basis for a just settlement of the Palestinian problem." *Pravda*, on October 21, 1981, reported the joint Soviet-PLO support for the international conference and the granting of official diplomatic status to the PLO mission in Moscow.

84. Cited in report by Bernard Gwertzman, *New York Times*, August 13, 1981.

85. The text of the former presidents' comments is in the *New York Times*, October 12, 1981.

86. *Pravda*, August 26, 1981.

87. *Pravda*, March 29, 1981.

88. This, of course, had happened during the 1973 Arab-Israeli war. Cf. *Izvestia*, January 8, 1981.

89. Tass, November 1, 1981 (*FBIS:USSR*, November 2, 1981, p. H-3).

90. Cf. *Izvestia*, October 31, 1981.

91. Cf. Moscow Radio, in Arabic, November 8, 1981 (*FBIS:USSR*, November 9, 1981, pp. H-1/H-2).

92. As might be expected, Moscow was highly critical of Pakistan's increasingly close military tie to the United States (Cf. *Pravda*, September 27, 1981).

93. Cited in AP report, *Baltimore Sun*, November 24, 1981.

94. Cf. Freedman, *Soviet Policy Toward the Middle East Since 1970*, pp. 421–423.

95. For the text of the communique, see *Pravda*, January 17, 1982.

96. *Izvestia*, April 15, 1982. Moscow Radio, in an Arabic language broadcast on April 14 (Alexander Timoshkin commentary), cited the shooting as proving that the American-Israeli "fiendish alliance" was the number-one enemy of Islam (*FBIS:USSR*, April 15, 1982, p. H-1).

97. For Moscow's highly negative reaction to this development, see the Moscow Radio Arab language broadcast on May 28, 1981, as reported in *FBIS:USSR*, June 1, 1982, p. H-3.

98. For a description of the increasingly severe problems facing the PLO in Lebanon on the eve of the war, see David Butler, "In the Same Trench," *The Middle East* (June 1982), p. 6. See also his report, "Shiites in Beirut Clashes," *The Middle East* (February 1982), p. 14.

99. Cf. remarks by Taha Ramadan, first deputy prime minister of Iraq, Baghdad Radio, June 1, 1982 (*FBIS:MEA*, June 2, 1981, p. E-2).

100. The Moroccan Foreign Minister, Mohammed Boucetta, paid a visit to Cairo on June 7, 1982, thus further ending Egypt's ostracism. Egyptian President Mubarak's attendance at the funeral of King Khalid of Saudi Arabia later that month had the same effect.

101. Cf. *Pravda*, May 26, 1982.

102. Cf. Robert O. Freedman, "Soviet Policy Toward Syria Since Camp David," pp. 28–30.

103. Cf. Voice of Palestine, June 2, 1981, cited in *FBIS:MEA*, June 3, 1982, p. E-1.

104. For a detailed analysis of the difficulties inherent in the Soviet-PLO relationship, see Galia Golan, *The Soviet Union and the Palestine Liberation Organization* (New York: Praeger, 1980).

105. For Israeli military analyses of the war, see *Israel Defense Forces Journal*, vol. 1, no. 2 (December 1982), pp. 11–28; and Chaim Herzog, *The Arab-Israeli Wars* (New York: Random House, 1982), pp. 339–359. For a view from the Palestinian side, see the special issue of the *Journal of Palestine Studies*, no. 44/45 (Summer/Fall 1982) devoted to the war, especially the chronology, pp. 135–192.

106. For a detailed analysis of Soviet policy during the Israeli invasion, see Robert O. Freedman, "Soviet Policy Toward the Middle East in 1982," *Middle East Contemporary Survey, 1982*, forthcoming.

107. Kaddafi went so far as to state that Soviet-Arab friendship was going up in flames the same way Beirut was (Cf. Tripoli *JANA*, June 26, 1982) (*FBIS:MEA*, June 26, 1982, pp. Q-2,3).

108. In response to a letter from Brezhnev, Reagan had reportedly warned against outside powers getting involved in the fighting. (Cf. report by David Shipler, *New York Times*, June 30, 1982, citing Israeli Prime Minister Menahem Begin, who also said he had received two messages from Moscow asking Israel not to hit the Soviet Embassy in Beirut, and report by Hedrick Smith, *New York Times*, June 11, 1982.)

109. For an analysis of the economic benefits to Moscow of arms sales, see Andrew J. Pierre, *The Global Politics of Arms Sales* (Princeton, N.J.: Princeton University Press, 1982), pp. 78–80.

110. For the best analysis of Soviet strategy during the war, see Golan, *Yom Kippur and After.*

111. *Pravda*, June 15, 1982.

112. For the Brezhnev warning of July 8, see *Pravda*, July 9, 1982. For the Brezhnev appeal to Reagan while Israeli troops were moving to crush the PLO in early August, see *Pravda*, August 3, 1982.

113. *Izvestia*, September 10, 1982.

114. Cf. Dmitry Volsky, "Fez and the Bekaa Valley," *New Times* (Moscow), no. 38, 1982, pp. 7–8.

115. For an analysis of the status of the Soviet Middle East peace plan prior to the Israeli invasion of Lebanon, see Freedman, "Moscow, Washington and the Gulf," pp. 132–134.

116. Cf. *Middle East Journal*, vol. 37, no. 1 (Winter 1983), p. 71.

117. Cf. *Pravda*, September 11, 1982. The summit did agree, however, that any Arab countries that wished to renew ties with Egypt on a bilateral basis could do so.

118. *Pravda*, September 16, 1982.

119. *Pravda*, September 21, 1982.

120. *Pravda*, December 4, 1982.

121. *Pravda*, January 13, 1983; Tass, January 13, 1983 (*FBIS:USSR*, January 14, 1983, pp. H-1/H-2).

122. Tass, January 13, 1983.

123. UPI report, *Washington Post*, December 5, 1982.

124. Cf. report by David Ottaway, *Washington Post*, December 30, 1982, and comments by Yasir Arafat as recorded in the *Washington Post*, January 18, 1983.

125. Cf. report by Edward Walsh, *Washington Post*, January 5, 1983, and *New York Times* report, January 8, 1983.

2

U.S. Policy on the Middle East in the Period Since Camp David

Barry Rubin

The signing of the Camp David accords by Egypt, Israel, and the United States marked a major triumph for U.S. diplomacy, but it did not, in hindsight, initiate a new era for U.S. policy in the Middle East. Although the agreements greatly contributed to the maintenance of regional peace and sealed a new, closer relationship between Washington and Cairo, events elsewhere in the area were already beginning to distract the attention of the United States. The Soviet invasion of Afghanistan, the Iranian revolution and the subsequent hostage crisis, and the election of Ronald Reagan put different priorities on Washington's interests.

In the most direct fashion, the 1978 Camp David talks tied up the attention of U.S. policymakers at the very moment when they needed to be realizing the importance of developments in the Iranian revolution. But the failure to make progress on the treaty after the initial signing on April 25, 1979, dissolved into the taking of American hostages on November 4. This preoccupied the United States until the January 20, 1981, release of the prisoners. The Soviet invasion of Afghanistan was another shock that brought great-power conflict to the center of the table. By this point, the Reagan administration was putting far more priority on three other areas: the primacy of the Gulf, the primacy of the Soviet threat, and the primacy of a military response. Attempts to respond unilaterally to Soviet actions, and to create sentiment in the region for such efforts, preoccupied the Reagan administration during its first year.

Thus, the transition from the Carter to the Reagan administration brought with it a switch from attempts at making controlled changes to increase regional stability to a defensive posture of avoiding seemingly unpleasant changes. The Nixon Doctrine, in which the United States, then preoccupied with Indochina, sought local friends to manage stability, was replaced when Iran crumbled. The emphasis on regional issues, which dominated the Carter administration, reverted to a globalist approach focusing on East-West conflicts.

Certainly, the new emphasis on the Gulf was created by changes in economic power and strategic priorities set off by the rapid increases in the price of petroleum set by the Organization of Petroleum Exporting Countries (OPEC). The West, though not necessarily the United States, became more and more dependent on Middle East oil, enhancing its strategic importance. The infusion of money gave the oil-producing countries more leverage, and the social changes wrought by this cornucopia—and illustrated by the shah's fall—made stability there a much higher priority.

The number of regional crises during 1978–1981 was indeed daunting. War in the Sahara pitted Morocco against Algerian—said by some to be Soviet-backed—Polisario guerrillas. A sporadic conflict set the Saudi-allied Yemen Arab Republic (North Yemen) against the Soviet-allied Peoples Democratic Republic of Yemen (South Yemen). The Soviet fleet grew larger and extended its operations in the Indian Ocean, while finding new port facilities in the region. The Iran-Iraq war constantly seemed in danger of spreading, and a victory by either side would have posed an additional danger to the conservative Arab oil producers in the Gulf. The relationship between the USSR and Libya tightened, and Muammar Kaddafi's own ambitions toward Chad, the Sudan, and other places posed problems. There were clashes between U.S. and Libyan aircraft over the Libya-claimed Gulf of Sidra, and attacks on U.S. embassies in Pakistan and Libya, as well as in Iran, implied both growing anti-Americanism and a decline in local perceptions of American strength.

Thousands of Soviet and Cuban troops were in Ethiopia, with its strategic position along the Red Sea, shoring up the military dictatorship there and fighting Eritrean nationalist guerrillas. Another 90,000 Soviet troops were engaged in turning Afghanistan into a satellite, while the march of Soviet troops to Pakistan's border required major U.S. assistance to that country. The November 1979 attack by Islamic radicals on the holiest site in Islam—Mecca—provoked concern, probably exaggerated, over Saudi stability and heightened the panicky belief that a tidal wave of Islamic fundamentalism might further inflame the so-called "arc of crisis," a term coined by Carter's National Security Adviser Zbigniew Brzezinski. And there were the hostage crisis, the continued civil war in Lebanon, and a whole range of Arab-Israeli conflicts, including a border war in southern Lebanon, the

Israeli bombing of the Iraqi nuclear reactor, and frictions on and over the West Bank—not to mention the assassination of Egypt's President Anwar Sadat.

There was no shortage of issues capable of causing sleepless nights for those charged with defining and implementing U.S. foreign policy. In addition, U.S. policy toward the Middle East was no longer of secondary importance, but rather set the tone for U.S. policy in general. This was certainly true of Washington's transition toward a more militant and interventionist position that was seen between 1979 and 1981.

The Aftermath of Camp David

U.S. hopes that other Arab countries could be drawn into the Camp David framework were consistently disappointed, in part because they had been overestimated from the beginning. Immediately after the accords were signed, Secretary of State Cyrus Vance visited Jordan, Saudi Arabia, and Syria to drum up support. Not only were these states uninterested in participation, but they also moved to isolate Egypt.

President Carter also visited the Middle East in March 1979 to provide the last-minute impetus for approval of the accords in Egypt and Israel. These agreements, he stressed in a speech in Cairo, were part of a broader policy to obtain a comprehensive peace settlement. "Only the path of negotiation and accommodation," the president said, "can lead to the fulfillment of the hopes of the Palestinian people for peaceful self-expression." Camp David, he argued, gave them an opportunity for participation, a way to turn the autonomy process into a means for achieving self-determination.[1]

He did not use similar words in Israel, where the possibility of a Palestinian state was rejected by the government of Prime Minister Menahem Begin. If Egypt had to be assured of U.S. concern for improving its inter-Arab position, Israel had to be convinced of the United States' ability to keep its guarantees. He represented, Carter told the Knesset, "the most powerful country on Earth. And I can assure you that the United States intends to use that power in the pursuit of a stable and a peaceful Middle East."[2] Yet the United States took a back seat after the signing of the treaties in Washington on March 25, 1979, allowing Israel and Egypt to attempt to resolve the issues through bilateral talks. The United States tried to strengthen the new triangular relationship with aid money for both Egypt and Israel, using behind-the-scenes attempts to prepare the diplomatic stage for the next step.

The economic efforts proved far easier to carry out than the diplomatic. Assistance given to Egypt was designed to replace Arab funds withdrawn because of Camp David and to cement the U.S.-Egyptian relationship. As the perceived need for military leverage in the region grew, this provided another reason for assistance to Cairo. By the time the treaties were signed, the United States was providing $1 billion a year to Egypt in economic assistance. Cairo was the site of the largest Agency for International Development (AID) mission in the world. The United States also agreed to provide Israel with oil, if necessary until 1990, in exchange for returning the Sinai oil fields to Egypt. In April 1979 President Carter asked Congress for $4.8 billion in aid for Egypt and Israel: $300 million in economic development loans and grants and $1.5 billion in military credits for Cairo; $800 million in military grants and $2.2 billion in military credits for Jerusalem.[3]

Progress on autonomy proved more difficult. Veteran Democrat Robert Strauss became the president's roving Middle East envoy, but he needed time to learn his new job, which he resigned in November 1979. Although many Israel-Egypt exchanges were held, there was little apparent progress. Continued Israeli settlement on the West Bank made concessions on the part of the Begin government seem unlikely. At the same time, Washington explored ways of gaining some PLO involvement in the talks, seen also as the key to involving other Arab states in negotiations. The Arab states suggested that a possible UN Security Council resolution could reaffirm Resolutions 242 and 338 and add language to them recognizing Palestinian rights, a reprise of a 1977 effort that failed to gain PLO approval. Part of these 1979 efforts involved meetings between UN Ambassador Andrew Young and PLO representatives at the United Nations. When these were revealed publicly, Young was forced to resign in August 1979 after Israel protested.[4]

On another front, in August the United States put forward its own draft blueprint for autonomy, but the Israelis objected to Washington's interpretation as being closer to Cairo's, which favored legislative powers for the autonomy council. Meanwhile, Sadat became worried that pressing autonomy too quickly might slow Israel's withdrawal from Sinai. Both countries thus rejected the U.S. effort. The resignation of Israeli Foreign Minister Moshe Dayan in October 1979 removed one of the main architects of Camp David; Carter's Middle East envoy, Robert Strauss, resigned in November to run the President's reelection campaign.

Some American policymakers felt that U.S. pressure on Begin for concessions on autonomy would make his coalition shakier and more intransigent; others believed that only a real drive on the issue could show the Arab world that autonomy was no mere front for creeping annexation. At any rate, the U.S. strategy became one of taking technical questions first and leaving the thornier political issues for a later stage. By the spring of 1980, Sadat judged that the U.S. election campaign made the rest of the year unlikely to produce progress—or at least progress favorable to Egypt—and he sought to postpone serious efforts until after the November 1980 balloting. Momentum was lost, and the newly elected Reagan administration had to spend many months oulining its new policies and organizing itself. The May 1980 deadline envisioned after Camp David was not met, despite the continuing efforts of Strauss's replacement, Ambassador Sol Linowitz. Even two years later, after Israel completed its withdrawal from Sinai, agreement on autonomy seemed very distant.

The underlying problem was that Egypt and Israel had different visions of what they wanted. Cairo was aiming at a Palestinian state or some sort of West Bank/Gaza federation with Jordan. The Begin government was essentially unwilling to give up the territories, wanted to continue controlling the territories, and preferred to annex them. The United States did not have a clear goal in mind and was blocked by the positions of its two partners and by the intransigence of the other Arab states and the PLO as well. Without the support of these political factors, the Carter administration could not generate the political capital necessary for a breakthrough. Other issues, in the Middle East and elsewhere, made it difficult to maintain the concentration that had produced the Camp David success.

A related effort was the periodic U.S. attempt to resolve the Lebanese civil war. In September 1979, Washington proposed a peace conference on Lebanon involving all belligerents. The following month, Ambassador Philip Habib took the first of his many shuttle trips to secure peace in that country. Again, it was difficult for Washington to decide on a desired outcome, and the complex, conflicting objectives of the warring parties prevented any progress on the issue in 1979 or in the Reagan administration's 1981 efforts.

U.S.-Iranian Relations and the Hostage Crisis

The victory of the Iranian revolution and the triumph of its most radical Islamic wing under Ayatollah Ruhollah Khomeini changed Iran from a close ally to a self-defined enemy of the United States. Anti-Americanism lay at the heart of the revolution, since the United States was deemed responsible for the shah's political rule, Iran's cultural upheaval, and all internal opposition to the course of the revolution.

The Carter administration, however, thought it possible for a reconciliation after the shah's fall. A good amount of wishful thinking was involved in this process, but there was also the very real objective of preventing Iran from turning toward the USSR. U.S. gestures in this direction were not well received in Iran, however. Those moderates there who most wanted a better relationship were by that very view discredited.[5]

Although it was the admission of the shah to the United States for medical treatment that triggered the takeover of the U.S. Embassy in November 1979 and the holding of American diplomats as hostages for 444 days, the reasons for this kidnapping lay in internal Iranian politics. Washington's greatest policy failure in coping with the Islamic republic, as it had been in dealing with the revolt against the shah, lay not in a refusal to use force or to find some way to control the process, but in an inability to understand the course of developments in Teheran.[6]

Thus, dependence for embassy security on assistance promised by Prime Minister Mehdi Bazargan's government showed ignorance of the obvious powerlessness of that regime. The encounter between Brzezinski and moderate Iranian officials in Algiers only convinced the militants in Iran that their government was about to betray the revolution by improving relations with the United States. They decided to take drastic action precisely to forestall any rebuilding of ties between the two countries. After negotiations began over the hostages' release, Washington had great difficulty in understanding where power lay within Iran.

Almost immediately after the taking of the embassy, President Carter ruled out any immediate rescue attempt. A belief that the crisis would not last a long time, coupled with the country's post-Vietnam mood, seemed to rule out precipitate military action. Instead, the U.S. effort was limited to a range of punishments and diplomatic efforts that included appeals to the United Nations and to European and other allies for support, economic reprisals, including the freezing of Iranian assets, and the dispatch of naval forces to the Indian Ocean.

There was great hope on more than one occasion in the spring of 1980 for a breakthrough in the negotiations. Having exhausted these options, the United States tried a rescue attempt in April. While the overall plan was sound, technical shortcomings forced the cancellation of the mission; through criminal carelessness documents were left behind that allowed the Teheran government to uncover and destroy U.S. intelligence assets in the country.

For the next six months little happened. Finally, in mid-September, possibly under the pressure of Iran's increasingly severe conflict with Iraq, Ayatollah Khomeini put forward his conditions for the return of the hostages. This led to an acceleration of negotiations in October and November. On November 2, Iran's newly convened parliament approved an Iranian bargaining position. The change in Iran's position was due to changed circumstances: a governmental structure had been created and the country's internal political struggles had largely been resolved. In the face of the Iraqi invasion of mid-September 1980, continued holding of the hostages became a burden on Iran. The war had made the U.S. sanctions effective, even though earlier Iran's high oil income and its lack of need for military spare parts had meant that the embargo and the freeze on their overseas assets had little impact. In retrospect, the United States simply waited Iran out, but it did not gain the political advantage of this strategy because of the attention and urgency Washington focused on the issue.

The partly coincidental reactivation of the hostage issue just before the U.S. elections also influenced the American presidential contest. Iran's attempts to manipulate U.S. politics were too hesitant and clumsy to influence the campaign directly, but the high visibility of the issue in the closing days of the campaign, coupled with the Carter administration's inability to make progress and widespread—though inaccurate—public suspicions of White House manipulation, damaged the Democratic candidate.[7]

After Carter's electoral defeat, serious U.S.-Iran talks began. When Iran raised its demands, Washington took a tough stand. If this was the Iranian position, said the U.S. team, then an agreement was impossible. Since the Carter administration was leaving office on January 20, 1981, this was the deadline for a solution. Faced with the war, financial shortages, and the need to turn its attention to other matters, the Teheran regime began to make concessions. The offer of an acceptable deal by the State Department, whose position had not shifted since September, and the likelihood that the Reagan inauguration would bring additional delays to the negotiating process, or a tougher line, were other factors influencing Teheran to move toward a settlement.

Finally, the agreement was completed. The final snags were cleared away and the fifty-two hostages were released at the very moment that Carter was leaving office. The arrangements involved the return of about $11 billion of Iranian assets frozen by the U.S. government, with only $5.1 billion actually going back to Iran. Of the remainder, Iran used about $5 billion to pay off loans from U.S. Banks, and another $1 billion was put in a special fund to cover claims by

American companies. The United States also promised not to interfere in Iran's internal affairs in the future nor to block any legal action by Iran through the U.S. court system to try to regain the wealth of the shah's family.

Essentially, Iran and the United States returned to the prehostage situation on these issues though, of course, a great deal of bitterness had been engendered by the crisis. The alliance of the shah's era was gone, and even fairly normal relations would be difficult to attain.

In the United States, President Carter's electoral defeat seemed to mark at least a temporary loss for the liberal model of American foreign policy in terms of encouraging overseas reform and human rights, flexibility toward change and nationalism, and sensitivity toward foreign perceptions. In addition, reliance on indirect rather than direct applications of American power, as symbolized in the Nixon Doctrine, was struck a severe blow by the collapse of the shah's regime. If Washington could not depend on Iran to maintain Gulf stability—a stability further endangered by the replacement of the shah by the Khomeini regime (both as example and as an exporter of radical Islamic revolution)—then it would have to directly take on this responsibility, many people reasoned.

Strategic Responses in the Gulf

Even before Ronald Reagan's November 1980 electoral victory, the Carter Doctrine demonstrated increasing concern with the Gulf region. The undeniable economic and strategic importance of the area, the potential for greater instability created by the Iran-Iraq war, and the growing potential for Soviet influence in the region all raised its priority in the eyes of American policymakers.

The invasion of Afghanistan seriously undermined efforts at détente and, along with the Iranian revolution, encouraged establishment of a new chain of American strategic relationships in the region. There already had been an increase in U.S. military aid to Egypt, including the agreement to supply F-16s. Saudi Arabia was to be supplied with even more advanced weaponry, including equipment necessary to enhance the effectiveness of F-15s already sold to Riyadh and to provide an improved intelligence capacity for both Saudi Arabia and the United States with AWACS early-warning planes.

In January 1980, Brzezinski said the United States should form a "cooperative security framework" of Middle East nations against the Soviet Union. A few months later, Defense Department teams were sent to Saudi Arabia, Oman, Somalia, and Kenya to seek possible new facilities for U.S. use. A base was already being enlarged on the

British-owned island of Diego Garcia. The U.S. naval detachment in Bahrain was enlarged, navy and marine forces were sent into the Indian Ocean, and plans were accelerated for a Rapid Deployment Force to deter any further Soviet advances or to intervene in regional upheavals.

The Afghanistan invasion, said President Carter, was "the most serious threat to world peace since the Second World War."[8] His reaction was contained in the 1980 State of the Union message and became known as the Carter Doctrine. "The steady growth and increased projections abroad of Soviet military power," he said, combined with "the overwhelming dependence of Western nations, which now increasingly includes the United States, on vital oil supplies from the Middle East" to cause a serious threat to American interests. "The denial of these oil supplies—to us or to others—would threaten our security and provoke an economic crisis greater than that of the Great Depression 50 years ago, with a fundamental change in the way we live." This required an increase in American military strength, an ability to project it into the area, a regional security framework, and a serious warning to the Soviets that any aggression in the region would be met with a strong U.S. response.[9]

A belief that U.S. credibility in the area must be heightened and that rapid support should be shown to past allies can be seen in the dispatch of American military supplies to North Yemen when its border was attacked by pro-Soviet South Yemen in March 1979 and in the decision to supply Morocco with defensive arms in its battle against Polisario guerrillas in October 1980.

Thus, many of the attitudes and basic policies produced by the Reagan administration were prefigured by earlier decisions, though there were also major changes of emphasis and content, as well as in rhetoric and ideology.

Reagan Administration World View

Ronald Reagan came to the presidency in January 1981 with a view that foreign problems were caused by American weakness and Soviet machinations. He believed that the United States could have stopped the Iranian revolution and saved the shah. The Reagan team stressed terrorism as a major political threat and saw Moscow as a major force behind this problem.

If an imbalance in will and force between the United States and the Soviet Union was the cause of America's perceived decline, the new administration would answer this with a massive military buildup and a declared willingness to intervene in Third World conflicts. If

Washington's credibility in the eyes of allies was in question, then strong support for friends was necessary to persuade them of America's reliability. Similarly, those aligning with the USSR must be shown that there would be costs in raising Washington's ire.

Libya seemed a particularly attractive example for this new approach, as an anti-American country friendly toward Moscow and as a source of terrorism and instability as well. Yet even though the administration spoke a great deal about the threat posed by Muammar Kaddafi's regime, made some initial explorations of the possibility of overthrowing him, shot down two Libyan fighter planes in the Gulf of Sidra, and began a boycott of Libyan oil, regional events were not noticeably affected. Indeed, local commentators pointed out that allowing Kaddafi to portray himself as an Arab hero confronting a superpower only enhanced his position at home and in the area.

This illustrated the perennial difficulty of turning ideology into policy. New U.S. governments go through learning experiences in which their original plans to reshape the world give way to the press of reactions to events, the limits of means and options, and the erosive power of a career staff waging bureaucratic warfare.

Compared to the Carter administration, the Reagan team was far less concerned with the Arab-Israeli conflict, which it tended to see as an unfortunate distraction from greater threats centered in the Gulf and from the Soviets. For the first fifteen months of the Reagan administration, up until the Israeli withdrawal from eastern Sinai in April 1982, U.S. policymakers therefore saw no urgency in pushing the autonomy negotiations forward.

The fundamental problem for the Reagan administration was that there was no likely solution to the problem that seemed satisfactory. Washington could not accept Begin's definition of autonomy, because this would undermine U.S. interests in the Arab world. Similarly, any admission that autonomy was impossible would destroy the Camp David framework and the Israeli-Egyptian rapprochement. Although Reagan in his 1980 campaign had expressed some preference for a Jordanian solution for the occupied territories, this seemed foreclosed by Amman's disinterest in any such commitment.

American negotiations with the PLO were out of the question for a variety of reasons—past U.S. pledges to Israel, domestic political pressures, PLO intransigence, the frustrations of earlier failures—and also because the administration's strong stand against terrorism and its perception of the PLO as a Soviet ally did not make such a step seem logical. U.S. policymakers, having no preferred solution, were not going to invest political capital or take strategic risks in pressing for major advances in negotiations. Further, the new administration did not understand the centrality of the conflict in the thinking of Arab governments.

The autonomy talks generally were allowed to take their own course, and no special U.S. representative was appointed until early in 1982. Meanwhile, the administration pressed ahead in its attempts to construct a strategic alliance in the Gulf aimed against the USSR. There was some behind-the-scenes cooperation—the Saudis, for example, built bases larger than necessary to accommodate assisting forces in an emergency. Nevertheless, publicly the local states were much more interested in their Gulf Cooperation Council efforts than in tying themselves to a U.S.-led alliance and far more concerned about closer threats like Iran and the possibility of internal upheavals than about a Soviet threat.

To a large extent, then, the United States and the Arab countries were talking at cross purposes. While some observers saw the Reagan policy as a return to a 1950s-style emphasis on the East-West conflict and the construction of regional defense pacts, in reality it was designed as a unilateralist approach to the area, largely leaving out any important role for local allies—a part sought by Egypt and Israel, viewed ambiguously by Saudi Arabia, and shunned by Turkey and Pakistan.

Equally, it proved difficult for Washington to coordinate regional policy with its European and Japanese allies, who were far more dependent on Middle East oil than was the United States, but who contributed little to its defense. The European initiative for Arab-Israeli peace, rejected by the United States as being outside the Camp David framework, seemed to reach a dead end. On the other hand, European agreement to participate in the multinational force to maintain peace in the Sinai was a diplomatic success for the United States.

The economic importance of the Middle East continued to grow for the United States. American imports from the region in 1980 totaled $31.5 billion, and exports reached $15.3 billion.[10] The latter figure, large as it was, meant a significant trade deficit. Some of this money was returned in the form of Arab, particularly Saudi, investments. The imports were almost entirely in the form of petroleum. While U.S. dependence on Middle East supplies was extremely significant, the oil glut of 1981–1982 and the opening of new sources of production opened the possibility for changes in these trends.

U.S. investments in the area reached $7.7 billion in 1981, of which $5.3 billion were in Saudi Arabia alone. These shifts, already visible in earlier years, seemed gradually to exercise more leverage over American policy. Yet aside from the U.S. commitment to Saudi security, the impact of these developments were not as clear-cut as many observers stated. American objectives remained the maintenance of regional peace and stability, and the changes in the focus of U.S. policy had more to do with the emphasis on the Gulf than on any tendency to see the area through Saudi eyes.

Coping with Crises

A series of events during 1981–1982 tended to bring Arab-Israeli conflict issues to center stage and provoked a rising degree of tension in U.S.-Israeli relations. This chain of mini-confrontations, culminating in the June 1982 Israeli invasion of Lebanon, provoked a major new U.S. initiative toward the Arab-Israeli conflict.

The earlier episodes included the April 1981 movement of Syrian antiaircraft missiles into Lebanon; the June 7, 1981, Israeli raid destroying the Iraqi nuclear reactor near Baghdad; a July–August battle between PLO rockets and Israeli air power on the Lebanon-Israel border; the July 17, 1981, Israeli air raid on PLO offices in Beirut, which resulted in large-scale casualties; the controversy over AWACS sales to Saudi Arabia; the Israeli step toward annexation of the Golan Heights in December 1981; and the Israeli firing of West Bank mayors in March–April 1982.

The assassination of Egyptian President Anwar Sadat in October 1981 also provoked concern in Washington. His successor, Husni Mubarak, seemed likely to continue the general lines of Sadat's policy—particularly on Camp David—but was much less eager to identify Cairo as a U.S. surrogate in the region and more concerned with Egypt's reintegration into the Arab world and nonalignment. Clearly, while the hope of closer cooperation with the rest of the Gulf was the main idea of the Reagan administration, in practice the links with Egypt and Israel remained the centerpiece of the U.S. position in the area.

Early signals from the Reagan administration seemed favorable to the programs of Prime Minister Menahem Begin's government. Nevertheless, Washington's prime emphasis on maintaining quiet on the Arab-Israeli front—the fear that trouble there might result in war or weaken any impetus toward a strategic consensus in the Gulf—took the upper hand. The U.S. government alternated between the view that the Begin coalition was a prime threat to the U.S. standing in the Arab world and concern that pressure on Israel might only heighten the likelihood of precipitate action on the part of Jerusalem.

In the case of the Syrian missiles, the administration's original hard line against Damascus, the USSR's main ally in the Arab world, was quickly replaced by Ambassador Philip Habib's shuttle mission to avoid any conflagration. The U.S. government credited Saudi Arabia with having played an important role in defusing the crisis, a conclusion contributing to even closer bilateral relations.

The attack against Iraq embarrassed the United States, since it used American-built planes. This resulted in a temporary embargo on the sale of such equipment by the United States to Israel; the embargo was extended after the Beirut raid of July 1981. The skirmishes and shellings on the Israel-Lebanon border resulted in a U.S.-organized cease-fire involving the PLO, though this did not seem to alter American views on the question of broader negotiations with that organization.

The Gulf and Arab-Israeli policies most notably came into collision in the fierce battle over the sale of AWACS advance-warning radar planes to Saudi Arabia. The Saudis requested the planes after the onset of the Iran-Iraq war. Four planes with necessary support personnel were sent to Saudi Arabia under American control, and in October 1980, Riyadh announced its interest in purchasing the aircraft.

In addition, the Saudis wanted to improve their already purchased F-15s with bomb racks, auxiliary fuel tanks, and air-to-air missiles. Originally, this equipment—which could extend the range of these planes and make them more useful as offensive weapons—was denied by the United States lest the planes be used in any future war with Israel. This decision, made by the Carter administration when it was trying to win Israeli support for Camp David, was reversed by that same government as part of its turn toward a Carter Doctrine approach in the Gulf. The $2 billion sale, it was argued by supporters, would enhance Saudi security and protect the oil fields. These were prime U.S. interests as well, since the continued supply of Saudi petroleum was a major strategic and economic requirement of the West. The intelligence gathered, they said, would be available to the United States to monitor Soviet, Iranian, and other activities in the region. Bilateral relations with Saudi Arabia would be strengthened and U.S. credibility with the Gulf states would be enhanced.

Opponents of the sale saw it as endangering America's most advanced and secret technology by putting it in the hands of an unstable regime. Indeed, the continued large-scale sales of arms might undermine the Saudi monarchy, as had happened in Iran. Israel's security could also be threatened, since the planes could allegedly overlook that country's air activities and might be used to coordinate Arab air forces in any future conflict. Moreover, opponents of the sale contended, Saudi Arabia was doing little to help U.S. regional efforts or to further the Camp David peace process. Finally, by making it more likely that Saudi forces would be drawn into an Arab-Israeli war or that Israel might attack Saudi Arabia, the sale could have an effect opposite to that intended.

The sharp struggle in Congress finally ended with a narrow victory for the Reagan administration in October 1981. Washington sought to assuage Jerusalem with promises of further aid and an agreement on future security cooperation, though the latter quickly collapsed after Israel's change in the Golan's status. Despite these corollary actions, the decisions on AWACS and the air-force equipment for Saudi Arabia did not represent any clear turning point toward supporting the Arab position on the conflict and distancing America from Israel, though individuals on both sides purported to see this.

During the summer of 1981, Saudi Crown Prince Fahd introduced an eight-point proposal, which came to be known as the Fahd Plan. While calling for a return of the territories occupied by Israel in the 1967 war and endorsing a Palestinian state, the Fahd Plan also held out the possibility of Saudi recognition of Israel. This initiative was rejected by Israel and by most of the Arab world as well at a summit meeting in Fez, Morocco, some months later. President Reagan gave a mild but not uncritically positive statement on this program in the fall of 1981. The Israeli government saw this as an antagonistic move, whereas some Arabs unfairly blamed the United States for the plan's failure to receive endorsement at Fez.

Israel's invasion of Lebanon in June 1982 led to some dramatic developments in U.S. policy. Washington's lukewarm attitude toward the attack in its opening days, along with the disorganized and weak response of the Arab states, the PLO, and the Soviets, allowed Israel to carry its offensive on to Beirut.

Israel's victory brought benefits for the United States; these included the defeat of Syrian and PLO forces, their likely withdrawal from Lebanon, the election of a pro-Western regime there, and the demonstration that the United States held the cards in the Arab-Israeli conflict. But there were also costs involved: Arab claims that America was implicated or supportive of the attack threatened Washington's position in the region. Efforts were needed to reduce the negative impact and to take advantage of the opportunities opened by the invasion. These measures included Ambassador Philip Habib's negotiations for a cease-fire, PLO evacuation of Beirut, and the removal of foreign forces from Lebanon. The United States was once again at the center of events, showing its power and leverage through its influence on Israel and "honest broker" position between the parties.

The second element in this process was the long-awaited declaration of a U.S. position on the Arab-Israeli conflict through President Reagan's speech of September 1, 1982. Reagan carefully voiced support for Israel's security, while advocating a federated Jordanian-Palestinian state to govern the occupied territoreis. Israel's invasion of Lebanon seemed to have stimulated Amman to move toward a "Jordanian solution" if it could receive an Arab mandate. Another summit at Fez refused to provide this, however, and issued a watered-down version of the Fahd Plan. Nevertheless, it did not attack Reagan's plan and represented another Arab step toward eventually dealing with Israel.

While Reagan's efforts to gain some mandate for Jordan continued, the show of friendship toward the Arabs represented in the new Reagan position—for example, the call for a freeze on construction of new Israeli settlements in the occupied territories—helped shore up the reinforced U.S. regional position. A demonstration of U.S. desire to make progress on the issue was as important as—and more realistic than—any proximity of a dramatic breakthrough.

Gulf Security Efforts

The administration's continued stress on the Gulf was shown by President Reagan's October 1, 1981, remark at a news conference— "Saudi Arabia we will not permit to be an Iran." This implied that Washington would intervene not only against any Soviet advance on the Gulf—the Carter Doctrine—but also in the event of internal revolution in the Saudi kingdom.

Whether such outside U.S. military intervention would change the course of a domestic Saudi struggle or stir even wider turmoil and anti-Americanism remained open to question. Further, the United States was still far away from any realistic ability to project such force. Still, agreements signed by the Carter administration with Kenya, Oman, and Somalia seemed likely to furnish some facilities. Supplies were stored aboard naval vessels in the area, and there was the possibility for the United States to employ the Egyptian installation at Ras Bannas. Nonetheless, all these potential staging points required a great deal of expenditure and construction to make them useful.

American links were also strengthened with Pakistan, now a frontline state given the Soviet presence in Afghanistan. Some U.S. officials thought that Pakistan could play some role in Gulf security. Yet critics warned that the Pakistani government might itself prove to be an unstable pillar to lean on even in the more immediate context. U.S. aid to Pakistan had been cut off in 1979 because of that country's nuclear program, which congressional observers believed was aimed toward production of atomic weapons. The White House overcame this obstacle and offered Pakistani leader Zia al-Haq far more than an original Carter administration offer that he had labeled "peanuts." The most important item in the arms supplies were F-16s.

Although the Reagan administration naturally continued a hostile position toward the Soviet presence in Afghanistan, it did not provide much assistance to the nationalist guerrillas there, although some weapons had been supplied covertly even before the Carter administration left office. As with its predecessors (ironically in view of its strong anti-Soviet posture), the Reagan White House seemed content with mostly symbolic measures. Perhaps it cynically believed that the Afghans were already tying down Soviet troops but could not actually win the conflict.

Conclusions

By the fall of 1982, the United States seemed reasonably well covered against any direct Soviet offensive in the Middle East, but the possibility of internal upheavals or regional disputes disrupting American interests remained high. The RDF had still not found, or been assigned, a clear role, and the "strategic consensus" enjoyed only limited success.

Nevertheless, political developments in the region worked to the advantage of the United States. The specter of an Iranian victory in the war with Iraq raised particular concern among the Gulf Arabs and pushed them toward de facto cooperation with the United States. Arab-Israeli tensions, while creating many headaches, had weakened forces historically hostile to the United States and strengthened relatively moderate trends in the Arab world. U.S. credibility on the issue was maintained by President Reagan's September 1982 peace proposal.

The real test of Reagan's administration would be how it would react to—and be altered by—a large-scale crisis. This, in turn, would be affected by the nature and location of such a problem. Unfortunately, the lessons of the post–Camp David period for the United States took place in an atmosphere of great frustration and tension. Historic progress was achieved at Camp David, but attempts to move toward a comprehensive peace or steady progress were stymied. The Reagan administration avoided activism in dealing with this problem as long as possible, but in the face of necessity finally picked the most plausible approach.

Focusing on the less likely possibility of Soviet intervention in the region, however, did not greatly contribute toward solving the more immediate existing and future problems. During the last three decades, Middle East regimes have been destabilized by internal revolutionary forces, often in the form of military coups. Old regimes, unable to adjust to changing social realities and intellectual currents, fell by the wayside. The strain of arms races, the development of large military establishments, and the pressures of maintaining a militant foreign policy have contributed to this process.

Even before the tidal wave of oil income hit the Middle East following the 1973 war, it had become clear that the region's rapid development had brought political problems in its wake. The migration of peasants into the cities, increasing expectations, and demands of classes outside the political power structure (including the military caste) had brought to power radical military-dominated regimes. Despite their rhetoric, however, these did little better than their predecessors in solving their countries' social and economic problems.

Such factors remain the principal threats to individual countries. Now required are American strategies to encourage flexibility and adjustment to these forces. The attractiveness of good relations with the United States lies in the fact that America can help provide tools—including military ones in reasonable quantity and variety—to help nations defend and develop themselves. Nonetheless, by the 1980s it had become clear that the United States could not simply establish a pax Americana over the region. Ironically, the peak of American strength, in the 1950s, coincided with the greatest level of instability in the area.

Yet the weakness and shortcomings of other factors in the region pressed America's standing as the only force capable of mediating the Arab-Israeli dispute and of serving as protector of the Gulf states against some of the threats they faced. These "natural" advantages of the United States were illustrated by the evolution of the Iran-Iraq war and of Arab-Israeli hostility. It appears that the Reagan administration was lucky rather than skillful in benefitting from these developments.

Notes

1. U.S. Department of State, Bureau of Public Affairs, "President Carter's Trip to the Middle East," Selected Documents, no. 10 (Washington, D.C.: U.S. Government Printing Office, March 1979), p. 3.

2. Ibid., p. 10.

3. U.S. Congress, House of Representatives, Committee on Foreign Affairs, "Economic Support Fund Programs in the Middle East" (Washington, D.C.: U.S. Government Printing Office, April 1979), pp. 22–23.

4. William Quandt, "The Middle East Crisis," *Foreign Affairs*, vol. 58, no. 3 (1980), pp. 547–549.

5. *Washington Post,* October 23, 1979.

6. U.S.-Iran relations are discussed in more detail in Barry Rubin, *Paved with Good Intentions: The American Experience and Iran* (New York: Oxford University Press, 1980), and in "American Relations with the Islamic Republic of Iran, 1979–1981," *Iranian Studies,* vol. 13, nos. 1–4 (1980), pp. 307–320.

7. See the *New York Times*/CBS poll, *New York Times,* November 16, 1980.

8. *New York Times,* January 21, 1980.

9. *New York Times,* January 22, 1980.

10. For an analysis of U.S.-Arab trade, which forms the vast bulk of U.S. trade with the Middle East, see Charles Issawi, "The Historical Development of U.S.-Arab Economic Relations," *Arab-American Affairs,* no. 3 (Winter 1982), pp. 20–21.

Part 2

Regional Perspectives

3
The Post–Camp David Arab World

Shireen T. Hunter
Robert E. Hunter

The most frequently recurring image in the Arab world long has been that of leaders who—having only a short time before been seriously at odds with each other or even mortal enemies—are then seen warmly embracing in a surge of Arab brotherhood. Sometimes these manifestations of brotherly affection among Arab leaders are accompanied by declarations of impending mergers between, or unification of, their countries. Thus during the past twenty-five years or so there have been more than a half-dozen merger attempts involving two or more Arab countries. Yet these manifestations of Arab brotherhood and unity generally do not last long, and very often the images of Arab leaders in friendly embrace are replaced by images of anger and the trading of acrimonious charges and countercharges.

Of course, this characteristic of Arab politics makes a full grasp of its complexities very difficult for outside observers, and even for those Arabs who have not mastered the art of politics. However, these rapidly changing patterns of Arab politics do not stem primarily from the whims of Arab leaders—although individual desires sometimes play a role. Rather, they are essentially the result of much more significant factors, such as the Arab countries' geostrategic situations; their economic resources; their social, political, and religious makeups; their national aspirations; and their historical experiences—including long-standing rivalries with both Arab and other neighboring countries. These changing patterns reflect the impact of international factors on regional developments, including the effects of superpower rivalry and East-West confrontation.

In fact, during the four years that have elapsed since the signing of the Egyptian-Israeli peace treaty, the Arab political scene has to a remarkable degree reflected the close interaction of all these factors.

The events of the last few years have illustrated how close and intricate the interaction has become, not only among developments occurring in the traditional regions of the so-called Arab heartland but also in peripheral areas. Events in places like Chad and Ethiopia, not to mention Afghanistan and, of course, Iran, are having a major impact on developments in the Arab world proper. But nowhere during the past several years has the interaction been greater than in developments in the zone of Arab-Israeli conflict and in the Gulf.

The origins of this close interaction date from the Arab defeat in the 1967 Six-Day War and the subsequent Khartoum Conference of Arab heads of state, during which, for the first time, one group of Arab countries (Saudi Arabia, Kuwait, Libya) undertook major financial responsibility vis-à-vis their weakened neighbors (Egypt, Syria, and Jordan).[1] By doing so, these countries became more directly involved in the Arab-Israeli conflict, at the same time earning themselves a greater say in the formulation of Arab policy toward Israel. They also acquired a greater capacity to influence the content and direction of the foreign policies—both regional and international—of those Arab countries involved in physical hostilities with Israel.[2]

Two further, almost simultaneous, developments brought the Gulf countries (including, to a lesser degree, non-Arab Iran) into the mainstream of Arab politics and made them significant players on the Middle Eastern and international political scenes. They were the British military withdrawal from the Gulf and changes in the international oil market—the latter culminating in the Arab oil embargo and the oil price explosion of 1973. The combined effects of these two developments were: (1) a tremendous increase in the value of the Gulf countries to the industrial world, and (2) a heightening of their prestige and influence both regionally and internationally—influence that essentially derived from the vast financial resources they had accumulated as a result of the rise in oil prices.

The growing importance of the Gulf to Western industrial countries meant that the region became the focus of even greater East-West conflict. The survival of the pro-Western regimes of the Gulf gained primary importance to the West, and Western countries increasingly evaluated events in other parts of the Arab world and its periphery in light of the impact of those events on Gulf security. The Soviet invasion of Afghanistan, Iran's weakness, and Moscow's efforts to enter Gulf security discussions sharpened Western concern.

The interaction between the Gulf and other parts of the Arab world—in particular, the zone of Arab-Israeli conflict—was increased as a result of yet another development. This time the tendency was to *reduce* the independent influence of the Gulf countries and to set limits to their impact on the evolution of Arab policies—particularly those relating to such fundamental issues as the Arab-Israeli conflict. What occurred was the massive emigration of labor from poorer Arab countries to the Gulf following the development boom created by the oil-price increases. Among these immigrants were large numbers of Palestinians, although Palestinian immigration at least to one Gulf country (Kuwait) had started long before these developments. The consequences of large numbers of Palestinians in the Gulf countries (even though they could not become citizens) were a need for greater sensitivity on the part of their governments in dealing with the Palestinian problem and limitations imposed on their freedom of choice regarding policies toward the Arab-Israeli conflict. The impact of the Palestinian factor was further strengthened by the fact that since 1967 the PLO had grown into a considerable, albeit factionalized, military and political force in the Arab world. The presence of large groups of nonindigenous Arabs in the Gulf states also meant that the hitherto traditional and closed Gulf societies became much more permeable to the political and ideological currents of the larger Arab world.

Notwithstanding these close interactions and intricate linkages, the state of the immediate regional environment itself has affected the behavior of Arab countries, in particular those of the Gulf. Whenever the latter have felt less threatened by the regional environment (e.g., after the oil revolution of 1973), they have pursued a more active policy both regionally and internationally, one aimed at exerting more influence in determining the direction of Arab politics. But whenever the regional environment has appeared threatening and hostile (e.g., after the fall of the shah), they have opted for a more cautious and less active stand.

The Political Landscape of the Arab World and Its Periphery in 1979

During the five years (1973–1978) of active diplomatic effort at regional and international levels—an activity dubbed petro-dollar diplomacy—the Gulf countries, led by Saudi Arabia, had managed to bring about considerable changes in the pattern of inter-Arab alignments, changes favorable to their own interests. They had also helped change the international posture of a number of key Arab countries, bringing them closer to their own stands (e.g., moderate Arab influence on Egyptian attitudes toward the Soviet Union beginning as early as the late 1960s). In the context of the Arab-Israeli conflict, the Gulf countries had also managed to win far greater sympathy—if not yet active support—for the Arab cause among European and Third World countries, thus enhancing their legitimacy and prestige in the Arab world. Relations with those Arab countries that were not actually won over (e.g., Syria) were nevertheless tolerable, with few exceptions, because of extensive use of the Gulf countries' financial resources.

The situation in the peripheral countries, particularly Iran in the Gulf region, was also satisfactory to the Gulf Arabs. They were not completely comfortable with the growing power of Iran, the largest and most populous (but non-Arab) regional state, but nevertheless viewed Iran as maintaining a regional environment that was essentially compatible with the security interests of the Gulf Arab countries and their friends elsewhere in the Arab world. For example, even though many Gulf Arabs resented Iran's military assistance to Oman to combat the Dhofar rebellion and protested against it, they nevertheless benefitted from its results. Iran also kept in check Iraq's growing power, which—although the Gulf Arab countries never would admit it—was more threatening to the security and territorial integrity of at least the smaller Gulf countries than Iran had ever been or could be.[3] Moreover, Iran had greatly improved its relations with most of the Arab countries and had adopted a more pro-Arab stand—at least on the surface—on the Arab-Israeli conflict. In fact, Arab-Iranian relations had improved to such a degree that there was talk of a Cairo-Riyadh-Teheran axis developing in the Middle East. This is not to say that competition was not high—particularly between Iran and Saudi Arabia—or that strong misgivings and disagreements did not persist; but as far as the fundamentals of regional security were concerned, there was a large degree of community of interest among these countries.

Cracks had begun to appear in this rather nice picture by mid-1978. On the one hand, President Sadat had engaged in his own independent Middle East diplomacy with Israel, effectively cutting off his Gulf friends (but not the shah, who supported him). On the other hand, Iran was undergoing unprecedented social and political turmoil that for the first time in twenty-five years put in serious doubt the survival of the Pahlavi regime. By March 1979, when the Egyptian-Israeli peace treaty was signed, the situation in the Gulf had deteriorated even further as a result of the shah's collapse.

Although one of the primary preoccupations of Middle East analysts has been deciding on the degree of impact of the Iranian revolution on Gulf security, the extent to which the Iranian revoution has also affected regional attitudes on a number of other important issues, including the Egyptian-Israeli peace treaty, has not been sufficiently appreciated. It is not the intention of this paper to compensate for this neglect, but it is nevertheless necessary to address the impact of the Iranian revolution on the Gulf and on other parts of the Arab world.

Iran's Revolution, Iraq's Ambitions, and Gulf Politics

The revolution in Iran had three important consequences for the Gulf Arab countries: it removed Iran's much resented yet highly stabilizing influence from the Gulf region; it turned Iran into a source of instability (though mostly indirect); and it created opportunities—actually irresistible temptations—for Iraq to try to establish its hegemony in the Gulf and its predominant influence in the Arab world.[4] Developments both in the Gulf and other parts of the Arab world seemed to favor Iraq.

On the Gulf front, Saudi Arabia and smaller Gulf countries experienced the shock of the Iranian revoution and its reverberations within their own countries. For example, in November and December 1979 Saudi Arabia was shaken by the seizure of the Grand Mosque in Mecca by a group of Islamic (Sunni) fundamentalists and by the Shia riots in its eastern provinces. Kuwait, Bahrain, and the UAE also had their share of Shia agitation. In addition to the impact of the Iranian example of the Gulf's Shia population, there was the newly-forged alliance between revolutionary Iran and the PLO (particularly its more extreme factions), as well as with other radical Arab countries, such as Libya—a combination that led to a serious deterioration in the state of the regional environment.[5] Furthermore, in the aftermath of the shah's downfall, the Gulf countries, particularly Saudi Arabia, were feeling extremely insecure about their relations with the United States and were gripped with anxiety regarding the U.S. attitude should they themselves be threatened by an Iran-like situation.[6] On the Arab-Israeli front, meanwhile, Egypt's peace treaty with Israel had removed it from the Arab military equation with Israel and had left Syria feeling exposed and insecure.

Under these circumstances, Iraq seemed to be the only country in the Arab world with enough physical strength, when combined with a clear sense of direction, to be capable of unifying Arab ranks and charting a new Arab security and political strategy both toward Israel and in the Gulf region.

Despite its apparent aloofness from Arab and international politics, Iraqi leaders—in particular Saddam Hussein—have been paving the way for Iraq's reemergence since at least 1973. For example, Iraq had begun quietly to work with a number of West European countries, particularly France, and had expanded the scope of its economic and military cooperation with them.[7] These activities gained much faster tempo in 1979 as a result of the increase in Iraq's oil revenues and the assumption of total power by Saddam Hussein. During this period, Iraq also had quietly begun to improve its relations with a number of Arab countries, essentially through economic assistance, with Jordan being the best example. Iraq also followed the same policy toward a number of Third World countries, a move that illustrated the breadth of Iraq's ambitions, which reached far beyond the Arab world.[8]

Thus Iraq was poised to assume a larger role in the Arab and Third worlds, even had the Iranian revolution not happened and had it not so drastically changed regional conditions. This would have been so not only as a result of Iraq's conscious policy but also because Egypt's removal from the Arab scene after Camp David had created a vacuum that Iraq was only too eager to fill. But it was the Iranian revolution and the apparently total collapse of the Iranian armed forces that propelled Iraq so rapidly into a leadership role during 1979 and 1980, until the start of the war with Iran.

To begin with, Iraq organized the Baghdad Summit meetings of Arab heads of state in November 1978 and April 1979. Later, in February 1980, Saddam Hussein introduced his own version of a Pan-Arab charter, urging the Arabs to steer clear of superpower links and to opt for strict nonalignment. Parallel with the introduction of his charter, Saddam Hussein apparently informed the Gulf countries that Baghdad's own special relationship with Moscow was over, a move that had already been indicated by Iraq's negative attitude to the Soviet intervention in Afghanistan during the Islamic Conference in January 1980.[9] The purpose of the charter was quite clear: to prevent a formal alliance between the Gulf countries and the United States and thus to make Iraq the final arbiter of Gulf affairs. Considering that this was the time, following the Soviet invasion of Afghanistan, when the United States had enunciated its new strategy for the defense of the Gulf—a strategy that included very close military cooperation with Gulf and some Arab and African countries—Iraq had to move quickly. In its proposed charter, Iraq—in a veiled manner—offered its military assistance and protection to other Arab countries, especially those of the Gulf area.

On the Arab-Israeli front, as well, as early as September 1978 Iraq seized on Syria's sense of insecurity after the signing of the Camp David accords and set out to improve its relations with Damascus. Progress was rapid, and in October 1978 Iraqi and Syrian leaders declared that, ending a decade of hostility, they would merge the two countries. In the months that followed, they made considerable progress towards political and economic cooperation, but their negotiations bogged down on the issue of the unification of their two Ba'ath parties. The ideological differences proved to be much more serious and intractable than had been imagined. Even so, ideological hagglings were in reality the outward manifestation of a much more important power struggle between Iraqi and Syrian leaders. For example, as a prerequisite to unity the Iraqis demanded that Syria reestablish the legitimacy of the Ba'ath party, which in fact meant that the Syrian leadership should dissolve itself and hand power to the founders of the Syrian Ba'ath. Since Iraq had given sanctuary to these leaders who had fled from Syria, such a move would guarantee Iraq's influence over the Syrian leadership.[10] It is no wonder, therefore, that despite the Syrians' desire to gain increased military support and strategic depth to correct the balance of power with Israel, they refused the deal.

Then, in July 1979, a coup attempt was uncovered in Iraq, and the Iraqis accused Syria's President Hafez Assad of having been involved. Consequently the unity talks collapsed. In view of the depth of the historical and ideological rivalry between Iraq and Syria, the possibility of Syrian involvement in the Iraqi coup attempt cannot be ruled out. Nevertheless, some Arab sources believe that Iraq might have exaggerated the July plot when it realized that there would be no return to Orthodox Ba'athism in Syria and consequently no Iraqi control of Syrian politics.[11]

Another factor that must have contributed to the failure of Iraqi-Syrian rapprochement was the opposite directions in which the two countries were moving in regard to their superpower connections. Despite occasional strains in its relations with the Soviet Union and flirtations with the United States, culminating in the Carter-Assad meeting of May 1977, Syria essentially remained committed to close relations with the Soviet Union, while Iraq was loosening its Soviet ties and drawing closer to the West.

After the failure of the Syrian venture, Saddam Hussein concentrated his attention even more on Gulf affairs and pursued with more determination the forging of a closely knit relationship with Jordan. For its part, Syria shortly afterwards turned to Libya and in September 1980 entered into a "union"—illogical and unlikely as it may sound— with that country.

The resurgence of Iraq as the strongest regional power in the Gulf and its hyperactive diplomacy, combined with the other factors referred to earlier (e.g., the Iranian revolution, the Camp David accords, and the relative erosion of the Gulf countries' confidence in their alliance with the United States), led the Gulf countries, including Saudi Arabia, to adopt a very cautious, noncommittal, and almost reactive policy. This underlying caution characterized their policies toward matters of regional security and the Arab-Israeli conflict. Thus for over a year the Gulf countries echoed Iraq's call to keep the Gulf free of superpower presence and to develop a self-reliant military force for the Gulf's defense. The only exception was Oman's Sultan Qabus (who incidentally fancied himself as the guardian of the Strait of Hormuz), who openly advocated a policy of cooperation between the Gulf countries and the United States. Whatever one might think of Qabus, he nevertheless very clearly saw through Iraq's designs and openly said that the kind of "military self-reliance" that was accepted by the Saudis was "little more than reliance on the Iraqis."[12]

The caution about superpower involvement demonstrated by the Gulf countries did not mean, however, that they were happy with growing Iraqi power or that they did nothing to organize themselves more effectively. Quite the contrary: security and other cooperation among the Gulf countries was stepped up. For example, in October 1979 the Gulf leaders gathered in Taif, Saudi Arabia, to confer about regional security; Iraq was not invited to the meeting. It was clear at the time, however, that Iraq could not be kept out of Gulf affairs much longer. In fact, Saudi Arabia had already gone a long way to improve its relations with Baghdad, but it must be remembered that Saudi-Iraqi relations have never been as bad as Iraq's relations with the smaller Gulf countries, particularly Kuwait. In fact, as a result of Iran's growing power, by the mid-1970s Saudi Arabia and Iraq had begun limited and discreet cooperation on internal security issues and certain aspects of regional politics.

As far as the stance of the Gulf countries during this period toward the Arab-Israeli conflict was concerned, and particularly the stance of Saudi Arabia, developments in the Gulf exerted considerable influence. For instance, although it is impossible to determine what Saudi attitudes would have been toward the Camp David accords had there not been an Iranian revolution, it is nevertheless true that the heightened state of regional instability and Iran's new links with the Palestinians and radical Arab states (such as Syria and Libya) made it much more difficult for Saudi Arabia to be accommodating. At least rhetorically, the Saudis even tried to outbid the radicals, and King Khalid called for a holy war against Israel. For similar reasons, plus the presence of large number of Palestinians in their midst, other Gulf countries took an uncompromising stand vis-à-vis Camp David. This situation was to change, however, after the outbreak of the war between Iran and Iraq.

The Iran-Iraq War:
Impact on the Gulf and Arab Politics

By September 1980, all outward indications were that Iraq was the up-and-coming power in the Arab world and certainly the new regional "superpower" in the Gulf region. Yet despite all the appearances of strength and force, Iraq had serious internal problems. These essentially derived from Iraq's ethnic and religious makeup and the nature of its leadership—problems that predated the Iranian revolution, but nevertheless were exacerbated by it. Iraq's single most serious problem—as perceived by its leaders—was the danger of rising fundamentalism among its Shia population. Official Iraqi statistics indicate a 50/50 balance between the Shia and Sunni populations, whereas the opposition groups claim that the Shias constitute 80 percent of Iraq's population. A more realistic estimate is somewhere between 55 to 60 percent. But the Shia-Sunni balance becomes particularly significant if one excludes the non-Arab, but Sunni, Kurds; the Shia Arabs then have a clear majority. Nevertheless, despite their numerical majority, the Shias in Iraq have always been an underprivileged class—economically and politically. Rather than rectifying this condition, the growing tendency of the Ba'athist regime, and particularly the Takriti clan, was to concentrate power in the hands of its closest allies, diminishing even further the level of Shia participation in Iraq's political life. Moreover, the secular and socialist character of the Ba'athist ideology was not very appealing to the Shias, particularly the clerical establishment. Consequently, during the 1970s there were several Shia riots in Iraq (e.g., 1974, 1977, 1979), which the government blamed on Syrian and Iranian instigation. There were also Shia underground opposition groups (e.g., Al Dawah, or "the call," and the Mujahadeen). The Iraqi leadership treated the Shia dissidents very harshly. According to Hana Batatu, Saddam Hussein has admitted to having killed, between 1974–1979, 500 of Iraq's prominent Shias, including the foremost Iraqi religious leader, Imam Baghir Sadr.[13]

Needless to say, the Iranian revolution gave a new impetus to Iraq's Shia dissident movement. Moreover, given the animosity between Saddam Hussein and Ayatollah Ruhollah Khomeini, Iran started to agitate among the Iraqi Shias. But the possibility of an Iranian-type revolution in Iraq was only one—and certainly not the most important—reason for Iraq's attack on Iran in September 1980. Iraq's other principal objective was in fact to cut Iran down to size once and for all, for instance, by separating Khuzistan from Iran and thus guaranteeing Iraq's future supremacy in the Gulf. Given Iran's chaotic state, the disintegration of its armed forces, and the international hostility it faced because of the still-continuing American-hostage crisis, the Iraqis decided that the time had come to strike.

Iraq expected a quick victory, a sort of *blitzkrieg* that would bring Iran to its knees and also get rid of Khomeini, but this was not to be the case. The war proved to be, if not the undoing of Saddam Hussein, at least the shattering of his grandiose ambitions. At the beginning of the war, the Gulf countries faced the awkward situation that their short- and long-term interests would suffer no matter who won. A victory by Iran most probably would embolden it to export its revolution more aggressively to other parts of the Gulf, thus increasing the threat of instability and subversion. By contrast, a victory by Iraq, making it the overwhelmingly superior regional power, would seriously reduce the Gulf countries' freedom of action in regional and inter-Arab matters. Moreover, some Gulf countries (such as Kuwait) could not be sure that, after victory over Iran, Iraq would not press its territorial claims on other countries.

But the expected *blitzkreig* turned into a trench war, a situation that, once the danger of the war's expansion to other parts of the Gulf had passed, best suited the Gulf countries' interests. The war kept Iran and Iraq occupied with a militarily and economically debilitating venture and provided the Gulf countries with additional time to coordinate and organize their efforts to deal with their security problems. It also gave them an opportunity to gain leverage over Iraq through giving it financial assistance (estimated at a total of $20–$30 billion) and other forms of indirect aid to help it in its war effort against Iran.

The Gulf Cooperation Council

Efforts to develop some kind of collective security arrangements among the Gulf countries date from the late 1960s. These efforts failed because of Arab-Iranian rivalry and mutual distrust. As noted above, after the Iranian revolution Iraq took the lead in organizing Gulf affairs and tried to chart a nonaligned course for the Gulf countries within the framework of its Pan-Arab charter. But after Iraq became preoccupied with its war with Iran, the other Gulf countries stepped up their efforts to forge closer cooperation and coordination of military, security, and other policies. The culmination of these efforts was the creation of the Gulf Cooperation Council (GCC) in the winter of 1981.

The GCC is characterized by its members as their first step toward the integration of economic, social, political, and military policies.[14] Important as the GCC's projected economic integration might be, however, it was not the real impetus for its creation. First was the integration of the internal security apparatuses of the Gulf countries and later their military and defense establishments. As early as 1980, Saudi Arabia—the prime mover—started negotiating with other Gulf countries to conclude bilateral security agreements, and it has already signed such an agreement with Bahrain. Saudi Arabia in fact wants to create a kind of Gulf Interpol, using its own extensive security network. Its General Intelligence Department has installed a large computer-assisted surveillance system ordered from the United Kingdom in 1975, which became fully operational in 1981. It involves twenty-seven computer-linked branch offices connected to two main centers in Riyadh and Jeddah through scrambled radio links. The branches are sited at airports, frontier posts, and major industrial complexes and in all the main towns. According to experts, this system could easily be extended to cover the other Gulf countries by the addition of a few extra terminals. Such a linkage has already been achieved with Bahrain.

Saudi Arabia also has been behind the move to integrate the Gulf's defense establishments. Defense ministers of the Gulf countries have met in Riyadh several times. Apparently they have agreed in principle on a broad, mutual defense plan aimed at integrating their air defenses and creating a Gulf early warning system plus a command, control, and communications capability that would include the Saudi Airborne Warning and Control System (AWACS). They seem also to have agreed to establish a coordinated arms-procurement policy, so that the six states would have compatible arms systems, and a domestic Gulf defense industry and to integrate units from each of the six armed forces into a Gulf "rapid deployment force" to meet local threats.[15]

The GCC's security and military dimension acquires particular significance in light of U.S.-Saudi military-cooperation agreements. It is evident that a more integrated Gulf security and military network would facilitate the linking of U.S. and local strategies for the defense of the Gulf. Nonetheless, there may be problems ahead even though the Gulf countries have rushed into making extensive commitments because of their feelings of insecurity, and the future course of Gulf cooperation might not be all that smooth. For example:

- There still are territorial disputes and other rivalries among the GCC members.[16]
- There are significant policy differences among the GCC members. For instance, Kuwait's more determinedly nonaligned posture is in sharp contrast with Oman's pro-Western stance.

- There are misgivings among at least some GCC members that the whole setup might just serve to legitimize Saudi hegemony over the southern littoral of the Gulf. (We should not forget that Saudi Arabia did not recognize the UAE until 1974, three years after its creation.)
- There is the Iraqi factor, although for the time being it is somewhat less important. Iraq is a regional power but not a GCC member. After the creation of the GCC, Iraq's foreign minister said that this type of cooperation should be carried out within the context of the Arab League. Consequently, once Iraq recovers from the effects of war—although this will take some time—it certainly would not accept its exclusion from Gulf affairs. The Iraqi problem would become much more serious in the event of Saddam Hussein's fall. In fact, this fear has led Saudi Arabia, at least, to think about bringing Iraq into the Gulf defense system.
- There are misgivings among other Arabs regarding the GCC. Some feel that the GCC is only a rich man's club and point to the absence of the two Yemens. Others feel that it is undermining the Arab League. And yet others think that it is just a cover for a greater Western presence in the Gulf.

Notwithstanding these negative considerations, as long as present conditions of instability continue to persist, the Gulf countries will probably continue to develop the GCC. This trend in turn will enhance Saudi Arabia's leadership role in the Gulf. However, neither the integration of Gulf security and defense nor the imposition of Saudi influence will be easily achieved.

Changes in Gulf conditions as a result of the Iran-Iraq war also led to a more active Saudi policy on the Arab-Israeli front. Thus, unlike 1979 and 1980 when Saudi Arabia scrupulously followed the Arab consensus against Camp David, in 1981 the Saudis took a major initiative and promoted the Fahd Plan at the Fez Summit in November. Although the Fahd Plan ran aground on the hard rocks of Arab politics, it was significant in that it showed some Saudi willingness to risk getting its fingers burned in the business of talking about peace making in the Middle East.

The creation of the GCC provoked a negative reaction on the part of the radical Arabs. Some of them, worried by increased intra-Gulf activity and signs of greater Western presence in the Gulf, took countermeasures of their own. In August 1981, for instance, South Yemen (PDRY), Libya, and non-Arab Ethiopia met in Aden and signed a mutual cooperation agreement. The participants did not say that they were planning to create a network of facilities to rival those of the GCC (possibly to be used by the Soviets), but the PDRY president did say that the conference was aimed at preventing U.S. and Western military activity in the region.[17] Given the geographic location of the Aden group, it is unlikely that they could develop into anything like the GCC, but they are likely to cooperate more closely with one another. Thus the effect of the GCC's creation, combined with other developments, has been to further polarize Gulf and Arab politics.

Developments in the Gulf led to the polarization of Arab politics on other fronts as well and made it more difficult for the Arabs to reach consensus on other important issues, such as the Arab-Israeli problem. The Fahd Plan, for example, was a casualty of this polarization.

The Arab-Israeli Zone

Even prior to the Lebanon war, a number of important events affected the political scene in the Arab-Israeli zone, which had remained relatively stable since the signing of the Egyptian-Israeli peace treaty. Events in the Gulf continued to affect this zone, the most significant result being the growing rift between Syria and most of the Arab states.

Syria has been the only Arab country actively to support Iran in its war with Iraq, although Libya and to a lesser extent, Algeria, have also shown sympathy for Iran. The underlying reason for Syria's behavior is, of course, the deep-rooted historical and ideological rivalry between it and Iraq.[18] Therefore, under no circumstances could Syria let Iraq become too strong and influential in the Arab world. But the fact that during the period under discussion Iraq had begun to move closer to moderate Arab states and the West, and farther away from the so-called Steadfastness Front, made it even more important for Syria to check the increase in Iraq's power.

Although Syrian policies might have contributed to Iraq's poor showing in the war, they also had certain costs. For example, when Israel annexed the Golan Heights in December 1981, President Assad toured Arab countries to harness Arab support for Syria. He even suggested reconvening the suspended Fez Summit, but his efforts met with total failure. Perhaps even more important, there were indications that the members of the Gulf Cooperation Council might stop their financial assistance to Syria should it continue its policies. Such a step would have seriously complicated the problems of President Assad, who already had internal unrest and, according to some reports, problems in the Syrian armed forces. It was unlikely that Syria's political gain could have compensated for a cutting-off of Gulf money from other sources, including Syria's ally Libya, with the latter's having felt the pinch of the global oil glut and falling prices. Syrian policy in regard to the Gulf war thus illustrated how the interests and aspirations of an Arab country in the Arab-Israeli zone could be affected by its behavior in regard to Gulf affairs.

A more significant development in the Arab-Israeli zone was the assassination of President Sadat and the assumption of power in Egypt by Husni Mubarak. President Sadat's policy of making peace with Israel had brought Egypt many benefits: the recovering of lost territory, including the valuable Sinai oil fields; an outpouring of Western (particularly U.S.) military and economic assistance; the reopening of the Suez Canal; a sharp increase in tourism; and most important, the reduction, if not total elimination, of the danger of another costly war with Israel.

Yet Sadat's policies also imposed certain costs, the most important of which was Egypt's almost complete isolation within the Arab world, symbolized by the removal of the Arab League headquarters from Cairo. The Egyptian public found this situation emotionally hard to deal with, particularly as time went on and the Arab position vis-à-vis Egypt did not soften. This was so because many Egyptians saw the country's leadership role in the Arab world taken away—in their view—by "lesser" countries such as Iraq and Saudi Arabia. It is true that Egyptians consider their country to be the heart and soul of the Arab world, but they also have understood that to realize its full potential Egypt needs that Arab world.

Sadat's policy of close identification with the West also was not pleasing to many Egyptians who took a certain pride in the country's early traditions of nonalignment. In fact, they resented Sadat's ending Russian influence only to replace it with U.S. influence, although they very much welcomed the former development.

Sadat's assassination by Muslim fundamentalists graphically illustrated the existence of popular dissatisfaction with certain aspects of his basic policies. It also illustrated the inherent fragility of Middle Eastern societies and political regimes even when they do not show outward signs of instability. When Mubarak took power there were grave uncertainties regarding both his capacity to rule the country and the direction in which he might point Egypt. Uncertainties in both regards considerably subsided after Mubarak showed dexterity in dealing with Egypt's opposition groups by adopting a firm attitude towards extremist groups—particularly the Muslim fundamentalists— while at the same time reaching out to other opposition groups.

Consequently, those groups that were highly critical of Sadat were willing to give Mubarak a chance.

After assuming the presidency, Mubarak also made several statements regarding the future economic and foreign policies of Egypt, in order to please his public. For example, he declared that the open-door policy and foreign investment associated with it should benefit the majority of the people and not just a small minority and should increase the country's productive capacity. In regard to foreign policy, Mubarak emphasized the importance of Egypt's relations with the Arab countries, reaffirmed Egypt's attachment to the principle of nonalignment, and even declared his readiness to improve relations with the Soviet Union.

Despite these statements, however, Mubarak did not take any actions (except for freeing a number of political prisoners and an ending of propaganda attacks on other Arab leaders) that could be considered major departures from the policies of the Sadat era. For this reason, Mubarak's statements were considered essentially to have been devices to buy time and to avoid hard choices, particularly as long as the Sinai withdrawal was not completed. Even after its completion, Egypt has faced a number of hard choices regarding economic policy and internal political organization, but—until the Lebanon war of June 1982—its foreign-policy choices became much simpler as a result of developments on the Gulf front.

Until the Lebanon war, the most difficult foreign-policy problem for Egypt was considered to be how to reconcile the requirement of maintaining cordial relations with Israel with the improvement of its relations with the Arab countries. It was largely believed that the Arab countries—even the moderates—would demand some cooling of Egypt's relations with Israel and its distancing from the Camp David process before they could readmit Egypt into the Arab fold. This Arab attitude in turn would have caused Egypt an extremely difficult problem in trying to balance these contradictory pressures.

But events in the Gulf, notably Iraq's poor showing in the war with Iran and the increased fears of the Gulf Arab countries about the repercussions of a possible Iranian victory, suddenly put Egypt in a somewhat more favorable bargaining position vis-à-vis the rest of the Arab world. In fact, Egypt gained a position in which it could demand some limited concessions from the Arab counries before it rejoined the Arab world. This is what Mubarak did—although not exactly in these terms—by asking the Arab countries to join Egypt in efforts to restore the rights of the Palestinians. He also seized the occasion of the death of Saudi Arabia's King Khalid to visit Riyadh and talk with King Fahd, with whom Mubarak had maintained contact during the period of strained Egyptian-Saudi relations.

In fact, despite the Lebanon war and continued Egyptian-Israeli relations, Iraq—the country that organized Arab opposition to Egypt in 1979—began moving towards reestablishing diplomatic relations with Egypt. Iraq has needed military supplies (Iraq concluded a $1 billion arms deal with Egypt), but most important it has needed direct military assistance, and Egypt was the only Arab country capable of giving it such aid.

In 1982, following Egypt's regaining of the entire Sinai, Jordan and Morocco sent congratulatory messages to Mubarak. Official statements from the Gulf Arab countries were muted, but the state-controlled media published favorable articles about Egypt. In fact, the Gulf countries had some real need for Egypt's return to the Arab fold. Iraq's poor showing in the war with Iran weakened Saddam Hussein's regime, with which the Gulf Arab countries had managed to establish more-or-less friendly relations. Should Saddam Hussein's regime fall and be replaced either by an Islamic fundamentalist or a more radical Ba'athist regime, this would greatly increase the Gulf countries' vulnerability. Thus they would value having Egypt more involved in Gulf affairs as a stabilizing force. Moreover, before the Iran-Iraq war the Gulf countries to some extent were counting on Iraq—albeit reluctantly—to help them organize against internal subversion or other regional challenges to their security. But Iraq's poor showing in the war demonstrated the limits of its military power. In these circumstances, the only Arab country that could effectively help the Gulf Arabs has been Egypt.

Despite these considerations, however, the Gulf countries may not be able to reestablish diplomatic relations with Egypt in the immediate future, because of the large number of Palestinians in the Gulf countries and the governments' fears of Palestinian reprisal, especially following the Lebanon war. In fact, as Naef Hawatmeh, the radical Palestinian leader, put it even before the war: "The Saudis fear Iran, but they also fear a great deal the Palestinian and Arab reactions."[19] Even though this diagnosis applied to even a greater extent to other Gulf countries and they may not be capable of immediately restoring diplomatic relations with Egypt, unofficial cooperation between them and Egypt probably will increase. Indeed, in December 1982, military delegations from both Iraq and the United Arab Emirates visited Egypt to negotiate arms deals,[20] and in January 1983, Iraqi Deputy Prime Minister Tariq Aziz, after publicly offering to discuss the restoration of ties with Egypt, met Egyptian Minister of State for

Foreign Affairs Butrus Ghali in the first high-level meeting between the two countries since Camp David.[21]

Before the Lebanon war, the combination of changes inside Egypt and those in the Gulf region, plus the final Israeli withdrawal from the Sinai, eased the way for some Arab-Egyptian reconciliation, but at the same time deepened divisions in the Arab world between the moderate and radical Arabs. It also led to renewed maneuvering between opposing Arab camps in order to preempt others' initiatives, particularly in regard to the Palestinian issue and Arab-Israeli relations. Thus, Saudi Arabia started talking to other Arab governments in order to organize a meeting of Arab heads of state that would approve the Fahd Plan. The radical Arabs also met in Algiers to try to map out a strategy to confront the Saudi initiative.

A particularly uncertain point in the midst of all these changes was the position of the PLO. When there was more-or-less unity among Arabs of whatever stripe in opposition to Egypt's role in Camp David, the PLO could count upon a large degree of latitude in setting its own course in balancing diplomatic approaches with terrorism. But if the moderate Arab states—especially those inovlved with the GCC, but also including Syria's archenemy, Iraq—were tempted to seek some Egyptian involvement with Gulf problems, the PLO's position had to be affected to some degree. The likelihood was that some of its elements would advocate a more rejectionist position out of a fear that one or more moderate Arab states would slacken their active opposition to Camp David.

The Lebanon War

These developments in Arab politics—especially involving linkages between the Gulf and the Arab-Israeli zone—were overtaken by Israel's invasion of Lebanon in June 1982. The war and events ensuing from it have had major consequences for the inter-Arab balance of power and politics, although their full and long-term implications have yet to become clear. Nevertheless, the behavior of the Arab countries, both during and after the war, has confirmed the underlying theme of this article—namely, the close linkage between Gulf politics and those of the Arab-Israeli zone, and the predominance of regional factors in the political calculations of individual Arab governments.

Thus the Gulf Arabs—including Iraq—remained largely silent and inactive during the Lebanon war, although Saudi Arabia did appeal to the United States to defuse the crisis. To be sure the experience was humiliating, and there was little of a practical nature that individual Arab states could have done. But in terms of marshalling Arab support, both Syria and the PLO suffered from their own past policies: the self-imposed "odd man out" stance of Damascus and the PLO effort over the years to pressure Arab states for support, despite competing preoccupations like Gulf security. The predominance of regional considerations also meant that, after the war, not only did Iraq continue to woo Egypt, but also Saddam Hussein hinted—in discussions with a U.S. congressman—that Iraq was prepared, under certain circumstance, to recognize Israel's right to exist.[22]

For its part, Egypt demonstrated during and after the war that it was principally concerned with preserving its treaty with Israel and its close relationship with the United States, despite its vulnerability to charges that peace with Israel paved the way for the latter's invasion of Lebanon. Egypt did prevent a return to negotiations under the aegis of Camp David while Israel continued to occupy parts of Lebanon, but it did not shape its overall stance in Arab politics based on that consideration.

Likewise, despite the depth of bitterness lingering from the Lebanon war, the moderate Arabs did feel a need to respond to the peace plan advanced by the United States in September 1982. In part, there was growing understanding of the difficulties of countering Israel through military means; but concerns about Gulf security also led the moderates of the region once again to give the Americans the benefit of the doubt. Still, the Arabs' capacity to unite behind a pragmatic stand different from their traditional one proved limited, although the Arab summit at Fez, Morocco, in September 1982 was on the surface a great show of Arab unity.[23] Moreover, limitations on united Arab action also applied to the GCC, whose council failed to agree on a security pact and whose agreement on defense fell short of the idea of a Common Defense Council, as advocated by Saudi Arabia.[24]

However, while the Lebanon war did not alter the basic aspects of Arab politics, it did have a number of important consequences for the inter-Arab balance of power and for the international dimensions of Arab politics, creating a much more fluid situation in the whole Arab region.

The most significant consequence was the withdrawal of the PLO from Beirut and its military disintegration, developments that led to its even deeper fractioning and created serious uncertainties regarding its future. This could lead Saudi Arabia, a major key to progress in Arab-Israeli peacemaking, to be more forthcoming in support of U.S. efforts. Not yet clear are the full implications of Lebanese events for the PLO's political prospects, incluiding the question of its leadership. Thus far, Arafat seems to have maintained control, as illustrated by the decision in early 1983 to hold a meeting of the Palestine National Council in Algiers instead of Damascus. However, there is no guarantee that he will be able to continue to do so. In fact, the PLO could well split into two or more factions, each following a different agenda and each supported by different Arab countries. Particularly in the absence of progress on Arab-Israeli peacemaking, this could mean more violence, potentially against Western assets in the region and against moderate Arab regimes.[25] In any event, the end of the Lebanon war does not mean an end to problems of Palestinian nationalism.

The other important consequence of the Lebanon war was the relative weakening of Syria—as noted in its endorsement of the declaration of the Fez Arab summit, whereas it had derailed the Fahd Plan a year earlier—and the improvement in Jordan's position. The latter, however, was essentially due to the central role assigned to Jordan in the U.S. peace plan of September 1982, plus the apparent desire of PLO Chairman Yasir Arafat to gain something politically from the defeat in Beirut, both within Arab politics and within the PLO itself.

Of course, Syria does remain an important force in the area, particularly in its capacity to obstruct peace efforts through mischief making in Lebanon and manipulation of certain elements of the PLO based in Damascus. Syria's weakening, however, did benefit Iraq, since Damascus has moderated its opposition to Baghdad. For example, Syria did not object when the Fez Summit pledged Pan-Arab support to Iraq against Iran.[26]

Egypt's position and influence in the region did suffer somewhat, partly because of the predominant role assigned to Jordan in the new U.S. plan and partly because of Egypt's continued relations with Israel. However, with the withdrawal of foreign forces from Lebanon, Egypt would have a chance to exploit the underlying movement taking place in Arab politics before the war, especially its renewed acceptability in the Gulf for security purposes and as a potential counterweight to Iraq. Indeed, as mentioned above, even as negotiations for the withdrawal from Lebanon were in their early stages, several Gulf states moved to reestablish ties to Egypt.

Conclusions

In general, events in the Arab world since the signing of the Egyptian-Israeli peace treaty in March 1979 (plus the Iran-Iraq and Lebanon wars) seem to bear out the following observations:

- The Gulf Arab states are more preoccupied with their own security than they had been before and also are more able to engage in some fledgling cooperation that could proceed further if events warrant and politics permit.
- Iraq's role has changed radically, as its potential as the Gulf "superpower" has been badly damaged—indeed, as its Gulf neighbors (plus Jordan) have become concerned, by contrast, with excessive Iraqi weakness.
- The course of the Iran-Iraq war, plus the potential for some progress within the context of the U.S. peace plan of September 1982, could place Egypt in a better position within the Arab world than was true for the first few years following President Sadat's trip to Jerusalem. However, a lack of progress on Arab-Israeli peacemaking could cause increased internal strains in Egypt and weaken its position in the Arab world, thus nullifying positive gains for Egypt from developments in the Gulf. The combination of such factors could face Egypt with extremely difficult foreign-policy choices.
- Syria continues to be "odd man out" within Arab councils (though it still has its limited partners, the PDRY and Libya). Currently it also has limited options for pursuing its interests. However, Syria could gain from a combination of military recovery, Lebanese stalemate, and lack of progress towards Arab-Israeli peace.
- By contrast, Jordan now has greater options with regard to the Arab-Israeli conflict because of PLO political weakness after the Lebanon war, greater Saudi interest in the peace process, and the nature of the U.S. peace plan. However, Jordan's position could become less favorable in the absence of progress toward peace and with the potential radicalization of the Palestinians.
- The moderate Arabs are in a better position than they have been in the last few years. The failure of the rejectionists to help Syria and the PLO in the Lebanon war was a key factor. The moderates' situation could improve further if there is progress towards peace, but it could deteriorate under the opposite conditions.
- Nevertheless, there is still no prospect of a broader Arab unity that could submerge traditional rivalries. Consequently, general polarization of the Arab world is likely to continue, even though a total failure of U.S. peacemaking efforts could temporarily recreate a semblance of Arab unity. In the region as a whole, the key conundrums are the position of Iraq within the Arab constellation, which is dependent on the outcome of the Iran-Iraq war, and the evolution of the PLO.

• In the long run, the Lebanon war and its aftermath could have very serious consequences for all Arab governments, moderate and radical alike. Arab impotence, not only in preventing Israel's incursion but also in protecting the lives of innocent civilians, has damaged the legitimacy of Arab governments. With this crisis of confidence among the Arab populace, such extremist ideas as Islamic fundamentalism may very well gain further credence. Whether this happens will depend largely on the outcome of the Iran-Iraq war and on progress—or lack thereof—toward peace in the Arab-Israeli conflict.

Notes

1. However, since the mid-1950s and increasingly so afterwards, the Gulf had become a focus of Arab—especially Egyptian—politics for a variety of economic and political reasons. The Gulf countries were the last Arab countries to gain independence and thus became the focus of Arab nationalism and anticolonialism. Economically, too, the wealth of the Gulf countries was strongly enticing to countries like Egypt with ambitions for Arab leadership. For a discussion of the impact of econmic factors on relations between the Gulf countries and the rest of the Arab world, see Emile Bustani, *Marche Arabesque* (London: Faber & Faber, Ltd., 1961); David Hirst, *Oil and Public Opinion in the Middle East* (London: Faber & Faber, Ltd., 1966); and Robert Stephens, *The Arabs' New Frontier* (London: Temple Smith, 1971).

2. From the very beginning Saudi Arabia, Kuwait, and Libya exacted a price from the so-called front-line countries, and in particular from Egypt, for the financial support given to them, and "the price was a political one: concessions on the part of Egypt and its willingness to reassess its dominant political posture in the region in exchange for economic support." Nazli Choucri, *International Politics of Energy Interdependence: The Case of Petroleum* (Lexington, Mass.: D. C. Heath Co., 1976), p. 93.

3. Iraq's expansionist ambitions vis-à-vis other Gulf countries were clearly demonstrated by its territorial claims and attacks on Kuwait, first in 1961 and then in 1972. In recent years, Iraqi pressure on Kuwait has continued with less-serious border skirmishes. For example, Iraq has pressured Kuwait to lease to it the island of Bubian. Moreover, Iraq tried to achieve its territorial ambitions under the guise of pan-Arabism and as a step towards greater Arab unity. Any Iranian effort, however—as illustrated by the case of the three uninhabited islands (Abmusa and the Tumbs)—would face the tremendous barrier of Arab nationalism.

4. See Shireen T. Hunter, "The Real Nature of Iran's Threat," *Los Angeles Times*, June 15, 1982, p. II-7, and "The Arab Threat to Iran," *Baltimore Sun*, August 4, 1982, p. A-11.

5. Since the mid-1950s, Iran's relations with the Arab countries have essentially been determined by the latter's ideological orientation and partic-

ularly by their position vis-à-vis the East-West conflict. Thus after entering the Baghdad Pact, Iran became a principal target of Nasserite propaganda and subversion. Later, Iraq, Syria, and Libya joined the anti-Iranian campaign. By contrast, Iran had good, or at least tolerable, relations with moderate Arabs. After the revolution, as well, the same pattern has persisted in Arab-Iranian relations, this time with the moderate Arabs' coalescing against Iran. See Shireen T. Hunter, "The Gulf War: Where do Arab Interests Lie?" *Monday Morning,* March 9–15, 1981, pp. 56–57.

6. According to Arnold Hottinger, the Saudis suspected that "at a certain point the Americans decided to do away with the Shah and establish a silent pact with Khomeini. In their view this is the only explanation for the Shah's sudden fall. And it inevitably raises for them the question of whether Washington may not one day find it expedient to topple the Saudi regime." "Does Saudi Arabia Face Revolution?," *New York Review of Books,* November 1979.

7. See Edith Penrose and Ernest Benn, *Iraq: International Relations and National Development* (Boulder: Colo.: Westview Press, 1978), pp. 436–439.

8. For example, between 1976 and 1980, Iraq had committed $1.25 billion in loans and oil credits to Arab and Third World countries through the Iraq Fund for External Development. See "Iraq Fund's President for External Development Gives Views on OPEC and the Third World," *OPEC Bulletin,* vol. 11, no. 18 (September 1980), p. 18. Moreover, the IFED was not the only channel of Iraq's economic diplomacy.

9. See "New Roles for Old Drivers," *The Middle East,* no. 66 (April 1980), pp. 19–20. The text of the Arab charter introduced by Iraq:

A Charter for Action

1. The presence in the Arab homeland of any foreign troops or military forces shall be rejected and no facilities for the use of Arab territory shall be extended to them in any form or under any pretext or cover. Any Arab regime that fails to comply with this principle shall be proscribed and boycotted both economically and politically, a well as politically opposed by all available means.

2. The recourse to armed force by one Arab state against another Arab state shall be prohibited, and any dispute arising between Arab states shall be resolved by peaceful means in accordance with the principles of joint Arab action and the higher Arab interest.

3. The principle embodied in Article 2 shall apply to the relations of the Arab nation and its constituent states with neighboring countries, with recourse to armed force in any disputes arising with these countries prohibited except in the case of self-defense or the defense of sovereignty against threats that affect the security and vital interests of the Arab states.

4. All the Arab states shall collaborate in opposing any aggression or violation by any foreign power directed against the territorial sovereignty of any Arab state or the waging of war against any Arab states. All the Arab states shall act together in facing up to and repelling such aggression or violation by every available means including military action, collective political and economic boycotts, or action in other fields as the need arises and in accordance with the dictates of the national interest.

5. The Arab states reaffirm their adherence to international law and practice insofar as concerns the use of air space, waterways, and land routes by any state not in a state of war with any Arab state.

6. The Arab states shall steer clear of the arena of international conflicts and war, and shall maintain strict neutrality and non-alignment vis-à-vis any party to a conflict or war, provided that none of the parties in such conflicts and war shall violate Arab territorial sovereignty or the established rights of the Arab states as guaranteed by international law and practice. The Arab states shall prohibit any involvement by their armed forces, partially or totally, in wars or armed disputes in the area or outside it on behalf of any state or foreign party.

7. The Arab states undertake to establish close economic ties between each other in such a manner as to make possible the creation of a common foundation for an advanced and unified Arab economic structure.

8. In putting forward the principles of this charter, Iraq reaffirms its readiness to assume the commitments implicit in it towards all Arab states or any party that adheres to it, and is prepared to discuss it with the other Arab states and would welcome any suggestions that would reinforce its effectiveness.

10. See *The Middle East*, no. 64, February 1980, p. 15.

11. Ibid., p. 14.

12. See *The Middle East*, no. 66, April 1980, pp. 19–20.

13. Hana Batatu, "Iraq's Underground Shi'a Movement: Characteristics, Causes, and Prospects," *Middle East Journal*, vol. 25, no. 4 (Autumn 1981), pp. 578–594.

14. For example, all the existing joint Gulf organizations, such as Gulf News Agency, Gulf Television, Gulf Labor Organization, and Gulf Organization for Industrial Consulting, will be subsumed by the GCC. There are also plans for the unification of economic laws, the issuing of credit cards, a Gulf Common Market, and a unified currency.

15. See *Strategy Week*, vol. 8, no. 6 (February 15–21, 1982), pp. 1–2; and March 15–21, 1982, p. 3.

16. For example, when last March Bahrain launched its coastal patrol boat *Hawar* in the Fasht al-Dibal region, Qatar—which claims sovereignty over the area as well as Hawar Island after which the boat is named—protested against Bahrain's action. Ibid.

17. *Christian Science Monitor*, August 20, 1981.

18. Historically Syria has tried to acquire a leadership role in the Arab world by promoting the concept of greater Syria, while Iraq pursued similar ambitions by promoting the idea of the Fertile Crescent. Syrian-Iraqi divisions later widened as a result of a schism within the Ba'athist movement. For an examination of the Syrian role, see Chapter 5 by John Devlin.

19. *Washington Post*, April 18, 1982.

20. UPI report, *Washington Post*, December 5, 1982.

21. AFP (Agence France Press) Report, *Washington Post*, January 8, 1983.

22. See report by Maamoun Youssef, *Washington Post*, January 3, 1983.

23. For a discussion of the Fez Summit, see Chapter 1 by Robert O. Freedman.

24. The failure was due partly to suspicions of Saudi Arabia on the part of smaller Gulf countries and partly to fear of Iranian retaliation. See *Strategy Week*, vol. 8, no. 46 (November 22–28, 1982), p. 2.

25. The Palestinians might reach the conclusion that the only way to get the West to act in their favor is to hit the West where it hurts most, namely in the Gulf, by undermining pro-Western Gulf regimes. See Shireen T. Hunter, "Lebanon's Waves in the Gulf," *Christian Science Monitor*, June 30, 1982.

26. Syria's change of attitude, however, was also due to strains in its relations with Iran, emanating among other things from disagreements regarding the nature of the future Iraqi regime should Saddam Hussein fall.

4
Iran and the Middle East in the Khomeini Era

Robert G. Darius

Events in Iran since the beginning of the ongoing Iranian revolution have increased the West's interest in Iran and its institutions while intensifying the level of stereotyping prevalent toward Iran in particular and Islam in general. Despite increased interest, Iranian affairs still remain shrouded in mystery for most people in the West.

Since its inception the Islamic Republic of Iran has been influenced heavily by the personal traits, likes, and dislikes of the frail, implacable, 83-year-old Ayatollah Ruhollah Khomeini, who remains the central figure of the revolution, "the sole source of political legitimacy. When he dies, many believe, Iran could fragment into a factional background, perhaps a civil war."[1] Civil war is a real possibility and a worst-case scenario, but other alternatives abound.

The wealthy, the educated, and much of the Western-oriented, upper middle class have fled Iran; some have joined the opposition and most have become disenchanted with the clergy-dominated Islamic Republic. The armed forces are stronger but are still indecisive and weak. The clergy command mass support among the poor, illiterate, religious masses who form the vast majority of the population. The age-old religious institutions, which the former shah ignored, permeate all levels of society and provide the mullahs with an excellent existing political/religious structure for maintaining power. Mullahcracy, along with upheavals, is probably the most likely scenario in Iran, at least for the foreseeable future. As James A. Bill points out, "the central and pivotal role" of religious leaders in the Iranian revolution "cannot be overemphasized."[2] Indeed, it was the Shia religious leaders who "directed and then took control of the revolution."[3] "From their mosques, schools, cells (hojrehs), and holy shrines, the Shi'a clerics personally and effectively put together an opposition organization that stretched from one end of the country to the other. It was this organization that mobilized the population and that was ultimately responsible for the collapse and destruction of the Pahlavi regime."[4]

Is the demise of mullahcracy in sight, as many Iranians in exile claim? Probably not. Major revolutions with popular, mass participation have usually been followed by prolonged periods of upheaval, as illustrated by the French and Russian revolutions. Historians will be in a better position to judge the Iranian revolution; at this stage one can only conjecture about its ultimate direction. But the revolution certainly has occasioned a deep and profound internal socioeconomic upheaval, with potentially far-reaching implications for other states in the Gulf area and in the Middle East. As William Quandt points out, this revolution was "unquestionably the most disruptive upheaval in the Middle East in the last generation." In contrast, the Egyptian-Israeli peace accord was "a welcome development" for the West.[5]

Ever since the departure of the former shah in mid-January 1979 and the return of Khomeini on January 31, 1979, he has remained the key source of power in Iran. The struggle between Mehdi Bazargan's "moderate" de jure government, on the one hand, and the de facto government of the *Komitehs* and the extremist mullahs on the other, ended after the seizure of the U.S. Embassy and the detention of U.S. diplomatic personnel as hostages. This event illustrated Khomeini's commitment that Iran should be free from the "hands of foreigners" and that diplomatic immunity was synonymous with "capitulations" of the pre-1928 era. But the hostage crisis primarily served as a vehicle in the internal struggle between "moderates" and "extremist fundamentalists." Toward the end of 1979, economic problems, the dual layer of government, the process of drafting the Islamic constitution, and ethnic unrest indicated the tempo of revolutionary upheaval, as well as rising political discontent in Iran.

The de jure Bazargan government was only a facade, since real power lay in the hands of the clergy and their *Komitehs*. The seizure of the U.S. Embassy and the taking of the hostages provided Khomeini an opportunity not only to use anti-American feelings to mobilize the population but also to neutralize the so-called Westernized liberals who were allegedly prepared "to compromise with imperialism."[6] Such was the fate of Bazargan's government.

The ongoing Gulf war has also worked to the advantage of the extremist Muslim fundamentalists by enabling them to divert public attention away from divisive domestic issues and toward national unity against Iraq, the enemy—a development illustrating the complex relationship of internal-external events as they have affected Iran in recent times. As R. K. Ramazani points out, "The interplay between domestic and foreign policy should be considered in regard to the foreign policy of all countries. . . . "[7] In the case of Khomeini's regime, the crucial link between domestic and external policies can be illustrated as follows:

- The general disparity of wealth, the high level of corruption, brutality, death, midnight door knocks by the secret police, and other characteristics of the former regime also apply in the new regime. Violence, injustice, and suffocation of basic human rights today in Iran is unsurpassed, while a new "dynasty" rising from the bosom of the mullahs is trying to solidify its rule in that country.
- Underlying cleavages among such groups as urban and rural; wealthy and poor; Shia and Sunni; minorities and majority; left and right; conservative religious masses, the middle class, and the tribal elements remain the principal sources of upheaval in Iran.
- The historic vestiges of Kurdish, Baluch, Azerbaijani, and ethnic-Arab divisions and grievances have not and probably will not disappear from Iran's political scene in the 1980s. These traditional divisions can only be swept under by sheer force, if a strong central government could emerge in Teheran that could handle them. Such a government is not foreseen. So ethnic, tribal, and ideological unrest and discontent will grow as long as the central government remains weak. The distant provinces of Iran lack the national control through the rural police (the gendarmerie) that was effective under the former shah, and Khomeini has so far been unable to reorganize the gendarmerie into an effective force. The *Pasdaran*—young, fervent supporters of Khomeini—have taken over the role of the gendarmerie, but so far have failed to establish order in Iran.
- Fear, frustration, and uncertainty have resulted in a massive "brain drain" of professionals (estimated to be in excess of 200,000 people), with many others waiting to escape from Iran. The result has been a shortage of professionals to manage the country. Without the return of at least some of them, Iran will remain crippled.
- Khomeini's regime decimated and purged the top military leaders who served the former shah and initially may have served Khomeini, leading to disintegration and demoralization of the higher echelons of the military. However, as a result of the Gulf war, Khomeini has begun to rejuvenate the armed forces.

- Khomeini's "Islamic" economic system is a shambles. Unemployment; underemployment; inflation; shortages of goods, services, and housing; the collapse of the industrial sector; and drastic cuts in oil production illustrate the faltering economy. Whether Khomeini can remedy these problems in the foreseeable future is doubtful.
- The underground opponents of the Islamic Republic killed about 1,000 leading clergymen in the year after the 53 U.S. hostages were released. The clergy's grim response was to execute at least 2,150 people during the same period. The swift death sentences were carried out primarily against the Mujahedeen Khalgh and others who allegedly or actually violated Islamic tenets, including those against adultery and drug dealing.[8]
- Security is lacking in Iran. The execution of members of the Bahai sect and the Mujahedeen Khalgh continues, based on various charges such as espionage on behalf of foreign powers. The *Pasdaran* (revolutionary guards) are busy fighting the Iraqis, the Kurdish rebels, various bands of Baluch, and their own personal enemies, as well as "pro-American and counterrevolutionary mini-groups,"[9] as they are discovered by the *Pasdaran* and *Savama*'s security forces in Teheran and other areas of the country. Kurdish rebels, monarchists, army deserters, and some members of Mujahedeen Khalgh have joined forces in the Kurdish areas against Khomeini.[10] The Kurdish-leftist alliance illustrates again the discontent among ethnic and ideological groups in Iran.
- Terrorist attacks against mullahs and their representatives continue by Marxists, supporters of the *ancien regime,* and ideological or ethnic dissidents. The immediate objective of the opposition is revenge. For example, according to the clandestine Free Voice of Iran Radio, the opposition group that calls itself the Revenge Committee took credit for the attack on Mohammad Khamene'i, Majlis deputy and brother of President Khamene'i, on January 10, 1982.[11] The bloody feud will continue during the 1980s, particularly among the large, extended families in Iran.
- The "Great Satan" theory helps the clergy escape from "the realities of domestic disunity, of ideological divisions, and of basic structural flaws in the Iranian society. . . . "[12] Eventually the leaders of the Islamic Republic must confront Iran's internal problems, instead of blaming the United States and—to some extent—the USSR as the "satans." Defiance of the West has been a principal source of support for Khomeini, as it was for Nasser in Egypt, and as it is for Kaddafi in Libya. Such negative

rhetoric fails to solve the internal problems of Iran, but it helps reinforce populist support for Khomeini.

- President Seyyed Ali Khamene'i stresses Iran's refusal to approach the United States to obtain advanced technology. Apparently the United States still is considered "an oppressor, hegemonist, and imperialist power,"[13] while less pejorative terms are used to describe the Soviet Union.
- Foreign Minister Ali Akbar Velayati stated in mid-January 1982 that Iran will refuse to normalize relations with the United States because of alleged U.S. support for Kurdish rebels, Marxists, and other leftist elements that oppose Khomeini. He added, however, that Iran wishes to improve its ties with the USSR, the Gulf states, and West European countries.[14] Apparently the Soviet Union already provides sizable aid to the Tudeh (Communist) party, which, however, is mistrusted by members of the ruling Iranian elite.[15]
- Khomeini has been a proponent of the Steadfastness and Confrontation Front of Libya, Syria, and the Palestine Liberation Organization (PLO). In addition, his support of Shia movements is illustrated by the support he extended to the Lebanese Shia Amal movement.
- Despite the fact that the Islamic Republic of Iran is an avowed enemy of Israel, has no diplomatic relations with it, supports the PLO, and publicly vows to liberate Jerusalem (the third-holiest city in Islam after Mecca and Medina), Iran's leaders reportedly purchased arms from Israel as early as August 1980.

In order to understand the foreign policy of the Islamic Republic of Iran toward the Mideast, one also must examine Khomeini's views of the Arabs, Israel, and the Palestine Liberation Organization in greater detail. In addition, the modifications in Iran's foreign policy must be analyzed in terms of domestic changes in Iran, its involvement in the Gulf war, and its isolation from the West.

Khomeini's Views on Islam and Nationalism

Iran's foreign policy since 1979 has been unconventional. The United States and the Soviet Union have been viewed as an "arch satan" and a "satan" respectively. Conservative Arab leaders are seen as "corrupt" and West Europeans as neocolonizers and "exploiters" of Third World masses. This negative rhetoric has left Khomeini's regime little room for friendship with most of the Middle East and the West; the only possible "friends" that remain are Cuba; North

Korea; Syria; Libya; South Yemen; a few nonaligned, revolutionary Third World states; and Eastern Europe.

Khomeini views Israel as an American creation and the United States as the principal supporter of Zionism and the so-called reactionary conservative leaders in the Middle East. He sees the Palestinians as freedom fighters who have suffered for decades from the "expansionist" policies of Israel. Indeed, Khomeini's *Weltanschauung* is a moralistic view of the world, seen in terms of "good" and "evil," "imperialism," "Zionism," superpower "intervention," and "exploitation." Undoubtedly, Khomeini's lifelong struggle against the former shah, his extensive residence in Iraq, and his identification with the poor Shia masses in Iran and Iraq have left a permanent impression. This mentality is the driving force in Iran's foreign and domestic revolutionary rhetoric. In some ways such rhetoric uses external powers as scapegoats to avoid dealing with Iran's immense internal problems and to consolidate the clergys' rule by directing the ongoing Iranian revolution toward mullahcracy.

The Islamic Republic's foreign policy has a strong moralist tone, based on Shia eschatology, Khomeini's naive *Weltanschauung,* and the strong undercurrent of Persian patriotism. Iran's adversaries are not only viewed as satanic in the moralistic context of personifying "evil" but also in the broader context of the term *shaytani kardan,* which means intervention from outside, beyond one's realm of authority and with malice aforethought. The Shia eschatology and belief system is the product of a national political culture that began in the Safavi era (1501–1736), based on the pursuit of a righteous life-style, as exemplified by the life of Prophet Mohammad, Prophet Ali, and Shia's twelve imams. Shia Islam also has been influenced heavily by Persian history and culture. In addition, the view of the leading clergy in Iran has been affected by great-power rivalries in Iran, as well as by the former shah's moderate policies toward Israel, South Africa, and the West. So, naturally, the fall of the shah and the establishment of an Islamic Republic led to a denunciation of these same policies.

Another aspect of Iran's foreign policy is the role of Islam and patriotism and the dilemmas they cause for Iran. They are—and will remain—the foundations of Iranian domestic and foreign policies and provide the basis for understanding the forces that operate in Iran. Shia Islam evolved as the state religion. Woven into the fabric of Persian patriotism, it has become the most potent cohesive force of the clergy who personify Shia orthodoxy and symbolize it for the Shia in Iran and elsewhere. For this reason, the Iranian revolution is more relevant for the Shia than for the Sunni.

When compared to Islam, neither secularism, socialism, nor communism seems to have great appeal or relevance as a model of social change and revolution in the Mideast, because each system is seen as an irrelevant imported ideology. Herein lies the pertinence of Islamic revolution as an indigenous model of political change in the Muslim world. Of course, just as one should not overestimate the likelihood of revolutions in the Middle East based on the unique Shia, Iranian experience, so likewise one should not underestimate the relevance of the broad appeal of the model of Islamic revolution as an indigenous method for political change. The Islamic model of revolution offers a grass-roots alternative, based on Muslim political theory, with which the masses can identify. It can provide a solid foundation for political legitimacy and for an acceptable relationship between those who govern and those who are governed. Indeed, the Islamic option can be a democratic model based on Islamic socioeconomic principles, rather than the rhetoric of Marxism, Leninism, the former shah's White Revolution, or Nasser's brand of socialism, with which the masses could not identify.

The resurgence of Islam, as illustrated and reinforced by Persian patriotism and the upheavals in Iran, is the most important single factor influencing Iran's policy toward the rest of the Mideast. Muslim religious activism of the Iranian brand concerns most of the Mideast states. As Charles Ebinger points out, "the thing that binds Saudi Arabia and Iraq together is fear of the spread of fundamentalist Islam out of Iran."[16] The fears of the "threat of the Khomeini revolution" have resulted in improved relations between Saudi Arabia and Iraq as well as Saudi Arabia and Bahrain and have reduced discord among many states of the Gulf region and the Arabian Peninsula.[17] Saudi Arabia has signed separate mutual-security pacts with Bahrain and Qatar, as these small Gulf states rushed in December 1981 to seek Saudi protection from the spread of the Khomeini-style revolution in the Gulf area.

Although Ayatollah Khomeini's Islamic Republic initially signaled a possible resurgence of Muslim fundamentalism throughout the Middle East, the resurgence appears to be less widespread and not as violent as the Iranian case suggested. Indeed, Iran's revolution is unique because of the evolution of Shia Islam, the history of Iran, and centuries of great-power rivalry in that country. These factors, together with the authoritarian rule of the Pahlavis, created an emotionally compressed sentiment that exploded when the former shah, with U.S. encouragement for human rights, took the lid off and then for various reasons could not decide to use his well-known authoritarian style to clamp that lid back on.

Islamic ideology pulls Iranians and Arabs together as "brethren" in Islam, whereas the forces of patriotism, ethnicity, and culture pull them apart, particularly when a war erupts between Arab Iraq and "Persian" Iran. Iran's foreign policy reflects the vicissitudes of the cohesion of Islam, which binds Iranians and Arabs, as opposed to the divisiveness of Persian patriotism and pan-Arab nationalism.

Because the basic political structure in the Gulf states is Islamic, the shah's secularization efforts failed. Saddam Hussein's efforts to create a secular structure, without a foundation in Islam, are likewise bound to fail. The Saudi structure historically has been based on Islam, which is also the basis of the government in Pakistan. The smaller states of the Gulf area also recognize the rising influence of Islam and have taken steps to base their domestic and external policies on Islamic precepts.

Khomeini's alleged quote that the Gulf should not be called "Persian" or "Arabian" but should be referred to as the "Islamic" Gulf can be seen as evidence of the "gulf" that distances Shia Iran from the Sunni Arabs. But this evaluation is an oversimplification, because the broader bonds of Islam usually override the Shia-Sunni schism. Beyond the level of patriotism, what has happened in the Gulf since the fall of the shah is, indeed, the creation of an "Islamic Gulf" in which the most dominant nations (Iran and Saudi Arabia) use the same scripture (the Koran) as the basis of their political legitimacy and mass support and as their primary source of authority. Both the House of Saud and the newly established House of Khomeini paraphrase the holy Koran as the basis of their internal and external policies. In this context, Iraq's secular brand of Arab socialism will find this area an inhospitable environment.

Islam is, indeed, the most virulent ideology in the Middle East today. But so is patriotism. Iran's foreign policy can be viewed in terms of its natural affinity with Arabs and Turks as Muslim "Brethren" versus Persian patriotism and pan-Arab nationalism that distances Iran from the Arab world.

Iran's Policy Toward the Mideast

The Phase of Euphoria

In the initial phase of the revolution, many Arabs welcomed Khomeini since he interjected Iran into the politics of the Arab-Israeli dispute. The breaking of diplomatic ties with Egypt, the severance of Iran's ties with Israel and the halt in the shipment of Iranian oil there, the Islamic Republic's explicit announcement of support for the PLO, and the clergy's hope that Muslims should move toward "freeing" Jerusalem represented Iran's broad foreign-policy rhetoric toward the Arab-Israeli dispute. In this context, the Islamic Republic was seen as a plus for the Arabs and a minus for Israel, because of the view that it could tilt the balance of power in favor of the Arabs.[18] Arab leaders regretted that the former shah had not taken similar actions, since he also was a Muslim leader.

Iran's relationship with Israel shifted from a discreet entente to open animosity. Iran's official Pars News Agency stated on February 18, 1979, that termination of all relations with Israel and full support of the PLO were the cornerstones of Iran's foreign policy. As a result of the Egyptian-Israeli peace accord, Israel probably had removed Egypt from its list of adversaries, but was now faced by Iran. Israel had to be concerned over the new strategic development on its eastern front. Iran, like Libya, considered the Camp David accords as anti-Arab and anti-Palestinian.

Yasir Arafat was the first foreign leader to visit Ayatollah Khomeini in Iran. During his February 1979 visit, Arafat said that Iran's Muslim revolution had "turned upside down" the balance of power in the Middle East. Arafat received a vague pledge from the ayatollah that Iran would "turn to the issue of victory over Israel" after the Islamic Republic consolidated its power.[19] This promise was based on Khomeini's view of the need to correct the injustices wrought on the Palestinians and the assistance of the Al Fatah group of the PLO to dissident Iranians before the revolution. Al Fatah was involved in the training of Iranian revolutionaries, particularly the Mujahedeen Khalgh, for several years. The PLO had supported anti-shah elements inside and outside Iran. The Palestinians were seen in Iran as poor, suffering people caught in the midst of "Zionist expansionism" and "U.S. imperialism," and as a people who had been "betrayed" and neglected by conservative Arab leaders who preferred to maintain themselves in power, rather than to assist their oppressed Palestinian "brethren."

It was only conservative Arab leaders who were alarmed over the appeal of Iran's model of revolution and its possible alignment with radical Arab states and over the implantation of a PLO mission in Ahwaz, Iran, close to the oil fields of the lower Gulf.[20] This event was seen as a psychological boost for the radical Arabs and as a potential source of a major shift in favor of revolutionary forces in the Middle East. With this exception, Arab sympathy for Khomeini and for the Islamic Republic of Iran was widespread in 1979. Posters of Khomeini in Palestinian camps, the generally positive attitude in the Arab world toward the Iranian revolution, and the identification of the poor masses, religious leaders, and many students with Islamic fundamentalism and Islamic revolutionary change were the hallmarks of the times. It was as if Iranians had miraculously joined the Arabs as Muslim brethren in the Mideast.

Beyond Euphoria

Events in Iran since the summer of 1979 have changed Arab views. The Arabs could not comprehend the killing and other injustices in Iran, since forgiveness is a cardinal principle of Islam. They thought that since the "enemy" was on his knees—as was the case with the pro-shah generals and leaders—forgiveness should supersede murder, revenge, and "instant justice" by the revolutionary zealots.

Even though Iran and Iraq adhered to a common anti-Zionist, anti-imperialist ideology and rhetoric, tempered by each side's national interests and historic experiences, the differences between them surfaced quickly. Iran's leaders considered Saddam Hussein a "usurper" of power who lacked popular support and political legitimacy, because the Iraqi people were not allowed to openly express themselves. Khomeini assumed that Iran's popular revolution could repeat itself in Iraq; he failed to recognize that Iran was quite different from Iraq and that the military, plus the forces of pan-Arabism, could unite to prevent an "Iranian-style" revolution there.

Iraqi leaders welcomed Khomeini's return to Iran. However, relations between Iran and Iraq deteriorated quickly after Iran's clergy renewed their claims to Bahrain as a province of Iran and urged the Shia in the Gulf area to rebel against their traditional, conservative Sunni rulers.[21] By October 1979, Shia demonstrations occurred in Iraq, Saudi Arabia, Bahrain, and Kuwait. These demonstrations caused Saddam Hussein to warn Khomeini that "Iraq's capabilities can be used against any side which tries to violate the sovereignty of Kuwait or Bahrain or harm their people or land. This applies to the entire gulf."[22] Hussein also added that "the Shah occupied three Arab islands in the Gulf. If the revolution is an Islamic one, then why have they not returned the islands to their Arab owners?"[23] In October, the Iraqi ambassador in Lebanon publicly stated that Iran "should restore all Iraq's rights in Shatt al-Arab by voluntarily agreeing to amend the Algiers agreement and deal with the Iranian nationalities with a spirit . . . which rejects fanaticism and persecution."[24] These heated verbal exchanges preceded attacks by the *Pasdaran* on the Iraqi Embassy in Teheran and the Iraqi Consulate in Khorramshahr and the occupation of Iraq's Consulate in Kermanshah. Escalated border incidents, the seizure of the hostages, Bazargan's removal from office, hard-line clergy domination, and the Gulf war followed.

Prelude to Gulf War. According to Claudia Wright, the fall of Mehdi Bazargan's government in November 1979, and its replacement by a revolutionary regime dominated by clerical factions, was the turning point in Iraqi-Iranian relations.[25] The removal of Bazargan and his cabinet members signaled to Iraq the end of moderation and the beginning of an inflexible foreign and domestic policy dominated by the extremist, hard-line clergy who espoused subversion in Iraq and in the rest of the Gulf states. By then Saddam Hussein preferred the return of anti-Khomeini forces led by the former shah's last premier, Shahpour Bakhtiar, to replace Khomeini's regime. So Iraq began to support anti-Khomeini forces both within and outside Iran.

Saddam Hussein was the first Arab leader to break relations with Khomeini, to deride his regime as non-Islamic, and to say that "the Koran was written in Arabic, and God destined the Arabs (not the Iranians) to play the vanguard role in Islam."[26] This comment failed to recognize that Islam was expanded greatly under Arabs and non-Arabs (Turks, Persians, and Berbers) and also showed Hussein's ethnocentric view that the real Muslims are first of all the Arabs.

The Gulf War. The Iraqi invasion of Iran on September 11, 1980— characterized by Saddam Hussein as "Qadisiyah," in reference to the Arab invasion of Persia in A.D. 637—began a chain of events that could have a deep and enduring impact on Iranian-Arab relations.

Despite Iraq's initial victories in the Gulf war, the Iraqi offensive was soon halted and Western expectations of a *blitzkrieg,* similar to the 1967 Mideast war, failed to materialize. Iraqi leaders could not maintain their successful penetration. They had underestimated the capability of the Iranian air force, the level of resistance in Iran, and the cohesive force of Persian patriotism. By November 1980 it was clear that Saddam Hussein had failed to achieve hoped-for-objectives. Indeed, it was difficult to determine if Hussein had limited objectives in mind to begin with. The stalemate situation in the Gulf war endured for a long time with both sides disclaiming any compromise.

What were Saddam Hussein's objectives in Iraq's ambitious invasion of Iran? Did Hussein hope to gain sovereignty over a long, thin slice of the riverbed in the Shatt al-Arab estuary as a minimum, or did he seek nothing less than hegemony in the Gulf? What were Ayatollah Khomeini's objectives during the war? Calling the Ba'athists a "godless" regime, Khomeini hoped to export the Islamic revolution, particularly to Iraq, which has a Shia majority ruled by a Sunni minority. Can Saddam Hussein, who has been called by his opponents "the butcher of Baghdad,"[27] last without popular support? If he loses the support of his army or if he fails to integrate the Kurds into the mainstream of Iraqi life, end the war with Iran, or win popular support among Iraq's Shia majority, can he survive as Iraq's leader?

Iraq is not the top candidate for stability in the Middle East. Chronic instability has characterized Iraqi politics since 1958. As Phebe M. Marr points out, in the past twenty years "at least 10 coups and attempted coups, two armed rebellions, and a full-scale civil war,"[28] have occurred in Iraq. So far the Khomeini regime also has been unstable. The ongoing revolution has been and could be used to justify the upheavals in Iran. But it is still questionable whether stability will return in the foreseeable future. As long as domestic turmoil prevails in Iran and Iraq, the likelihood of tension between them, in order to distract the attention of their people from domestic woes, remains high. This linkage between domestic politics and foreign policies played a key role in the Gulf war.

Saddam Hussein underestimated the power of Persian patriotism, which reawakened as a result of the Iraqi invasion and resolidified the support of Iran's masses behind Khomeini. Hussein also underestimated Iran's military capability. Iraq won many battles in the initial phases of the Gulf war, but ultimately could well lose the war. Such a fate appears inevitable if one correctly considers size, population, geography, military capability, and ideology as crucial factors in the war. Time also appears to be on Iran's side. Furthermore, the immediate dangers facing Iraq are greater than those facing Iran. The Gulf war did not divide Iran, as Saddam Hussein may have hoped; rather it unified Iran. As William O. Staudenmaier points out, "what started out as Saddam's qadisiyah may yet prove to be his Waterloo."[29]

Linkages and Reactions

The small conservative states of the Gulf (Bahrain and Kuwait in particular, because of their proximity) were alarmed by the possibility that the Gulf war could spill over into their territories. This concern was further fueled by Iran's revolutionary image of Islamic fundamentalism with which some religious ulemas, students, and the poor identify. Iran's revolutionary rhetoric further heightened—and continues to heighten—tensions in the area, as illustrated by the discovery of the small band of revolutionaries in Bahrain, dedicated to the overthrow of traditonal Arab regimes. Iran also has the capability of extending the war by attacking targets inside other Arab states that assisted Iraq, if Iran felt completely cornered, or if such action would bring Iraq to its knees. But this option appears less likely.

Arab leaders continue to denounce each other on the position each has taken concerning the Gulf war and the Camp David accords. Arab differences also reflect ideological differences and their ties with the Soviet Union or the United States. However, Saddam Hussein has so far succeeded in maintaining broad support among the moderate Arabs for his war against Iran. During 1980 he sought and created an "Arab entente," which consisted of Saudi Arabia, Jordan, and some of the small Gulf sheikhdoms, to support Iraq against Iran. Even though the support for Iraq was not "without limits or conditions,"[30] Saudi Arabia provided ample economic aid to Iraq, and Egypt sent Soviet arms through Jordan to Iraq. King Hussein deplored "collaboration" between some Arab governments and Iran against Iraq and called on Arabs to take a united stand against Iran's "crimes."[31] The first contingent of Jordanian "volunteers" to join Iraqi troops in the Gulf war against Iran left Amman on March 2, 1982.[32]

The increasing support for Iraq reflected the ties of Arab "brotherhood" and the reaction of the conservative Arab leaders to Khomeini's declarations to export revolution to the Arab world. Iraq's rival, Syria, supported by Libya, openly supported Iran. Iraq broke diplomatic ties with Syria and Libya, while Saudi Arabia broke diplomatic ties with Libya. Indeed, one result of the Gulf war was further disunity among the Arabs who opposed the Camp David accords. Another result was to open a new wound in the Mideast, which drew attention away from the Arab-Israeli dispute. Khomeini's 1979 promise to Yasir Arafat to turn Iran's attention to the Arab-Israeli dispute backfired because of the Gulf war. In fact, the war and Iran's revolutionary rhetoric reduced the likelihood of a successfully concerted effort to bring peace by those who opposed the Camp David accords. The Gulf war showed the difficulties in maintaining a unified Arab stand on the Arab-Israeli dispute, let alone the achievement of a unified Muslim, Mideast stand that could include Arabs as well as non-Arabs.

After the Israeli annexation of the Golan Heights, Hafez Assad of Syria indicated his interest in trying to resolve the Gulf war. Damascus radio, which expressed the official position of the Syrian government, reported on December 29, 1981, that it was time to end the war in order to conserve "Arab and Islamic energies to counter Israel's expansionist designs."[33] In reality, before Hafez Assad could have mediated between Iran and Iraq, he needed to improve Syria's relations with Iraq. At the same time that reports from Kuwait indicated that the then Crown Prince Fahd of Saudi Arabia was trying to reduce discord between Syria and Iraq and Syria and Jordan, Saddam Hussein denounced Assad's efforts toward Arab unity. In a broadcast in early Janaury 1982, Hussein said, "He who speaks about the Zionist annexation of the Golan Heights and wants the area liberated through participation by Iraq and other Arabs must stop backing the enemies of the Arab nation."[34] Saddam Hussein was referring to Syrian support for Iran in the Gulf war. Kaddafi, in a similar critical vein, sharply attacked Saudi Arabia. He said that the pro-American Arab states were "more dangerous than Israel and ought to be overthrown."[35]

Hafez Assad also accused the United States and Iraq of providing arms and support for the Muslim Brotherhood organization in its "subversive activities" in Syria. The large-scale uprising in Hama, north of Damascus, by the Muslim Brotherhood, in which weapons manufactured in the United States and cases of arms bearing the words "property of the Government of Iraq" were found,[36] was used by the president and secretary general of Syria's ruling Arab Socialist Ba'ath party as the alleged proof of U.S.-Iraqi involvement in the Hama uprising. Hama historically has been one of the centers of fundamentalist Muslim opposition to Assad, who seized power in a coup over twelve years ago.

The Iranian and Saudi press and radio corps have continued to attack each other since Khomeini seized power. Iran accused Saudi Arabia of mistreating Iranian pilgrims to Mecca and of providing military assistance to Iraq during the Gulf war. Saudi Arabia responded that Iran's leaders are "bringing destruction on their country and paving the way for outside intervention in the entire Gulf region"[37] and that "what the Iranians are doing is at variance with Islam in terms of actions, deeds, and thoughts," as reported in the Saudi daily newspaper, *Okaz*.[38] The *Al Jazirah*, another Saudi newspaper, predicted in November 1981 "a hot winter for Ayatollah Khomeini and his followers," which never materialized.

Ayatollah Khomeini denounced Prince Fahd's plan for a Mideast settlement as "inconsistent with Islam."[39] A Teheran newspaper also attacked Yasir Arafat for his favorable comments toward that Saudi peace proposal. Iran and Libya were critical of Prince Fahd's plan because it implicitly suggested the recognition of Israel in return for the establishment of a state for the Palestinians. According to Pars News Agency, Prince Fahd's proposal "would eventually establish Israel as the master of the Islamic and Arab worlds."[40]

Since January 1982, Iranian-PLO relations have been on the decline. Teheran has accused the PLO of contacting dissident Iranian leaders in France, and PLO leaders have criticized Iran for its reported military ties with Israel.[41] According to one report, there is considerable evidence that Iran received arms from Israel, an activity the report claims "may have started even before the war began in September 1980."[42] Apparently a former State Department official also has confirmed that at least one shipment had been sent to Iran from

Israel in August 1980. Israeli shipments reportedly included tires for F-4 fighter bombers, parts for M-60 tanks, an M-43 tank engine, plus engines for Scorpion tanks. These shipments may have helped turn "the tide of battle" in the Gulf war in November 1980 in favor of Iran. Former Iranian President Bani Sadr has confirmed the shipment of arms from Israel.

Khaled Al-Hassan, a leading PLO official, criticized Khomeini's alleged plot to topple the present government in Bahrain, stating that "this irresponsible act was aimed not only at Bahrain, but at other Gulf countries . . . and the Arab world should adopt a serious stand toward dangers menacing the Gulf."[43] Seyyed Ali Khamen'i, Iran's president, asserted that the "creation of the Bahrain problem" was aimed at diverting attention from the Israeli "annexation" of the Golan Heights. He denied that Iran had any role in the incident in Bahrain.[44]

Iranian leaders believe that the plight of the Palestinian people is at the core of the Mideast tragedy. In the initial phase of the revolution, Iran's leaders strongly supported the cause of the Palestinians. However, the prolonged Gulf war and the accusations concerning Iranian plots to overthrow the regime in Bahrain caused Iranians to grow cool toward the PLO. This attitude also developed because of the reported bond between Mujahedeen Khalgh led by Massoud Rajavi and the PLO. In the long run, it was PLO support for Iraq that was the principal factor in dampening Iran's attitude. But it should be noted that Iranian sympathy still remains with the Palestinians, particularly since the June 1982 Israeli invasion of Lebanon and the massacre of Palestinian men, women, and children in Beirut.

Iran condemned the Israeli bombing of Iraqi nuclear facilities, the Israeli overflight of Jordanian and Saudi air space, the Israeli bombing of civilian targets in Lebanon, the annexation of the Golan Heights, the June 1982 invasion of Lebanon, and its bloody aftermath, as well as the Camp David accords and the role of the United States as an "imperialist" power in the Mideast. Over 1,000 Iranians were dispatched to Lebanon as a symbol of support for the PLO. Some Arabs saw this as a friendly gesture despite the ineffectiveness of the Iranians in the chaotic war in Lebanon; other Arabs remained angry because Iran did not agree to end its war with Iraq, despite Iraqi promises to withdraw all of its forces from Iranian territory and end the war because of the Israeli invasion.

As Robert O. Freedman points out, "While in the Shah's day Iran was a key element of the American anti-Soviet alliance grouping, today it is a major factor preventing the formation of the anti-imperialist Arab unity which Moscow has been seeking."[45] In reality,

Khomeini's rhetoric and the Gulf war so far have increased the differences between Arabs who oppose the Camp David accords and have reduced the chances of the conservative Arab states to gain support for various initiatives to begin the process of a comprehensive settlement of the Arab-Israeli dispute.

Final Observations

Iran's anti-Soviet, anti-U.S., and anti-Israeli rhetoric since the shah's ouster failed to succeed in the Middle East. So far, Iran's foreign policy toward the Middle East has not accomplished its objectives of toppling conservative, pro-Western regimes; boosting the Palestinian cause; or "freeing" Jerusalem. Khomeini's words and actions instead contributed to the outbreak of the Gulf war, creating a new crisis in Mideast politics that could leave a deep scar on Iran's relations with the Arabs.

Saddam Hussein's knee-jerk reaction—to invade Iran—has proven to be the biggest blunder he has ever made. It was an opportunistic overreaction to Iran's upheavals and revolution. Khomeini's rhetoric of exporting the Islamic revolution and his actions in carrying the war into Iraq also could prove to be a blunder in the conduct of Iran's foreign policy. In a broader sense, the revolutionary zeal of extremists in Iran during the euphoric phase of the revolution is probably typical of any genuine revolution, as has been the overreaction of Iraq's leaders at the possibility of a revolution in their country.

The main event that influenced Iran's policy toward the Arab world was the Gulf war. Khomeini probably realizes now that Arab ties supersede Muslim ties and that in the final analysis, Iran—a non-Arab state—cannot gain support when it is involved in a war against an Arab state. These political realities should have a sobering effect on the clergy in Iran and could change Iran's revolutionary rhetoric toward the Mideast. But it is more likely that the hostility of Teheran toward the conservative, moderate Arab regimes will continue as long as Khomeini is alive or his policies are pursued. In the absence of Khomeini, Iran may possibly remain dedicated to the export of revolution or may moderate its policy. As long as Iran is dedicated to exporting revolution and fomenting the Shia in the Mideast, Arab-Iranian relations will remain cool. When the Gulf war finally ends, it is to be hoped that Iran will moderate its extremist rhetoric and improve its relations with the Arabs.

Iran's foreign-policy failures in the Middle East since the Camp David accords are a result of Khomeini's inflexible, dogmatic views. Khomeini has naive views toward the foreign-policy and defense challenges that Iran faces in being located directly below the Soviet Union, in an area of potential superpower conflict, and between two zones of conflict, the Arab-Israeli and the Indo-Pakistani. Being a religious leader with his own vision, Khomeini sees it as his religious duty to export the Islamic revolution to the Middle East, without regard for the consequences of his exhortations. The pro-Khomeini clergy has chosen to disregard the former shah's astute evaluation of Iran's role in the framework of political realities of East-West rivalry, Arab-Israeli conflict, Shia-Sunni cleavages, and Persian versus pan-Arab nationalisms. Khomeini has ignored these complex matters in favor of his personal preferences as to what should be, rather than what are, the political realities in the Mideast. As long as this trend continues, Iran will remain a source of tension and instability in the Gulf area and in the entire Middle East.

Notes

1. John Kifner, "Iran Pursues Grim Repression to Meet Guerrillas' Challenge," *New York Times,* January 18, 1982, p. 1.
2. James A. Bill, "Power and Religion in Revolutionary Iran," *The Middle East Journal,* vol. 36, no. 1 (Winter 1982), p. 22.
3. Ibid.
4. Ibid.
5. William Quandt, "The Middle East Crises," *Foreign Affairs,* vol. 58, no. 3 (1980), pp. 545–546.
6. Eric Rouleau, "Khomeini's Iran," *Foreign Affairs,* vol. 59, no. 1 (Fall 1980), p. 19.
7. R. K. Ramazani, "Who Lost America? The Case of Iran," *The Middle East Journal,* vol. 36, no. 1 (Winter 1982), p. 7.
8. Kifner, "Iran Pursues Grim Repression to Meet Guerrillas' Challenge," p. 1.
9. *FBIS*-MEA-82-004, January 7, 1982, vol. 5, no. 004, p. i.
10. *FBIS*-MEA-82-005, January 8, 1982, vol. 5, no. 005, p. ii.
11. *FBIS*-MEA-82-006, January 11, 1982, vol. 5, no. 006, p. i.
12. Ramazani, "Who Lost America? The Case of Iran," p. 21.
13. *FBIS*-MEA-82-005, January 8, 1982, vol. 5, no. 005, p. ii.
14. *FBIS*-MEA-82-008, January 13, 1982, vol. 5, no. 008, p. ii.
15. Barry Rubin, "U.S. Aid for Pakistan," *New York Times,* February 19, 1982, p. A31.
16. Cited in "Iraq's Ambitious War Aims," *Newsweek,* October 6, 1981, p. 38.
17. "Syria, in Bid to End Iran-Iraq War, Seeks Talks with Teheran," *New York Times,* December 30, 1981, p. A3.
18. Robert G. Darius, "The Iranian Revolution of 1978–79: Potential Implications for Major Countries in the Area," in Enver M. Koury and Charles

G. MacDonald, eds., *Revolution in Iran: A Reappraisal* (Hyattsville, Md.: The Institute of Middle Eastern and North African Affairs, 1982), pp. 30–48.

19. James M. Markham, "Arafat, in Iran, Reports Khomeini Pledges Aid for Victory Over Israel," *New York Times*, February 19, 1979, p. 1.

20. Ibid.

21. The fact that Saddam Hussein had expelled Khomeini from his place of exile in Iraq in 1978, however, set a personal tone of bitterness between the two leaders.

22. As quoted by Claudia Wright in "Implications of the Iran-Iraq War," *Foreign Affairs*, vol. 59 (Winter 1980/81), p. 278.

23. Ibid.

24. Ibid.

25. Ibid, p. 279.

26. Claudia Wright, "Iraq—New Power in the Middle East," *Foreign Affairs*, vol. 58 (Winter 1979), p. 260.

27. "Iraq's Ambitious War Aims," *Newsweek*, October 6, 1981, p. 37.

28. Phebe A. Marr, "The Political Elite in Iraq," in George Lenczowski, ed., *Political Elites in the Middle East* (Washington, D.C.: The American Enterprise Institute for Public Policy Research, 1975), p. 125.

29. William O. Staudenmaier, "A Strategic Analysis of the Gulf War," Carlisle Barracks, U.S. Army War College, Strategic Studies Institute, p. 31.

30. Claudia Wright, "Implications of the Iran-Iraq War," p. 285.

31. *FBIS*-MEA-82-004, January 7, 1982, vol. 5, no. 004, p. i.

32. "Jordanian Volunteers Leave for Iraq," *New York Times*, March 3, 1982, p. A5.

33. "Syria, in Bid to End Iran-Iraq War, Seeks Talks with Teheran," p. A3.

34. "New Denunciations Hinder Arab Efforts on Unity," *New York Times*, January 8, 1982, p. A3.

35. Ibid.

36. "Syria's Chief Says U.S. Sends Arms to Insurgents," *New York Times*, March 8, 1982, p. A3.

37. "Khomeini Rules Out Saudis' Peace Plan as Contrary to Islam," *New York Times*, November 18, 1981, p. A13.

38. Ibid.

39. Ibid.

40. Ibid.

41. "Alleged Iranian-backed Plot Criticized by PLO Officials," *Saudi Report*, vol. 3 (February 1, 1982), p. 9.

42. Phil Marfleet and Edward J. Mann, "Seeking Arms from the Devil," *The Middle East Magazine*, no. 87 (January 1982), p. 20.

43. "Alleged Iranian-backed Plot Criticized by PLO Officials," p. 9.

44. *FBIS*-MEA-82-005, January 8, 1982, vol. 5, no. 005, p. ii.

45. Robert O. Freedman, "Soviet Policy Toward Khomeini's Iran: A Preliminary Analysis," paper delivered to Middle East Studies Association, Washington, D.C., November 1980, p. 45.

Part 3

Domestic Perspectives
Since Camp David

5
Syrian Policy

John F. Devlin

At the time Anwar Sadat went to Jerusalem in November 1977, Syria's standing in the region had already started to drop from the best years it had known in its post-UAR (United Arab Republic) existence—the period 1971–1975, a high plateau of domestic political stability, economic prosperity, and success abroad. In September 1975, Damascus parted company with Cairo on the issue of a second-stage withdrawal of forces. In 1976 Syria felt compelled to intervene in the Lebanese civil war, which had begun the previous year, in order to prevent a situation that might invite Israeli military intervention. Although its initial moves were successful, at the end of 1977 it had become obvious that getting out would be much harder than marching in. Jordan, which in 1975 had been close to being in partnership with Syria to confine and influence the Palestine organizations, had begun to ease away from Syria and look for other regional partners.

Syria's changed regional fortunes were mainly due to Egypt. When Egypt chooses to lead the Arab world, its population, military strength, cultural influence, and intellectual leadership enable it to do so. When it does not choose to lead, other states compete for its mantle. None has succeeded. While one state or leader may achieve local superiority, no one has been able to truly equal the weight of an absent Egypt. As the prime minister of Bahrain said recently, "The truth is that Egypt is an integral part of the Arab nation, which cannot do without it."[1]

The strength of Egypt in inter-Arab affairs has been clear in respect to Syria. Though Damascus was a center of Arab nationalism, the home of many of those most influential in spreading that ideology, it was fragmented by the French. Syrian politicians spent the 1920s and 1930s trying to put it together again, but they did not succeed until the time of World War II. Independence came in 1946. Egypt and Iraq had the advantage of being unified political entities when their leaders, Gamal Nasser and Nuri Sa'id, competed for influence in Syria in the 1950s. Nasser won hands down, although he was compelled by Syrian enthusiasm to join the two countries as the United Arab Republic.

Syria seceded from the UAR in 1961; that failure destroyed the prestige of pan-Arabists in Syria and permitted the rise of "regionalists" to the top levels of the Ba'ath party.[2] These men were strong ideologues who believed in the concept of national liberation movements, and their active support of this concept was in good measure responsible for setting in train the events that led to the 1967 Arab-Israeli war. After that affair, Syria was very active in fostering Fedayeen activity in Jordan and through that country to the occupied West Bank and to Israel itself.

The actions of the leaders of post-UAR Syria have differed in two ways from those of the first years of independence; both are significant for the period discussed in this essay for they are characteristic of President Hafez Assad—though he differed from the colleagues he ousted in 1970 in several other respects. First, where pre-1958 Syria had been the object of the policy initiatives of its Arab neighbors, since the mid-1960s it has been an activist state, one that has chosen its own road and followed it, acting instead of reacting. It has sometimes done so in close collaboration with others, as with Egypt in 1973; sometimes in harmony with the larger part of the Arab world, as during and after the Baghdad Summit of 1978; sometimes virtually alone, as today by supporting Iran against Iraq. Second, where pre-1958 Syria was the center of the pan-Arab movement, since the mid-1960s the primary focus of its external interests has been its immediate surroundings—Iraq and the components of geographic, or Ottoman, Syria (Lebanon, Jordan, Israel, and the West Bank and Gaza).[3]

The Internal Scene

The activist style of external policy has been carried on against the backdrop of domestic successes and failures. At the time the Egyptian-Israeli treaty was signed, the Ba'ath party had been in power for sixteen years, Assad for eight and a half. He relied on the military forces as the strongest of three elements of support, the others being the civil bureaucracy and the party apparatus. For several years internal affairs had gone well for him; the Camp David accords and the treaty came at the end of a period of relative domestic quiet. The treaty also came at a time when Syria was well along in a process of change, affecting most areas of Syrian society. Syria has experienced progressively more serious internal political discord since 1977.

Syria in 1979 was a much altered society from the laissez-faire, heavily agricultural one controlled by Sunni families from the cities that prevailed in pre-UAR days. Half of its 8.5 million people were city and town dwellers; agriculture contributed less than 20 percent to the gross national product (GNP). Manufacturing and other industry accounted for a third, and services, mostly in the public sector, were approaching the point where they amounted to half of the GNP. Nearly 300,000 people worked for the government in one civilian capacity or another.[4]

The changes of the 1960s and 1970s had also brought new people into the governing system in large numbers. Much of the huge increase in Damascus's population is made up of newly educated persons migrating from the provinces to further a career in a government ministry or in the central organs of the Ba'ath party and its associated mass, or people's organizations. Provincial capitals have experienced the same phenomenon on a lesser scale. The changes have not gone smoothly in all cases. Syria in the late 1970s began to experience some of the less pleasant manifestations of a "multi-sided clash of values which, . . . ranges those who want change and modernization against those who want to retain or return to old ways. The subsets of this clash range newly liberated country people opposite formerly powerful city elements, Ba'athist socialists against private entrepreneurs, Alawites against Sunni Muslim traditionalists."[5]

Militant opposition to the regime appeared about two years before the signing of the Egyptian-Israeli treaty and took the form of assassinations of prominent Ba'athists, most of them Alawites. No major regime figures were hit; the victims included professional men such as university administrators and local officials. Mid-1979 saw a change in the type of violence: Sunni militants gunned down three-dozen cadets in a military school in Aleppo, Syria's second-largest city. The rest of the year featured rioting and fighting between militants and the regime's security forces. This cycle of violence culminated in strikes and demonstrations in Aleppo in March and April 1980, which the regime put down with considerable severity. Government attempts to find and root out the hiding places of the Muslim militants resulted in violent confrontations between security troops and Muslim militants in which some of the latter as well as mere suspects were shot out of hand.

While clashes between government and militants continued, a new opposition technique appeared in 1981—car bombs. On several occasions motor vehicles laden with explosives have been detonated in public areas or near government offices, with considerable loss of life. In February 1982, the most serious episode of insurgence broke out, when government forces seeking Muslim militants' hideouts in Hama ran into an ambush. The militants, well armed and well fortified in the alleys of the old city, responded to the clash by calling for a general uprising. It took the government forces two weeks to crush the rebels, and they destroyed large parts of Hama's old city in the process. Casualties were heavy, but significantly the revolt did not spread to other cities.[6]

The Hama events have been the catalyst for bringing into existence an opposition front. The National Alliance for the Liberation of Syria in its charter issued on March 11, 1982, states that "all patriotic parties, organizations and individuals have collectively agreed to conduct a serious and responsible dialogue to deliver Syria from . . . [its] ordeals, wreck the treasonous regime of Hafiz al-Asad and set up a constitutional parliamentary regime."[7] The constituent elements are the Muslim Brotherhood, the pro-Iraqi wing of the Ba'ath party, the Islamic Front, the Arab Socialist party, and a variety of independent political figures. The two religious organizations are the most important, and their influence is seen in the charter's provision that Islam "be the religion of the country and the Islamic Shari'ah the main authority for legislation and reform. . . . "[8] According to the *Economist*, there are nineteen elements in this front, a number that argues against its effectiveness.[9] The named organizations are, in addition to the Muslim ones, splinters from the Ba'ath socialist movement of the 1960s, plus some Nasserites; none of the secular ones have shown much influence or backing for many years.

The Iraqi Factor

It is no accident that the charter of the National Alliance was first broadcast over the Iraqi radio. Relations between the two Ba'ath states have been poor for years; each has supported forces opposed to the other's regime. One of two anti-Baghdad fronts formed in late 1980 had its birth in Damascus. However, the Camp David accords brought a temporary pause in Syrian-Iraqi animosity. Assad sent a message to the Iraqi president on October 1, 1978, ten days before Iraq called for an Arab summit. Iraq responded by sending a special envoy, and this exchange led to a meeting of the two presidents in Baghdad from October 24 to 26, 1978, at which they signed a charter for joint action "in the various political, military, economic, cultural, information and other fields, including a determination to seek . . . to bring about the closest form of unity ties between Iraq and Syria."[10] The summit itself followed a few days later, bringing together almost all Arab states. The participants were persuaded—by an adroit mix of timing, slight accommodation to other views, and veiled hints of Iraqi reprisal on the part of Saddam Hussein for failure to go along—to take punitive measures against Egypt if it actually signed a treaty.

Under the umbrella of this renewed burst of Arab solidarity, work on implementing the October charter went ahead speedily. The first stage of committee meetings ended early in 1979 with an agreement between the two sides to reopen the oil pipeline from Kirkuk to the Mediterranean terminals of Tripoli and Banias, which had been closed for four years because of a dispute over prices. Discussions continued—but at a reduced pace—during the spring, culminating in a three-day meeting of the heads of both countries in mid-June. This resulted in the establishment of a joint political command, which was an indication that fundamental differences between the two states prevented any progress toward unity. A month later, events within Iraq finished off any pretense that there would be continued improvement in relations between Baghdad and Damascus. On July 16, Saddam Hussein announced that President Bakr was retiring for reasons of health. Saddam replaced him in his three government and party posts. A week later, Saddam announced the arrest of some fifty people on charges of plotting against the regime. In August twenty-one of those charged were executed, another score jailed. Five of those killed were members of the highest government and Ba'ath party bodies. In the course of these events, Saddam hinted that there had been Syrian complicity in a plot, although no details of such complicity—or even of the plot—were made public. These events ended the experiment in working toward unity.[11] Nonetheless, the oil pipelines remained open, and Iraq continued to pay Syria its subvention promised under the November Baghdad summit until 1981, when Syrian support for Iran in the war with Iraq grew too open for Baghdad's taste.

For Baghdad, breaking with a potential ally on the west has turned out to be unwise in view of the course of events in Iran. In 1979 it probably did not seem to be risky: Iran was already falling apart, with extensive fighting in the Kurdish areas and lesser trouble elsewhere. Iraq clearly misjudged Iranian strength and will. However, Saddam had another potential ally to the west; he was successfully wooing Jordan's King Hussein away from the close association with Syria that had characterized the mid-1970s. King Hussein's last visit to Damascus took place in October 1979.

Syria's relations with Iran are important to its activist external role. The Alawite religious leaders in Syria and Lebanon have asserted that the stories of un-Islamic practices attributed to their sect are false, that they are true Muslims, Shia followers of the Twelfth Imam, i.e., of the same strain of Islam as Ayatollah Khomeini and most Iranians.[12] This assertion of a common religious heritage gives them a tie with the Iranian revolution. The Iranian connection with the Shia community of Lebanon, which is unqualifiedly Twelver in orientation, is another reason for good relations with the mullahs in Iran; a Lebanese Shia community actively opposed to Syrian interests could make Damascus's position in that country very difficult. And any enemy of Iraq is a friend of Syria—most of the time. For all these reasons, Assad started building relations with the Islamic government in Iran early in its rule. Syria's information minister went to Iran in April 1979. Iranian Foreign Minister Ibrahim Yazdi met President Assad in Damascus September 10, 1979; he was the first of many high-level visitors, including the once-prominent Sadiq Khalkhali and the current speaker of the Majlis, Hashim Rafsanjani.

As relations with Iraq worsened, Syria took steps to improve its ties with Iran. It received Khalkhali warmly on April 4, 1980, just a few days after an Iranian-sponsored attack on the life of Iraqi Deputy Prime Minister Tariq Aziz. Although Syria was careful to let Iraq know that its oil could continue to flow through the pipelines, its sympathies were clearly with the Iranians in the war that started in September 1980. It had, before supporting the anti-Baghdad front, given assistance to elements that joined that front and was growing increasingly concerned at Iraqi assistance to dissidents in Syria. Iraq, asserting that Syria was directly aiding Iran with arms, broke diplomatic relations with Syria—plus North Korea and Libya as well—on October 10, 1980.

Syrian support for the Islamic government in Iran remained largely political and symbolic throughout 1981. Iraq continued to charge that Syria was sending arms and instructors to Iran and, more seriously, that it allowed Iranian aircraft to use Syrian airspace and on one or two occasions even to land for purposes of an attack on military installations in western Iraq. Although the charges were sweeping, the Gulf states judged in January that Syria might be able to help in settling the Iraq-Iran war, for they raised the issue with President Assad during his late December 1981 tour of peninsula states.[13] Iraq rejected the notion of Syrian involvement.

Concerned at continued Iraqi aid in the form of explosives, arms, and money for dissidents and impressed by Iran's turning of the tide in its war with Iraq, Syria then turned to further improve its relations with Iran. In March 1982, Foreign Minister Khaddam led a high-level delegation, including the ministers of oil and foreign trade, to Iran. The two states concluded an agreement to exchange Iranian oil for Syrian phosphates and food. The quantities planned are large—some 9 million tons (180,000 barrels a day) of oil from Iran and 500,000 tons of phosphates to Iran for the first year.[14] Although Syria is a net oil exporter, it has used Iraqi oil to blend with its own crude for use in its refineries. The Iranian oil will be used for the same purpose.

Damascus followed up the deal with Iran by closing its border with Iraq on April 8, accusing the latter, as it had many times before, of shipping arms and explosives into Syria. The latest case was said to have occurred in the eastern province of Dayr al-Zur. Two days later Syria informed Iraq that no more oil could move through the pipeline for export. With some assurance of supply due to its agreement with Iran, Syria could risk not having access to Iraqi oil. The move hit Iraq where it hurts; the pipeline across Syria had carried between a third and a half of Iraq's 900,000-barrel-a-day 1981 exports, and Iraq's only secure oil outlet is now the Turkish pipeline route. The actions will not stop Iraqi support for Syrian dissidents, but Damascus clearly hopes that it will make Saddam Hussein's position less secure.

There are risks in the line Syria is following. Despite its good military showing, Iran is a divided, economically distressed country, not a good long-term bet. Syria's dalliance with Iran has brought a negative reaction from the Gulf states. They were ambivalent about the war between Iraq and Iran; a situation of stalemate meant that neither party could turn its full attention to them. But an Iran flushed with the success of battlefield victories will be attractive to the discontented in the Gulf states, especially the Shia. The question of cutting off aid to Syria because that country's "strong support for Iran has reached the level of an alliance" has been raised at the ministerial level of the Gulf Cooperation Council, the year-old organization of the six Arabian Peninsula states with Gulf coastlines.[15] Syria got only about $1 billion in aid from Arab states in 1981 (the Baghdad Summit had promised it $1.8 billion, and in 1979 and 1980 its receipts came near to that), and further cuts would be painful.[16]

Assad's strong anti-Iraq and pro-Iran stance runs risks, too, for Syria's good bilateral relations with Saudi Arabia. These go back many years; Syrians of differing political colorations have gone into exile there, but they have not used the kingdom as a base for anti-Syrian activity. The post-UAR Ba'ath in Syria has made no serious efforts to develop party units in Saudi Arabia, an attitude that is a by-product of their concentration of interest in Syria's immediate hinterland. On a personal level, President Assad's brother, Rif'at, has close ties with Abdallah ibn Abd al-Aziz al-Saud, deputy prime minister and second ranking member of the Saudi house. Rif'at Assad, in addition to being a close relative in a society where blood ties count for much, is one of the president's closest counselors and the commander of the large and well-armed defense companies, a principal internal-security unit. Saudi Arabia has been helpful to Syria in solving problems in Lebanon and in defusing crises with Jordan, in addition to being a source of money.

The Lebanese Entanglement

The strong influence that Saudi Arabia is able to exercise on Syrian external affairs is most evident in Lebanon. Much of the Arab world was opposed to the Syrian intervention in 1976 on behalf of the Maronites. The Saudis arranged a cease-fire and called a conference of the principal states concerned in Riyadh, where agreement was reached to put the Syrian forces in Lebanon under the umbrella of an Arab Deterrent Force (ADF), which included token units for a time from other states.

By the time of the Egyptian-Israeli treaty signing, Syria had long since shifted from its original defense of the Maronites to the side of the Palestinians and the Lebanese National Movement, the grouping of left-of-center, mostly Muslim, political organizations. Syrian units and Maronite forces fought fairly continuously in the weeks just before and after the signing of the treaty.

In February 1980 the Syrians made what turned out to be the last move to compel the feeble Lebanese government of President Elias Sarkis to enlarge its administrative and security responsibilities. Syria abruptly announced that it was withdrawing its ADF forces from Beirut, but the ensuing uproar of protest caused Syria to drop the plan. Although there was some repositioning of Syrian forces later in the spring, they still maintained a presence in Beirut. A demonstration that the Lebanese needed the outside forces to prevent chaos may well have been all the Syrians intended by their threat.

During 1980 developments took place within the Maronite community that were to lead to the Zahle confrontation and crisis of April 1981. In two steps, Bashir Gemayel established the total supremacy of his forces, the Phalangists, within the Maronite community. In a sudden move, Gemayel turned his men against the National Liberal party (NLP) forces of former President Camille Shamoun, destroying much of their power in a series of bloody encounters in and around Beirut.[17] Gemayel went on to unite all Maronite militias under his control, seizing the last of the NLP positions in Beirut in October 1980. As he had already ensured the enmity of the third and weakest of the Maronite factions, that of former President Suleiman

Franjiyah, by murdering his son and other family members in 1978, Gemayel stood supreme in Mount Lebanon. He controlled the only forces of any note between the mountain ridge and the sea and from Franjiyah's small fief in the north as far as the Damascus-Beirut highway.

With a unified force under his command, Gemayel set about expanding his power, a course that brought him into conflict with the Syrians and with other factions in the Lebanese arena associated with them. There was some fighting between Maronites and Syrians in the Bekaa Valley town of Zahle in December 1980, but it lasted only a few days (with snow blocking the direct routes between Zahle and the Maronite heartland, fighting could not be sustained). Early in April 1981, Phalangist militia made another attempt to establish themselves militarily in Zahle and to improve the road leading from it directly to Maronite territory. Undisputed control of Zahle would have put the Phalangists in a position from which to interdict the highway from the Bekaa Valley to Beirut and cut off Syrian forces there. It also was an effort to expand Phalangist control outside the Maronite heartland. The Syrians reacted with military operations aimed at pushing the Maronites out of Zahle and stopping their road building.[18] On April 28, Israeli aircraft flying in support of the Phalangists shot down two Syrian helicopters. Syria responded by moving surface-to-air missile batteries into the Bekaa Valley area near the Syrian border. Israel took the position that the missiles had to be removed, or it would take them out by force.

The United States dispatched Ambassador Philip Habib to try to bring about some accommodation. Habib shuttled around the area, principally to Syria, Israel, and Saudi Arabia, making little progress for some weeks. In time other interested parties got involved; there was an upsurge in fighting between PLO and Israeli forces, and events shifted Habib's focus to the issue of a cease-fire between Israeli and Palestinian forces in Lebanon. This was arranged on July 24 in an intricate manner that satisfied the political postures of the interested parties. Neither the PLO nor Israel would deal directly with the other: Israel dealt with the Lebanese government through Habib; the PLO made its agreement "through the representative of the U.N. Secretary General."[19] At the same time a committee of the foreign ministers of Saudi Arabia, Kuwait, Syria, and Lebanon formed by the Arab League arranged a cease-fire in the Zahle area; it also persuaded Pierre Gemayel (father of Bashir Gemayel) to issue a statement that the Phalange would "give all guarantees . . . that there are no relations with Israel."[20]

Predictably, the PLO and Israel disagreed over the terms of the cease-fire. The latter asserted that it applied to any action against Israel or Israelis anywhere. The former asserted that it applied only to actions initiated from Lebanon and across the Lebanese border. Nonetheless, the cease-fire essentially held until, in the emotionally charged atmosphere prior to the final return of Sinai to Egyptian control, Israel struck by air at targets in coastal Lebanon in retaliation for grenade attacks in Gaza, the murder of an Israeli diplomat in Paris, and the death of an Israeli soldier in Lebanon from a land mine. Syrian and Israeli aircraft clashed in a dogfight during the raids on April 21, 1982.

Israel's invasion of Lebanon has drastically altered the situation in that country and the prospects of the external Arab actors involved in it, notably Syria and the PLO. Israel had been prepared to hit the Palestinian forces in Lebanon since early 1982 and had come close to invading several times. In reaction to the injury of two persons in Jerusalem, Israeli planes struck into Lebanon on May 9. There was some response by fringe Palestinian groups, but the main PLO formations held their fire as their leaders had agreed. The terrorist attack on Israel's ambassador in London—ironically by men not affiliated with the PLO—called forth heavy Israeli air attacks into Lebanon on June 5. This time the Palestinians responded with extensive artillery and rocket fire on northern Israel, providing the Begin administration with its rationale for an assault to drive the Palestinian military forces beyond artillery range of Israel, about twenty-five miles.

The larger desire to destroy the PLO quickly took over, and Israeli forces drove beyond the twenty-five-mile line, penning the surviving PLO forces and the organization's leadership into West Beirut. This action brought Israeli forces into areas where Syrian troops were deployed; on the second day of the invasion Syrian and Israeli units clashed. The Begin administration's assertion that it would leave the Syrians alone if they did not shoot is belied by Defense Minister Ariel Sharon's words. The issue was not "whether the Syrians would be involved in the campaign," he said, "but of how to guarantee that their intervention should remain a military campaign inside Lebanon . . . and not turn into a comprehensive war."[21] Syrian forces fought well on the ground but were pushed back and lost substantial quantities of equipment in battles lasting through the first week of June. Indeed, Syria was compelled to accede to a cease-fire while Israel was still fighting the PLO—a development that damaged Syrian-PLO relations. Attempts by Syrian aircraft to intervene led to heavy losses and to the total destruction of the missile batteries in the Bekaa Valley without the downing of a single Israeli plane.[22] The USSR replaced much lost equipment, but that has been the only tangible effect of the 1980 Soviet-Syrian treaty.

The Begin administration's hopes of getting a strong and friendly government in Lebanon by promoting the fortunes of Bashir Gemayel died when he was assassinated. Amin Gemayel, the newly installed president, is more closely attuned than was his brother to the currents in Arab politics and to the need for conciliatory moves within Lebanon. He is also weaker, with little control over the Phalangist militia.

In the tortuous negotiations conducted by the U.S. envoy, Philip Habib, to end the summer's hostlities, Syria managed to get its small units in Beirut withdrawn intact. It also accepted by far the largest number of Palestinian fighting men evacuated from Beirut. At the same time it lost a good measure of the control it had had over Arafat and the PLO leaders. With military means no longer practicable as a tactic against Israel, the PLO is correspondingly less dependent on Syria, through which much of its material had come. Arafat is exercising his new-found freedom of maneuver with considerable vigor, with the result that there is an increase in friction between him and the Syrian leaders.

Lebanon's future is far from clear. The parliament that successively elected Bashir and Amin Gemayel was itself chosen in 1972 and contains many of the traditional political leaders. Amin has not shown his late brother's intent to reassert Maronite dominance over all Lebanon. So far, and it is very early in his term, he has worked only with the traditional political leaders. But the Lebanese civil war that began in 1975 was in good part a struggle on the part of nonelite elements in the Sunni, Shia, and Orthodox communities to reduce their own leaders' power and privilege and to lessen the Maronite community's dominant position, aiming for a system that would be closer to the current demographic reality that the Maronite community is only the second largest in Lebanon.

The political direction of the Shia community in Lebanon is critical for the future of the country and for Syrian interests there. The Shia is the largest community in the country; it is also the poorest, the one most afflicted by the fighting between Palestinians and Israelis, and the one that is least devoted to its traditional leaders, the al-As'ads (no connection with Syria's president). Its principal organization is Amal, founded by Imam Musa Sadr—of Iranian origin as are many Shia religious leaders—and now headed by Nabih Birri; it is an alternative to the al-As'ads.[23] A reconstituted state that gave due weight to the Shia community's numbers would be a great boon to its members. Together, the Maronite and Shia communities outnumber all other Lebanese; an alliance between them would constitute the basis for a new Lebanese state. Such a state would, however, require a reshaping of the 1943 national pact under which Lebanon's sects are accorded posts of importance and number in accordance with their share of the population as of 1932.

If Syria's future interests in Lebanon required it to deal only with the two largest communities, its problems would be much simplified. But central to Lebanon's future and to Syria's interest in that future is the disposition of the Palestinians. The PLO and its several factions are supported financially and materially by many Arab states.[24] Assad's government has extensive sway over the PLO, as it demonstrated when it forced that organization to boycott the Arab Summit in Amman in November 1980. Yet there are limits on Syrian actions in this area. Like other Arab governments, the Syrian regime survives because, even without public-opinion polls and other paraphernalia of multiparty states, it is sensitive to the basic desires of its people. Support for the Palestinian cause strikes an emotional chord in the body politic; Syrian governments may lead, persuade, even force the PLO, but they cannot abandon the cause. Although the Palestinian organizations have not formally abandoned their goal of recovering Palestine, the repeated answer of Yasir Arafat when asked why the PLO will not recognize Israel is that recognition would constitute giving up a trump card without gaining anything in return. This answer indicates that he and most Palestinians know that Israel is there to stay and that a Palestinian entity located in the West Bank and Gaza is the most they can hope for. Israel, however, continues to see the PLO as an organization dedicated to its destruction.

Syria has failed to achieve the goals for which it has striven in Lebanon. Damascus is within the range of Israeli guns in the Bekaa Valley; the country is at this writing partitioned into three major sections—the Maronite area, the Israeli-occupied south, and a small Syrian enclave in the north and northeast. Efforts by the United States and its European associates to bring about the withdrawal of Israeli, Syrian, and PLO forces are in process. They may succeed. Withdrawals are necessary for the establishment of a functioning Lebanese political system. Necessary—but not sufficient—because working agreements among Lebanon's own communities, their traditional leaders, and their would-be leaders are just as essential. And each of those elements is likely, in its own way, to look outside the country for support for its cause.

Syria and Israel—The Bilateral Connection

In some ways it is anomalous to speak of bilateral relations between two countries that are at war and do not deal directly with one another. But even in such conditions, the level of animosity or of tolerance for each other's behavior can and does vary. Relations between Syria and Israel were perhaps at their least contentious in the mid-1970s. Secretary Kissinger concluded an arrangement whereby the two parties indirectly acknowledged each other's zones of interest in Lebanon.[25] This particular arrangement proved fairly durable; trouble over the military operations around Zahle in 1981 was the first significant break in it.

Nonetheless, relations between Syria and Israel have hardened since Anwar Sadat's visit to Jerusalem, the Camp David accords, and the treaty. Syria was a charter member of the Steadfastness and Confrontation Front (along with Libya, Algeria, PDRY, and the PLO), which was formed to oppose the consequences of these moves. Syria saw the treaty between Israel and Egypt as a separate peace, one that would virtually eliminate the possibility of a broad approach to a settlement, a tactic in which Arab numbers would count. The semi-official newspaper *Tishrin* said, anticipating the signing of a treaty, "with the establishment of a separate peace there will emerge a new state of conflict in the area threatening all possibilities for establishing a genuine peace."[26] Israeli actions since the treaty have strengthened Syrian perceptions that Israel intends to use the separation of Egypt from "the battle" in order to encroach further on territory Syria regards as Arab. Among these actions are the spread of settlements on the West Bank and support for the "free Lebanon" that Saad Haddad proclaimed in the strip of land along Israel's northern border that he controls with forces armed by Israel.[27]

Of most direct concern to Syria is the question of the Golan Heights. Syria broke with Egypt over the question of a second-stage disengagement in 1975; Assad judged that the relative simplicity of the Egyptian position in Sinai could not be replicated in the Golan area. Israel holds very strongly to the view that Syrian forces must never have an opportunity to reoccupy the heights overlooking Jewish communities along the Sea of Galilee. Hence it was, at most, willing to consider returning in a second stage a very thin slice of territory; Assad considered it too small. At the time of the treaty the Israeli settlements in the heights had some 4,000 people. The numbers are now approximately thirty-one settlements and 7,000 people.[28]

Stating the issue in regard to the Golan is simplicity itself. Syria wants to regain the territory it lost in 1967; any such return must be linked to a solution that gives the Palestinians a state of their own. Otherwise they would remain a political burden on Syria and an overwhelming impediment to establishing a functioning political system in Lebanon. Israel insists on controlling the Golan area for reasons of security, and it has progressively hardened its position. In April

1979 then Agriculture Minister Sharon said that Israel would not return the Golan to Syria; Prime Minister Begin repeated the assertion the next month. Independently of the government, a movement for annexation of Golan gathered impetus, and supporters of the movement brought a bill for annexation before the Knesset where it was defeated on March 11, 1981. The bill was not sponsored by the Likud. Prime Minister Begin chose the time to make a move in regard to the Golan. On December 14, 1981, he pushed through the cabinet and Knesset a measure that provided that "the law, jurisdiction, and administration of the state [of Israel] shall apply to the Golan Heights."[29] The United Nations Security Council (Resolution 497) declared this move of no effect, a position for which the United States voted. A second resolution recommending that member states "consider applying concrete and effective measures in order to nullify the Israeli annexation" was vetoed by the United States.[30]

A follow-up to this Israeli move has embroiled the Druze residents of the Golan with the Israeli authorities. The latter have taken the position that the Druze should carry identity cards that indicate that they are residents of Israel, rather than the cards formerly issued to them, showing them under military occupation. The Druze, as a heterodox Muslim sect, have lived under many governments over the centuries. They cannot be sure that the Israeli one is the last, and they fear reprisals if at some future date Syrians should return.[31] There has been a general strike in response to efforts to compel Druze to accept the cards. The affair has reached a standoff as of this writing, but the last has not been heard of it.

The hardening of the Syrian attitude toward Israel and the tenser situation between Israel and Syria is best perceived by going outside the time frame of this paper. On March 8, 1972, President Assad said in a speech, "We support the Security Council resolution when interpreted as providing for the withdrawal of the enemy from the Arab territory occupied in 1967 and as a confirmation . . . of the rights of the Palestinian people."[32] This was the standard Arab interpretation of Resolution 242; the same terms for peace were spoken by Anwar Sadat before the Knesset on November 20, 1977. After the 1973 hostilities, Syria accepted UN Security Council Resolution 338, which by implication incorporates 242 and its recognition of Israel. In the past two years, Syria has denied that it has ever accepted 242 or recognized Israel.

Mid-1982 brought changes in this position also. Syria joined other Arab League states at Fez in September in a statement that included the words, "Guarantees for peace for all the states of the region"

(Article seven). Syrian Information Minister Iskandar Ahmad affirmed that Syria includes Israel among the states covered by this phrase.[33]

Syria is in no position to challenge Israel militarily. It has substantial ground forces tied up in Lebanon, its air force suffered heavy losses in combat with Israel in June 1982, and major internal-security concerns such as the February Hama uprising can require the use of regular troops. Moreover, use of troops in large internal-security operations may have affected military morale and discipline, though there is no evidence to this effect, merely assertions by interested parties. Nor can Syria expect help from other Arabs. Iraq is embroiled in war with Iran. Jordan's forces are small. Other Arab armies are inconsequential. While Syrian public statements do not admit that Arab forces, with Egypt out of the lineup, are not a match for Israel, there can be little doubt that Hafez Assad and his advisers are aware of the realities of the military balance between Syria and Israel (or between Syria with potential Arab allies and Israel). This appreciation colors Syrian responses to events in the area and continues to result in a cautious attitude toward Israel where military conflict might be involved. In Lebanon, the Syrians fought but made no effort to expand the fighting to the Golan area.

Syria and the Arab States

It is noteworthy that, despite its domestic difficulties and its relatively isolated position, Syria has been consistent in holding to its position among the Aab states. It is an aspect of being an actor in the Middle East scene, rather than a stage on which others tried to play roles as happened in the 1950s. This consistency has brought it into conflict with many Arab states. Egypt and Iraq have been discussed. The Assad regime appears convinced that Jordan is permitting the regime's militant Muslim enemies to operate from its territory. Damascus massed troops on the border in November 1980; after some days the Saudis were able to defuse a tense situation.

This determined approach has, for the period since March 1979, limited Syria's friends among Arab governments to Algeria, PDRY, and Libya; all remain grouped with the PLO in the Steadfastness and Confrontation Front opposed to treaty relations or dealings with Israel under conditions that have prevailed since the mid-1970s. Kaddafi has proved an erratic associate; the union between Libya and Syria that he proclaimed in September 1980 has not progressed beyond the stage of "promoting unitary meetings between the two fraternal countries," although the Libyan People's Congress called in January 1982 for specific measures to implement the agreement to unite.[34]

Kaddafi is also an unreliable source of funds, disappointing to Syria because his wealth was perhaps the most appealing aspect of the proposed union. Relations with PDRY are on both party and government levels, but the Syrians are careful not to show approbation for PDRY moves that might offend the Saudis. The latter are more important to Damascus than is the Marxist state in Aden.

Relations with the Great Powers

In Syria's relations outside the Middle East, the most striking single development of the period under consideration is the Treaty of Friendship and Cooperation between the USSR and Syria, signed on October 8, 1980. The treaty is similar to the one Moscow concluded with Iraq in April 1972 in most respects. It calls for the USSR to respect Syria's policy of nonalignment, "a major factor contributing to the preservation and consolidation of the international peace and security" and for Syria to respect the "peaceful foreign policy of the USSR." Article 5 requires the parties to consult "with a view of coordinating their positions" in the event of threats to either or to world peace. Article 10 is not found in the Iraq treaty. It states: "The high contracting parties shall continue to develop cooperation in the military field on the basis of appropriate agreements concluded between them in the interests of strengthening their defense capacity."[35]

What is most striking is not the content, although that is important, but that the treaty came about. The USSR since the 1960s has been urging such a relationship on Syria, but to no avail. Regimes in Damascus have been very conscious of not being beholden to outsiders and have been careful to make Syrian independence clear. Decisions such as the intervention in Lebanon in 1976 and the massing of troops on Jordan's border in 1980 were pointedly taken without consulting the USSR; in the former case Prime Minister Kosygin arrived in Damascus as the Syrian troops were moving. By the end of the 1970s, however, Assad's regime stood in great need of support because of the domestic and external problems discussed above. And it needed an assured supply of weapons if it was to avoid being hopelessly outclassed by Israel.[36]

An external backer is important to Syria even in its role as an activist state in its region. The United States in a way performed that role for a time after the 1973 war, virtually shutting the USSR out of the action. In Syria's perception the United States became less and less able and willing to deliver what Syria wanted in terms of regained territory from Israel. The USSR also has shown little capability to perform in that area, but it can and does supply, along with arms, political support for the Arab side in the confrontation with Israel.

The clause of the October 1980 treaty concerning military cooperation notwithstanding, there has not been any marked change in military relationshps since then. One small-scale joint military exercise was carried out in July 1981. Soviet military specialists continue to train and advise. Some of them have been targets of terrorist attacks. A new arms agreement may be in the works following the March 1982 visit of senior Soviet military officials.[37]

In the field of trade and technical assistance, Syria clearly prefers to deal with Western countries when it can. In 1979 Syrian trade with the communist countries amounted to only 17 percent of the total; it had been dropping steadily for years. Some of this drop was due to availability of hard currency in large amounts from the donations agreed to at the Rabat and Baghdad summits. A comparison of statistics for 1978–1980 shows that trade (in this case imports) from the socialist countries has a "relative resurgence" in years when Arab aid is reduced. A Syria short of hard currency must turn more to the Council for Mutual Economic Assistance (Comecon).[38] With a reduction of such Arab money in 1981 and probably in 1982, some rise in Syria's trade with Comecon countries is to be expected. But Western Europe should continue to account for about half the total.

Another aspect of Syria's external relations that deserves note is its readiness to turn to the United States for assistance in specific matters. The Assad regime knows that the United States has influence in Israel; the Habib missions of 1981 and 1982 showed that clearly, even if nothing else had for some years. The hope that "this time" the United States will see its and Syria's interests as the same recurs from time to time, as in the diplomatic exchanges over the matter of Israel's annexing the Golan. The U.S. association with Syria on this point did not last long. But it will happen again.

Conclusion

There has occurred over the three years since the signing of the treaty a confluence of developments concerning Syria. The most prominent are:

- Internal opposition is growing. Compared with 1979 the militant opposition is much stronger; government repression of it is greater; violence overall is much increased.
- In Lebanon, Israel's military success has destroyed much of what Syria hoped to achieve there. At this writing de facto partition

of Lebanon into a Maronite area, an Israeli-occupied area, and a Syrian-occupied area persists. Words of political accommodation are at least being uttered by Lebanese, but the future of the country is unclear.

- Syria is forging an open association with the Islamic government of Iran, a step increasing the enmity between it and Iraq and Jordan and one that could harm relations with its sources of funding among the oil-rich Gulf states.

Affecting Syria are two other trends in the Arab world: clear indications that Egypt's ostracism should end and substantially greater willingness to recognize Israel and in some fashion deal with it.

Singly, no one of these areas is likely to see major change. Taken as a group the chances are good that a major development or a shift from the patterns of the seventies is in the works.

- Internally, where the interaction of interests, values, and stresses will lead Syria is unclear. There may be a change of regime. There is certain to be continued struggle; if the national alliance can move its activities beyond Hama and Aleppo, it would be a sign of real strength.
- The whole question of Syria in Lebanon is bound up with the future of the Palestinians and the disposition of the Golan. Syria is likely to resist pulling its forces out of Lebanon unless such a move is linked to its other interests of regaining the Golan and definitively settling the Palestinian issue.
- Iranian forces have pushed the Iraqis back into Iraq, and Teheran is calling for the overthrow of Saddam Hussein. Syria's good relations with Iran have been used by the major Arab nations to obtain Iranian-government assurances that it would stop at the border. However, Iranian leaders continue to threaten invasion. But even the downfall of Saddam Hussein will not remove Iraq as a bitter and effective enemy of the Assad regime.

Whatever the outcome of these and other developments, observers should not expect that Syria's situation on the fifth anniversary of the Egyptian-Israeli treaty will be the same as it is on the third.

Notes

1. Interview with Eric Rouleau, *Le Monde*, March 19, 1982. Translation in Foreign Broadcast Information Service Daily Report, Middle East and Africa (hereafter cited as *FBIS*), March 23, 1982.

2. In Ba'ath parlance the entire Arab world is the "nation," *qawm* in Arabic; each country is a "region," *qutr* in Arabic. The party structure reflects this, with a national command for the whole and regional commands for each country, e.g., Syria, Lebanon, Jordan. Since the mid-1960s the Ba'ath party in Syria has been pan-Arab in words only.

3. The Syrian Arab Republic of today is but a part of the region known as Syria to the ancients and to the Ottomans. Divided into French and British mandates, the French area was further divided. France added to the Maronite Sanjak of Mount Lebanon other districts, largely Muslim in population, to comprise "Le Grand Liban." Cf. Elie Kedourie, "Lebanon: The Perils of Independence," *Washington Review of Strategic and International Studies*, vol. 1, no. 3 (July 1978), pp. 84–89.

4. For a discussion of these issues, see John F. Devlin, *Syria: Modern State in an Ancient Land* (Boulder, Colo.: Westview Press, 1983).

5. John F. Devlin, "Syria: A Clash of Values," *Middle East Insight*, vol. 2, no. 3 (May 1982), p. 30.

6. The question of numbers in this confrontation is tricky. Most information on the opposition comes from sources biased against Assad's regime—the Maronite Phalange's Voice of Lebanon Radio, the Iraqi government media, and spokesmen for the opposition abroad. Shaykh Ali Bayanuni of the Islamic Front claims the Syrian government killed 20,000 civilians and lost 10,000 itself in the Hama incident (*Le Matin*, March 22, 1982, translation in *FBIS*). Diplomatic observers are quoted as believing that 5,000 to 13,000 lives were lost (*Christian Science Monitor*, April 1, 1982). The Syrian regime has given no official figures; its concern has been to publicize support for itself by the Syrian populace.

7. Baghdad, Voice of Arab Syria, March 22, 1982 (*FBIS*).

8. Ibid.

9. The *Economist*, February 27, 1982, p. 51.

10. Baghdad Iraqi News Agency (INA), October 26, 1978 (*FBIS*). Also *Washington Post*, October 26 and 27, 1978.

11. Exactly what went on in Baghdad in the summer of 1979 has not been made clear. It is my belief that Saddam Hussein forced Bakr into retirement, perhaps because the older man was not functioning with full efficiency, perhaps because Saddam was overready to grab the reins. The "plot" may have been nothing more than differences over policy; Saddam is not receptive to views that differ from his. It may have involved the issue of union with Syria. Assad has charged that Saddam Hussein deliberately destroyed the unity process. Radio Damascus, December 13, 1981, transmitting the "text" of Assad's interview with Kuwait's *al-Ray al-Amm;* Assad speech, Radio Damascus, March 7, 1982 (both *FBIS*).

12. Hana Batatu, "Some Observations on the Social Roots of Syria's Ruling, Military Group and the Causes for Its Dominance," *Middle East Journal*, vol. 35, no. 3 (Summer 1981), p. 335.

13. Bahrain, Gulf News Agency, January 9, 1982, citing the assistant secretary general of the Gulf Cooperation Council (*FBIS*).

14. Radio Teheran, March 17, 1982 (*FBIS*); *Washington Post*, March 18, 1982; Radio Teheran, April 5, 1982 (*FBIS*).

15. *Al-Sharq at Awsat* (London), March 18, 1982, translation in *FBIS*.

16. Colin Legum, Haim Shaked, and Daniel Dishon (eds.), *Middle East Contemporary Survey, 1978-79* (London: Holmes and Meier, 1980), p. 217.

17. *New York Times*, July 9, 1980.

18. *Wall Street Journal*, April 9, 1981; *Washington Post*, April 10, 1981.

19. Salim al-Za'nun, speaking at a press conference in Kuwait, March 20, 1982, Damascus, Syrian Arab News Agency, March 20, 1982 (*FBIS*).

20. Beirut, Voice of Lebanon, July 7, 1981 (*FBIS*). Cf. also *The Economist*, July 18, 1981, p. 48.

21. Interview in *Yedi'ot Aharanot*, June 20, 1982 (translation in *FBIS*).

22. Israel had not pressed for the removal of the missiles, apparently confident that it could handle the threat they posed to Israeli air operations. Cf. interview with Chief of Staff Eytan in ibid, January 8, 1982 (*FBIS*).

23. Sadr founded Amal in the early 1970s. He disappeared while on a trip to Libya and is presumed dead.

24. See Chapter 8 by Aaron Miller.

25. *New York Times*, May 6, 1981.

26. Quoted on Damascus Radio, press review, March 9, 1979 (*FBIS*).

27. A principal reason for Israel's support of Haddad was to prevent guerrillas from gaining access to Israel's northern border.

28. *New York Times*, December 17, 1981.

29. Embassy of Israel, policy background paper, December 16, 1981 (Washington, D.C.).

30. Text in *New York Times*, January 21, 1982.

31. Cf. David Shipler's article in *New York Times*, April 19, 1982.

32. Radio Damascus, March 8, 1972 (*FBIS*); *New York Times*, November 21, 1977, for the text of Sadat's address.

33. Monte Carlo Radio, October 11, 1982 (*FBIS*), reporting a press conference with the minister.

34. Radio Damascus, April 10, 1982, citing a meeting of a Ba'ath delegation and a Libyan General People's Congress delegation; Radio Tripoli, January 5, 1982 (both *FBIS*).

35. Text of the treaty, Moscow TASS in English, October 8, 1980 (*FBIS, USSR*).

36. For an analysis of Soviet-Syrian relations during this period, see Robert O. Freedman, *Soviet Policy Toward the Middle East Since 1970*, Third Edition (New York: Praeger, 1982), pp. 247–264, 368–369, 380–381, 395–397, 406–408.

37. Beirut, Voice of Lebanon (Phalangist), March 26, 1981; Paris *al-Mustaqbal*, March 20, 1982 (both *FBIS*).

38. Economist Intelligence Unit, *Quarterly Report for Syria and Jordan, First Quarter, 1981*, p. 2.

6
Israeli Policy

Don Peretz

The victory of Menahem Begin's Likud block in Israel's tenth Knesset elections during 1981 confirmed that the landslide in the ninth elections of 1977 was no accident. The country was in the process of a fundamental change, a transition from the socialist ideology of Labor to the center-right perspective of Likud. The change affected the programs of political parties, as well as influencing a wide variety of internal and external government policies, attitudes of Israel's citizens, the country's value system, and its relations with Arab neighbors and countries beyond the Middle East, including Jews in the diaspora. Indeed, since 1977 the central government theme has become the territorial unification of Eretz Yisrael.

The "earthquake," as some journalists called the 1977 election, could be attributed to the electorate's disenchantment with Labor and the loss by the Labor Alignment of many traditional supporters to the newly formed Democratic Movement for Change (DMC). At first the large support accrued by the DMC was perceived as a protest vote against thirty years of Labor rule. During Israel's first thirty years and before, during the British Mandate, Labor's socialist Zionism formed the Israeli national ethos, established its value system, and its economic and social perspectives as well. But by the late 1970s it was clear that many of Labor's slogans had worn thin and that there was growing disaffection with its outlook. Indeed, it appeared that there was general disillusionment with the degeneration of the Labor bloc of parties, now grouped in the alignment, into just another political bloc intent on preserving its power and privileges.

Although 1977 marked the real shift in the political balance from Labor to Likud, it had been in the making for nearly two decades. A variety of internal factors had created the necessary conditions. They included Israel's changing demography, from a nation of largely

European immigrants to one of an Asian and African majority; the relative decline of nonurban sectors of the economy; industrial modernization; the growing emphasis on making Israel into a center of high-level science- and technology-based industry; and the attrition of the Labor Party's social-democratic ideology. The change in 1977 was not merely the transfer of government from Labor to Likud—it was the culmination of transformations in society that had begun a decade and more before political observers ever imagined that Begin would head Israel's government.

The Oriental Revolt

Some observers characterized the 1977 and 1981 elections as "the Oriental Revolt," an upsurge of ethnic issues as a factor of major political consequence for the first time. The complex of political, economic, and social tensions between Jews of European extraction and those from Asia-Africa (often called Orientals, Sephardim, or Easterners) had not figured prominently in previous elections. Initially, the new Jewish immigrants from Morocco, Tunisia, Algeria, Turkey, Iraq, and Iran were coopted by the Labor establishment. They voted Labor in large numbers and regarded its leader, David Ben-Gurion, as prophet, father figure, and political chief. But within a decade their dissatisfaction with what they perceived to be their secondary status led to a shift in voting patterns.

Labor, which was perceived as the "establishment," was held accountable for Oriental frustrations in achieving rapid enough upward mobility and for failure to meet demands for larger political representation, better housing, and better employment conditions. With Ben-Gurion's departure from politics in the 1960s, Labor lost one of its most alluring attractions; within Labor there was no individual to replace the glamour of "the old man." Instead, Ben-Gurion's charisma was taken on by the opposition leader, Menahem Begin, leader of the Herut party and of the Likud movement of which Herut was a part.

Since 1969 there has been a steady attrition of Oriental votes for Labor and an increase in their support for Likud. Among those born in Asia-Africa, 51 percent voted for Labor in 1969; 39 percent in 1973; 32 percent in 1977; and about 25 percent in 1981. In 1969, 32 percent voted for Likud; 43 percent in 1973; 46 percent in 1977; and about 60 percent in 1981. The shift was even more pronounced among second-generation Orientals. Those with fathers born in Asia-Africa gave 49 percent of their votes to Labor in 1969; 40 percent in 1973; 23 percent in 1977; and even less in 1981. Likud increased its strength among them from 37 percent in 1969 to 47 percent in 1973; 65 percent in 1977; and nearly the same in 1981.[1]

Even though Likud won its second Knesset election in 1981, it was still not regarded as the establishment. Labor was still the party of status, representing the Western elite that, at best, seemed to display paternalistic attitudes toward the Oriental immigrants. Party profiles drawn by Israeli pollsters showed Labor's supporters in the last two elections as mainly Ashkenazi, middle-aged or older, better-educated, white-collar workers of middle and upper income. Likud's constituency was largely Oriental, youths between eighteen and thirty, many of them religious, blue-collar workers with less education and income.[2]

These differences emerged as dominant themes in the 1981 election. Likud campaigners increasingly referred to Labor's discrimination against the Orientals, and many of their election advertisements hinted at Labor's "racism." Indeed, on occasion pronouncements by some Labor campaigners stirred Oriental dismay. Mordechai Gur, a former army chief-of-staff and a top leader of the Labor party, angrily threatened Oriental hecklers that "we will beat you as we beat the Arabs." Labor party leader Shimon Peres angrily called the hecklers "Khomeinistis" and advised them to go back to their home countries. A few days before the end of the campaign, a moderator of the most important Labor rally during the campaign declared that "the nice people," "the real fighters," and the "army officers" (most of whom were Ashkenazi) are with Labor, whereas the Likud camp is supported by "Chakchakim" (a derogatory term applied to Moroccan hooligans, or to hooligans generally).[3]

Until 1981 attempts to channel Oriental discontent and special concerns into ethnic separatist factions had not been particularly successful. But now the "ethnic challenge" shook the whole political structure, bringing havoc to Israel's third-largest faction, the National Religious party (NRP). When NRP chose its electoral list for the tenth Knesset, Orientals complained that only two of the top ten candidates were Afro-Asian. One of the young NRP leaders, Aharon Abuhatzeira, who was minister of religious affairs in Begin's coalition cabinet, demanded second place on the NRP list, as representative of the many Orientals who voted for the religious party. After the party yielded to this demand, Abuhatzeira raised his price and insisted that half the first ten positions on the list be Orientals. When the party rejected his demands, Abuhatzeira quit the NRP to form a new list of Oriental Jews called Tami, the Movement for Israel's Tradition. The top positions were filled with prominent Orientals who were among the few reaching high position in the political arena. By winning three Knesset seats in the 1981 election, Tami became the first successful Oriental Jewish party since the second Knesset. Within a few months of the election, Abuhatzeira used his new power to reenter the coalition government and to attain a new cabinet post, which he soon lost after being forced to resign when he was convicted for previous financial wrongdoings. Nevertheless, Tami remained an important member of the coalition, because its three Knesset votes were necessary to give Begin the majority required to keep power.

Four other ethnic lists ran in the 1981 election, but none won even a single seat despite the fact that Orientals were more than 45 percent of the over 1,900,000 voters. These lists included "respectable" figures, several of them former Knesset members who had served in established parties such as Labor, NRP, or DMC. They all made similar appeals to Oriental consciousness with promises to improve the status of Moroccan and other North African Jews, to rehabilitate the slums, and to attain better housing conditions.[4]

While Tami was a factor in diminishing the Oriental vote for NRP and in cutting its Knesset representation from twelve to six seats in 1981, the overwhelming majority of Orientals voted not for ethnic lists, but for Begin and Likud. Abuhatzeira's defection from NRP caused the greatest impact in the Oriental Revolt by capturing enough votes for three NRP seats. NRP lost the other three seats to Likud and to Tehiya, a right-wing party.

The era of shifting Oriental votes was also the time of a substantial increase in the Oriental population. Although by 1981 Orientals made up more than half of Israel's Jewish population, they still constituted less than half of the electorate because the percentage of children (nonvoters) in Oriental families was larger than in Ashkenazi families.

Attraction to traditional Labor values and symbolism was never great among Oriental Jews. Frontier pioneering, settlement in agricultural collectives (kibbutzim), or a strong labor-union consciousness did not attract them. Their values and national orientation derived more from those in the traditional societies of their origins; for instance, they tended to be more family than nation/state oriented, with primary loyalties to relatives and kin rather than to civic institutions. Attempts in earlier years to replace these so-called eastern values with those of Labor had little success. Often, rather than the eastern values being replaced, they were merely uprooted or dismantled. The psychological support given by the family and the close-knit community was often undermined, but new values were not absorbed.

One evidence of displacement has been the relatively high level of criminal activity resulting from economic and cultural insecurity and from social stress. Recent statistics show that Orientals make up more than 90 percent of the prison population in Israel and are involved much more in criminal behavior than Europeans.[5] Although there has been slow progress in integrating Oriental Jews into the mainstream of Israeli society, a large gap still persists. Israel's Central Bureau of Statistics reported in May 1982 that the gross income of Oriental urban wage earners was 40 percent lower per capita than that of salaried workers of Western origin and that the gap between rich and poor in cities was widening.[6]

Economic Dilemmas

Begin's government so successfully manipulated ethnicity in 1981 that ethnic concerns seemed to override class issues. The Likud government offered enough incentives to those at the bottom of the social scale to neutralize what was left of Labor's economic and social promises. However, there had been a decline in Likud's popularity between 1978 and 1980 when national attention focused more on economic than foreign affairs. After the euphoria wore off from Sadat's visit to Jerusalem in 1977 and from the peace treaty in 1979, more of the informed public turned their attention to internal problems. They saw that Begin failed to achieve most of the economic and social goals outlined in the Likud program that brought the party to power in 1977. Inflation had not been reduced; instead it escalated to an all-time high. There was little success in transferring huge components of the public economy, like Israel Chemicals or the aircraft industry, to the private sector. And the public payroll increased rather than diminished. Public-opinion polls during the year before the 1981 election indicated a significant loss of confidence in Likud.[7]

Begin's charisma was one of the "miracles" that saved Likud from suffering the fate of Labor in 1977. Another was that most of the Oriental voters who supported Begin were not directly affected by the unprecedented inflation, the increased unemployment, and the growth of the national debt. Deficiencies in these areas were more than balanced by increases in services in areas beneficial to the Oriental voter. Free public education was extended to the end of high school and Likud's housing program made available thousands of new apartments, mostly for those in lower-income brackets.

Disagreement within Begin's cabinet over economic policies resulted in the resignation of two finance ministers and a double reversal of policy in the two years before the election. The first finance minister, Simcha Ehrlich, leader of the Liberal party faction in Likud, resigned in October 1979. He was unable to cope with the rising security expenses, which he said resulted directly from the peace treaty and which he claimed would add 20 percent to the inflation rate. These costs included the transfer of major air bases and other important military installations from the Sinai to the Negev in southern Israel. To help meet these expenses the government imposed sharp reductions in subsidies for basic commodities. For example, the price of bread rose by 40 percent.[8]

One result of Ehrlich's attempts to find the balance between peace and austerity was mass demonstrations in which more than 1 million workers protested the subsidy cuts. Ehrlich was replaced by Yigal Hurvitz, an advocate of hard-line economic policy. He demanded even more subsidy cuts, a wage freeze for public servants, and reduction of the civil service by 20,000 workers. By the end of the year, the prices of many basic food items shot up by 100 percent. Under Ehrlich inflation reached an all time high of 138.4 percent, and the Israeli pound lost nearly half its value in less than a year. To mitigate the psychological effects of inflation, the government introduced a new unit of currency in 1980 called the shekel, which gradually replaced the pound at the rate of one shekel for ten pounds.[9]

Hurvitz was the second finance minister to go; he was replaced by Yoram Aridor a few months before the election. Aridor's first major act was to reduce taxes on consumer durables such as television sets and private cars, while instituting moderate increases in prices of a few basic commodities. Lower taxes on consumer goods, his supply-side argument went, would stimulate sales to a point at which total tax revenues would exceed collection of taxes at existing rates. Lower taxes obviously appealed to most Israelis, who are the world's highest-taxed citizens. With a per capita income of some $4,000, taxation came to 46.5 percent of the GNP in 1977.[10]

As the campaign progressed, Aridor appealed to the electorate by once again reducing prices on a number of food items, especially on the eve of Passover. Aridor's policies were attacked by several econ-omists. The governor of the Bank of Israel (the central bank) charged that the opportunity to stem inflation had been wasted because Likud failed to implement a comprehensive policy and demand had not been kept down along with prices. More serious budget cuts were necessary, he said, including some in the defense sector. The budget could be cut without lowering the standard of living or increasing taxes; one way would be to end the openhanded subsidies to export products that, he argued, should be forced to compete with imports. This would improve both productivity and efficiency.[11]

Labor's response to Likud's economic and social programs was hardly radical. Although the alignment still dominated the Histadrut federation of unions, it no longer seemed motivated by the socialist

Zionist ideology from which Labor had evolved. The party leaders and program rarely mentioned socialism, although Zionism was still an essential part of their credo. Rather, Labor proposed a mixture of administrative and mildly liberal measures to cope with the country's economic problems. In 1981 its economists advocated stabilization of the exchange rate, incentives to the export industry, long-term agreements to keep wages stable, and gradual alteration of the tax structure to control inflation. Differences between Labor and Likud on economic and social matters were more a question of degree than of radically opposed programs.

All economists agreed that a major cause of inflation was the government's excess expenditure and the creation of money to finance it. Disagreements were technical rather than ideological, over where to make the most drastic cuts. But even if government administration were curtailed, the bulk of expenditures would remain fixed in items including the escalating costs of imported oil, of debt financing, and of defense.[12] In Israel's early days when the population increased by scores of thousands a year, the cost of immigration was also a major stimulant to inflation, but immigration has declined in recent years so that it no longer drains the economy.

Each of Israel's wars was followed by a quantum leap in defense expenditures. Between 1975 and 1981 the cost of defense nearly doubled from $3,552 million to $6,056 million. Per capita defense expenditures increased by a third from $1,045 to $1,514. Because of increased government income this resulted in a decline in the percentage of government spending for defense from 50.1 to 30.6, and in the percentage of GNP for defense costs from 35.9 to 28.7.[13] Nevertheless, Israel remained among the nations with the highest defense expenditure in absolute terms, in per capita expenditure, and in percent of GNP. While rapidly increasing military costs and growth of defense industries helped to keep the wheels of the economy in motion, they failed to increase overall productive capacity.[14]

Each war also left its distinctive imprint on the economy. After 1967, there was a spurt of economic growth and an end to the recession that had plagued the country until months before the Six Day War. But the 1973 war caused a major economic decline from which, by the outbreak of the sixth war in 1982, there was no recovery. Called "Peace for Galilee," the 1982 war against the PLO in Lebanon proved to be one of the most expensive of Israel's military ventures. Economic costs were estimated at about $2.5 billion, of which up to $2 billion (10 percent of the GNP) was to replace war material for the Lebanon campaign. Other costs included a 20 percent decline in tourism during the high season of 1982, leaving a serious deficit in foreign currency. To help pay for the war, subsidies on basic foods were again cut and a special 4 percent income tax in the form of a compulsory loan was imposed. Inflation, which had decreased to 101.5 percent in 1981, shot back up to 130 percent. Industrial exports fell about 20 percent from the 1981 level during the three months of the war, and the indirect production loss was estimated at $400 million to $1 billion.[15]

A unique feature of the economic crisis is that much of the public is insulated against inflation, unemployment, and the decline in the value of currency. Most workers succeed in maintaining a relatively high standard of living despite the erosion of the public economy. The strong labor unions have achieved a kind of indexing that has linked wages and salaries to prices. Savings are protected through a variety of devices including foreign-currency accounts, pension funds, and saving schemes linked to the inflation rate. According to one economic observer, "the only unprotected lender has been, and continues to be, the state. Its loans were until recently only partially linked."[16]

The year after Israel's highest inflation, a poll testing the sense of economic well-being showed that the overwhelming majority of citizens did not consider themselves to be bad off, although the number who thought themselves well-to-do had declined. A larger number than ever considered themselves in a "middling" status. Few voters expected any serious alteration of personal economic conditions as a result of the 1981 election, and among those who did anticipate change, it was for the worst with either Labor or Likud.[17]

Foreign aid, especially U.S. government and private grants and loans, also helped to insulate Israelis from the high costs of security. The 1973 war marked a turning point in U.S. government assistance with an escalation from hundreds of millions to billions of dollars per year. The 1979 peace treaty resulted in another upward escalation when President Carter assumed responsibility for much of the expense in transferring Israeli bases from the Sinai to the Negev and in maintaining its qualitative edge in military equipment. Since 1973 Israel has been the largest single recipient of U.S. government assistance; in some years it received more than a quarter of all American foreign aid.[18]

Likud leaders like Begin and Minister of Defense Ariel Sharon saw no reason for Israel to be reticent or reluctant in accepting U.S. largesse. After all, they argued, Israel was America's only reliable ally in the Middle East and the principal guarantee against Soviet penetration of the region. At times, quarrels between U.S. and Israeli officials over American economic and military assistance became harsh as each side accused the other of ingratitude for what it had done to further the interests of the other. The increases in aid resulting from the peace treaty led to annual assistance from the United States in the vicinity of $2 billion; but by the end of 1982, Israel's request increased to $3.1 billion for the financial year starting October 1983, an increase of about $900 million from 1982. Finance Minister Aridor claimed that the request did not include assistance for the war in Lebanon, which he asserted "will be met by the Israeli public."[19]

Internal Politics

The peace treaty in 1979 also affected Israel's internal politics. Although Begin successfully won approval from 95 of the 120 Knesset members for the treaty, it sent tremors of dissidence through his Likud bloc, sparking the longest debate in Knesset history. Of the 18 negative votes, 7 came from Begin's Likud party (13 from the government coalition as a whole). At the other end of the spectrum, the 5 members of the Communist Democratic Front for Peace and Equality also voted against the treaty. By October several nationalist zealots who opposed Begin's policies as too compliant quit Herut to form a new party called Tehiya (Rennaissance). It included two Knesset members who left the Likud and several hundred sympathizers from the Gush Emunim (Bloc of the Faithful), the Land of Israel movement, as well as a few from the Labor movement who were opposed to territorial concessions.

The cabinet was also divided, especially by provisions of the treaty providing autonomy for Arab inhabitants of Gaza and the West Bank. Ex-general Ariel Sharon, then minister of agriculture, supported Gush Emunim in its demands for unrestricted Jewish settlement in the occupied areas. He was opposed by ex-generals Yigael Yadin, Ezer Weizman, and Moshe Dayan—the deputy prime minister and ministers of defense and foreign affairs, respectively

By August 1979, Dayan had resigned from the cabinet to protest Begin's policies related to the West Bank and the peace negotiations. Dayan felt that the peace process had been retarded by Begin's unwillingness to be more forthcoming. His letter of resignation stated, "The question of our relations with the Arabs of the areas, not with the PLO, seems in my view over many years as a key question to our existence and subject to solution."[20] Dayan was replaced as foreign minister in 1980 by Knesset speaker Yitzhak Shamir, a former leader of the underground Fighters for the Freedom of Israel ("Stern Gang"). He was one of the Likud minority who had voted against the peace treaty.

The next serious cabinet defection came in May 1980 when Weizman resigned, ostensibly to protest cuts in the defense budget. His resignation letter, however, expressed "reservations about the government's peace plan, its social policy and its style of functioning." Later, in his biography describing the negotiations with Egypt, Weizman stated that although both Begin and Sadat wanted peace, "Sadat wanted to take it by storm" whereas "Begin preferred to creep forward inch by inch. He took the dream of peace and ground it down into the fine, dry powder of details, legal clauses, and quotes from international law." Weizman was angered by his cabinet colleagues who he claimed were unprepared for Sadat's overtures. "I may be exaggerating," he wrote about the ministers, "but some of them acted as if peace had come at the wrong moment, bringing with it unnecessary headaches. Who needed it? . . . Peace was a couple of sizes too large for some of them. . . . Members of the cabinet, from the Prime Minister down, looked back with longing to the recent past, to their first months in office before Sadat's arrival in Israel. How idyllic it had all been. . . . The Egyptian President had spoiled the show for them."[21]

After voting against Begin's economic policies in the Knesset, Weizman was expelled from the Herut party, helping to reduce the coalition's narrow majority in Israel's parliament. For several months, Begin acted as defense minister himself, and then, in a controversial move, appointed Sharon to the post.

By the end of 1980 other defections reduced Begin's Knesset majority from seventy-seven to sixty-two. A fourth cabinet member, Justice Minister Shmuel Tamir, also resigned, because of the "intolerable situation" of his party, the Democratic Movement (formerly DMC), which had declined from fifteen to three seats. Because of internal disagreements, the DMC—which many voters in 1977 had perceived as the party of political reform—split into several factions, leaving only its founder, Deputy Prime Minister Yadin, and two others as Begin supporters. By the time of the 1981 election, Yadin formally disbanded his party, resigned from the Knesset, and decided to leave politics altogether. Expectations that the DMC would emerge as a strong third party—an alternative to Labor, Likud, or the religious bloc—were totally frustrated.

Election eve in June 1981 found a proliferation of electoral lists—thirty-one in all, more than in any previous election. Eleven had been on the ballot in 1977, six were formed as factions of parties represented in the ninth Knesset (like Tehiya), and fourteen were new. They included the previously mentioned Oriental lists and lists representing Russian immigrants, Arabs, the aged, and Rabbi Meir Kahane's Kach movement (affiliated with the U.S. Jewish Defense League). Twenty-one of the lists failed to receive the minimum 1 percent of votes required for Knesset representation. Only ten parties, three less than in 1977, received enough votes for representation in the new tenth Knesset. Despite the large number of parties, voting polarized between the two largest, Likud and Labor. Likud emerged with forty-eight seats and Labor with forty-seven. They were separated by less than 1 percent of the votes, as Likud received 37.11 and Labor 36.57 percent.

Two new parties emerged from the election, Abuhatzeira's Tami and Moshe Dayan's Telem (State Renewal list). But there was a sharp decline in support for nearly all other small parties. DMC disappeared; the NRP religious party, traditionally the third largest, lost half of its support; Communist strength declined; Labor's Arab affiliates lost their seats, as did other parties represented in the ninth Knesset such as Poalei (Workers) Agudat Israel, Shelli, Flatto-Sharon, and the Independent Liberals. In opposition, Labor could count on support only from Shulamit Aloni's Civil Rights Movement and the last remnant of the DMC, Shinui (Change), the liberal faction that broke away from DMC after DMC joined Begin's coalition in 1977.

Until the election Dayan's Telem list showed promise of substantial support. Polls late in 1980 showed that Dayan might receive as many as seventeen Knesset seats running as an independent candidate. But hopes that Telem would capture DMC and other middle-of-the-road votes vanished by June 1981. It seemed that the bitterness of the campaign persuaded many who had left the Labor ranks in 1977 to return (Labor received 12 percent more of the vote in 1981 than in 1977). Many liberal voters thought that a vote for one of the smaller parties like Shinui would ensure Begin's victory. Shinui's leader, Amnon Rubinstein, observed after the election that "fear of the rise of the Likud chased our supporters in droves to the ranks of Labor. We heard it from many of our friends who said, 'We would like to vote Shinui but are too scared.' "[22]

After the election and protracted negotiations Begin formed a new coalition supported by the three religious parties, NRP (six seats), Agudat Israel (four), and Tami (three), giving him a paper-thin majority of one in the Knesset. Shamir and Aridor were reappointed foreign and finance ministers respectively, and Sharon took over from Begin as defense minister. As the price for their support, the religious parties wrested several concessions, including new restrictions on Sabbath economic activity, greater financial aid to students in religious seminaries, exemption from military draft for "newly observant" students of Jewish theology, and a pledge to exclude conversions to Judaism made by nonorthodox rabbis for purposes of official identity (important for Jewish immigrants in obtaining citizenship and other privileges).[23]

Within a little more than a year, Begin increased his Knesset majority to sixty-four against an opposition of fifty-six by a series of shifts and turns. Compromises resulting in a further hardening on foreign policy and a tough stance in the West Bank convinced Tehiya to join the government. A new cabinet post, minister of science and development, was created for one of Tehiya's leaders, Yuval Neeman, an outstanding physicist and former president of the country's leading technical university. Telem disbanded and its two Knesset members joined Likud, one of them also receiving the cabinet post of minister without portfolio. The coalition majority would have been larger had not two Likud members defected to Labor, in part because of a dispute over Begin's West Bank and economic policies and in part because of hoped-for political benefits in shifting to Labor.

Although Labor and Likud received nearly equal votes in the 1981 election, Likud had the advantage in coalition building. Labor had only Shinui with two seats and the Civil Rights movement with one as close associates in a possible cabinet. With the trend toward the right in Israeli politics, Likud had more possibilities. It had more in common than did Labor with the religious parties and with Tami, Tehiya, and Telem. Labor had no charismatic personalities like Begin among its leaders, nor was its program greatly different on either domestic or foreign affairs. True, within the ranks of Labor there were doves, staunch trade unionists, and a generally liberal outlook, but the alignment was much more divided on most issues than was Likud or the whole Begin coalition of half a dozen parties. By 1981, there was no significant deviation in the coalition on Begin's intent to retain the occupied territories, negotiate with or recognize the Palestinians, and maintain the free-enterprise approach to economic problems, whereas Labor was divided on all these issues.

More importantly, public opinion over the years was moving more to the right than to the left. Polls consistently showed Begin far in the lead as the choice for prime minister, and his foreign policies, policies in the West Bank, and other world views were more acceptable than those of the diffused Labor leadership. Given Israel's severe foreign problems, the public generally yearned for strong leaders. Indeed, a poll taken by Dahaf in 1981 showed that 31 percent of the Jewish population was in favor of doing away with political parties, 55 percent supported restrictions on press freedom, 21 percent would prefer an undemocratic government with "acceptable" policies to a democratic government with "unacceptable" policies (20 percent were indifferent on the issue), 23 percent wanted to prohibit all strikes, and 41 percent favored a regime of strong leaders independent of political parties.[24] The author of an article in *Monitin*, explaining these results, observed that the democratic structures of Israeli society were never as deeply rooted as those in countries with generations-old democratic traditions. Most immigrants to Israel came from countries that were unfamiliar with democracy; the conditions in which the state evolved were not conducive to development of democratic institutions. At the heart of society, even among Ben-Gurion's close associates, were some individuals who found democratic procedures wearisome and would have been glad to see them go.[25] Still, as the poll indicated, such thinking remained clearly in the minority.

One result of difficulties in Israel, the political uncertainties, and the continued wars was a serious decline in Jewish immigration. According to a study published by the Falk Institute for Economic Research in Jerusalem, approximately 340,000 people emigrated from Israel between 1948 and 1979, an annual average of 225 emigrants for every 1,000 immigrants. The study found that after every wave of new settlers there occurred an increase in emigration, as newcomers who could not adjust left the country.[26] Some unofficial estimates placed the emigrants at over 500,000, based on the numbers of Israelis permanently settled in the United States. By the end of 1981 the situation reached crisis proportions when the government statistician revealed that for the first time since the establishment of the state in 1948, emigrants outnumbered immigrants. During 1980–1981 there was a net emigration of about 30,000 Jews, with an immigration of only some 21,000, leaving a net outmigration of 9,000.[27]

Israeli Arabs and the Arabs of the Occupied Areas

A dilemma of little concern to the Begin government was the situation of Israel's Arab minority, constituting some 16 percent of the population by the 1980s. Until the 1981 election there seemed to be a slow but steady increase of support by the country's Arab voters for Rakah, the New Communist list, which formed the core of the Democratic Front for Peace and Equality (DFPE). Between the elections of 1965 and 1977, the Arab vote for Rakah had increased from 23 to 51 percent. But in 1981, only 46 percent voted communist; the number of Arab votes for the Rakah-DFPE list decreased from 65,000 to 59,000, with a substantial return of Arab voters to labor. One explanation was that Israeli Arabs either feared or were disillusioned with the Begin government's indifference to their problems. Professor Moshe Sharon, a former adviser to Begin on Arab affairs who resigned because of the lack of an Arab policy, observed that to many in the minority Labor was the "best of bad alternatives." The Begin government's "almost total neglect" of the Arab sector led many to search for a moderate party that could understand their problems, according to Sharon.[28]

Corresponding to the decline in support for Rakah was a marked conservative trend among Israeli Arabs. Although many still identified themselves as Palestinians and linked this identity with sympathy for the PLO, polls indicated a decline in radicalization and in the intensity of nationalist sentiment. Many more were now willing to acknowledge Israel's legitimacy and to search for ways of accommodating themselves to the Jewish state.[29]

However, continuation of the Arab-Israeli conflict made life difficult for the minority. In the words of former Knesset member Abdel Aziz Zouabi, "my country is at war with my nation." The minority perceived itself as regarded by Jews as a potential fifth column and by the Arab world as "Jews." Although the economic situation of Israeli Arabs was generally better than that of Arabs in surrounding countries, their social isolation and lack of any political clout increased their alienation from the mainstream of Jewish society. For example, lacking veteran status, they experienced difficulty in obtaining improved housing, municipal services, and social benefits that were often linked to veteran status and taken for granted by the Jewish majority.[30]

After 1979 a number of issues widened the chasm between Israeli Arab and Jewish communities. While the majority of Jews, 70 percent, fully endorsed the peace treaty with Egypt, less than half the Arab public favored it. The gap also marked differences over Jewish settlements in the occupied areas and borders. Nearly three times as many Israeli Arabs as Jews opposed the settlements; two-thirds of the Arabs, but less than 2 percent of the Jews, would return all territory seized in the 1967 war in exchange for peace.[31]

The question of Palestinian identity was equally divisive. By large majorities, the Israeli Arabs showed their sympathy for Palestinian nationalism: 80.1 percent of the Arabs, but only 11 percent of the Jews, supported Israel's recognition of the Palestinian nation; 68 percent of the Arabs and 2.7 percent of the Jews called for Israel's recognition of the PLO; 64.3 percent of the Arabs and 5.4 percent of the Jews supported establishment of a Palestinian state in the West Bank and Gaza alongside Israel; 77.9 percent of the Arabs and 5.8 percent of the Jews supported the right of Palestinian refugee repatriation within the 1967 borders. In sum, Arabs fell outside the limits of the operative consensus, characterizing them as a "dissident minority" in the Israeli context.[32]

The war in Lebanon exacerbated the dilemma. Few Israeli Arabs did not have relatives among the Palestinian refugees in Lebanon; many were shocked by the events during the summer of 1982, especially by the massacre of Arab refugees in the Beirut camps. Most of them kept a low profile during the Israeli invasion, participating only in those antiwar demonstrations staged by the larger Jewish community.

On the government side, the Arab problem was perceived as a demographic threat, one in which the more rapid increase of Arab births threatened Zionist objectives. During 1982 Economics Minister Ya'acov Meridor warned about the threat of "creeping foreign ownership" (Israeli Arab) of land in Galilee and called for a change in the region's demographic trend. In a Knesset debate on the subject during July 1982, it was pointed out that Jews were only 40 percent of the population in central Galilee and that this proportion was "steadily and quite rapidly" declining. In many Jewish towns of the region, "non-Jewish elements" were buying up flats, public buildings, and commercial property.[33] The same demographic threat existed in Jerusalem, where a government housing official warned in 1982 that the number of Arabs would catch up to the Jewish population within eight years. Because of the difference in population growth (an Arab increase of 3.7 percent a year and a Jewish decline from 2.9 to 1.8 percent), Arabs would outnumber Jerusalem Jews within the decade. Jews presently form 53 percent (320,950) and Arabs 47 percent (283,600) of the population of greater Jerusalem, within an area from Ramallah up to Bethlehem.[34]

Problems of administration and the upsurge of militant Palestinian nationalism in the West Bank, Gaza, and the Golan area were a far more serious problem for the Begin government than were the Israeli Arabs after 1979. West Bankers were much more outspoken than Israeli Arabs in opposing the peace treaty, especially those provisions dealing with their future. Insistence by Begin's government on the right of continued Jewish settlement in the occupied territories stimulated increased protests by the Arab inhabitants. Minister of Agriculture Ariel Sharon pursued a policy of aggressive Jewish settlement, in accordance with the policies of Gush Emunim.

After Israel's supreme court temporarily suspended further confiscation of privately owned Arab land at Elon Moreh by Israel during 1979, the government announced that it would pursue its settlement policy on state lands. Opposition to government policy in the West Bank was one of the reasons for Dayan's resignation in 1979 and for Ezer Weizman's in 1980. By 1982 there were more than 100 settlements and over 25,000 Jewish settlers in the West Bank. Long-term government plans called for increasing not only rural but urban settlements and bringing the total Jewish population to some 300,000 by the end of the century.

Some observers perceived a scheme to absorb the West Bank without formal annexation, by integrating the economies, services, road systems, and administration of Israel and the occupied areas. With the Arab population on the West Bank only increasing at a rate of 1.4 percent per year, primarily as a result of a high rate of emigration (estimated at 100,000 since 1967), some observers even foresaw a shrinking of the huge Arab-Jewish population gap of 800,000 to 25,000.[35]

An extensive survey of the West Bank and its future prospects by Meron Benvenisti, former deputy mayor of Jerusalem, underscored the economic and social factors involved. "The economy of the West Bank may be characterized as undeveloped, non-viable, stagnant and dependent," he asserted. "It is an auxiliary sector of both the Israeli and the Jordanian economies." Because of the complex of restrictions in the area, there was little capital investment in the West Bank during the period of Jordanian control (1948–1967) and thus an undeveloped industrial base. Consequently the area provided an outlet for 25 percent of Israel's exports, according to the survey. Fifteen years of Israeli occupation brought significant changes to the West Bank occupational structure. Half the employed labor force there was working in Israel, where they provided a substantial proportion of workers in agriculture, construction, and service occupations. A total of some 75,000 West Bank Arabs in diverse categories of employment worked in Israel by 1981, more than 50 percent in construction.[36]

Over the years a dual administrative system had emerged, one for the indigenous Arabs, a second for Jewish settlers. The Jewish system was run largely by Gush Emunim; the Arab by the military authorities. Benvenisti concluded that "freezing" further Jewish settlement would not substantially alter the changing character of the West Bank. More important than the number of settlements was the shift of Israeli urban popualtion into areas that would guarantee continued control and create an "insurmountable political problem for any concession-oriented political party in the country."[37]

Arab opposition to these developments intensified after 1979, with increased protest demonstrations, noncooperation by mayors and village councils, and violent conflicts between Israeli military authorities and the inhabitants. Several West Bank leaders and mayors were arrested, imprisoned, or deported after being charged with collaborating with the PLO. In 1979, twenty-five Arab West Bank mayors resigned in protest against Israeli policies. After a terrorist attack on Jews in Hebron during 1980, two more mayors and a Muslim judge were deported to Lebanon. The Hebron incident sparked counter-terrorism when bombs were used in attempts to kill three Arab mayors. By 1982 there were major disturbances throughout the West Bank, more arrests, closings of Arab universities by the military authorities, and impositions of extensive curfews. In an attempt to counter the nationalist manifestations, which the authorities insisted resulted from PLO instigation, the government assisted in forming a number of Village Leagues. Attempts were made to legitimize the leagues by requiring West Bank Arab inhabitants to obtain vital documents through league intercession rather than through the customary municipal or village council offices.

Foreign Relations

Events and policies in the occupied territories, especially in the West Bank, have been interlocked with Israel's foreign policy during the three and a half years after the peace treaty. Although the Begin team waged a determined battle to maintain Israel's hegemony in Sinai and to prevent the loss of as much territory as possible in negotiations leading up to the treaty, they finally succumbed to Sadat's demand for return of "every inch" of the Sinai. In return for full normalization of diplomatic, economic, cultural, and other relations with Egypt, Israel agreed to fully withdraw all its military forces, bases, and civilians from Sinai. Within nine months of the treaty, more than two-thirds of Sinai was returned; within three years, all the peninsula was fully evacuated.[38] Normalization included opening the Suez Canal to Israeli ships for the first time and declaring the Strait of Tiran and the Gulf of Aqaba international waterways, assuring safe and secure passage to Israeli commerce.

Autonomy Disagreements

However, the West Bank and Gaza remained areas of contention. According to the 1978 Camp David Framework of Peace in the Middle East (which was reaffirmed in the treaty), following negotiations between Israel, the Palestinians, Jordan, and Egypt "the Israeli military government and its civilian administration would be withdrawn" from the occupied territories and an autonomous regime of the inhabitants would be established.[39] Egypt interpreted this to mean eventual Palestinian self-government; the Begin government insisted that autonomy not interfere with Israel's right to establish Jewish settlements in the territories and eventually incorporate them into Israel. In any case, since neither Jordan nor any Palestinian group chose to join the negotiations, they were little more than an exercise. Indeed, following the peace treaty Begin's concept of autonomy hardened. To Begin, autonomy applied not to the land but to its inhabitants. They would be authorized to establish control over their own domestic affairs in matters of education, social welfare, religion, and the like, under Israel's supervision. The land itself, according to Begin, was a Biblical heritage of the Jewish people and could not be alienated by turning it over to the Palestinian Arabs. Thus, Jews had every right to continued settlement in the West Bank, Gaza, and Golan and to exploitation of their agricultural, water, mineral, and other natural resources.

Jews living in the West Bank, or Judea and Samaria as the region was called by Begin, would not be included in the autonomy arrangement. This arrangement would ease Israel's burden, since local matters would be managed by the Arab autonomous administration rather than by the Israeli military government, which would be terminated. The autonomous administration would have limited authority, leaving concerns such as internal security, Jewish settlement, national lands, and even some economic affairs in Israeli hands.[40]

Begin's concept would assure that a Palestinian state would not be established in Judea, Samaria, or Gaza and that Jerusalem would remain united "forever as the capital of Israel, and Israel will never go back to the June 4, 1967 borders." This contradicted both Egyptian and U.S. positions, which envisaged some degree of Palestinian self-determination, either in association with Jordan or in some other form.[41]

This should have been no surprise to those familiar with Begin's ideological orientation. Surrender of any part of Jewish rights and/ or territory in mandatory Palestine was totally unacceptable to the Herut party that Begin established in 1948 and to the Revisionist movement from which Herut derived its ideology. The Revisionists had opposed exclusion of Transjordan, or Eastern Palestine, from provisions of the mandate applying to the Jewish homeland in the 1920s, and Begin opposed the UN partition plan in 1948, because it violated Jewish rights. According to Begin: "We want to bring about through the autonomy arrangements a situation whereby we will be able to live together, Jews and Arabs in an unpartitioned Eretz Yisrael." In this respect his position resembled that of the PLO, which also claimed that all of mandatory Palestine was one territorial unit and insisted on establishment of a single state in the whole of Palestine/ Eretz Yisrael.[42]

The issue of security, of secondary importance to Begin, was the primary reason for opposition to a Palestinian state by many Israelis who did not espouse Begin's ideology. Nonetheless, Begin also maintained that "If it [a Palestine state] were established in Judea, Samaria and Gaza, it would not only constitute a direct danger to Israel's security, but to its very existence." Such a state would become not only a source for terrorist activity against Israel but also a Soviet base to undermine Western interests in the region.⁴³

Even though a bitter diplomatic struggle was waged to retain a foothold in Sinai for security reasons, Begin's government perceived no historical or ideological obstacle to its surrender; thus a partially demilitarized Sinai, patrolled by a multinational force, could be turned over to Egypt in exchange for peace. However, the West Bank and Gaza were a different matter. Ideological commitment combined with a genuine security concern posed a major obstacle to resolving their future. Because it was difficult for Egyptian and U.S. negotiators in the autonomy talks during the years after the treaty to either put sufficient weight on Begin's ideological motives or to accept Israel's position, the talks dragged on, were frequently interrupted, and eventually petered out.

The policies used by Israel to implement Begin's ideology stirred intense opposition among the indigenous Arab inhabitants, which in turn caused deterioration of Israel's relations with Egypt and the United States. Measures taken to contain unrest and political dissidence in the occupied territoires, in addition to insistence on the proliferation of Jewish settlements, led to mistrust, accusations of faithlessness, and the breakdown of negotiations, not only on autonomy, but on other issues as well. Furthermore, the measures served to partially increase Israel's international isolation as it became the object of numerous UN General Assembly and Security Council resolutions castigating it for these policies. Beyond the UN, Israel was also criticized by the nonaligned nations, the European Economic Community (EEC), and diverse Western European countries.

The United States attempted to mitigate the effects of Israeli policy by approaching autonomy with step-by-step negotiations. Autonomy was divided into discrete subtopics: how the Palestinian council would be elected and who would be eligible to vote; how Jerusalem residents would participate; whether the autonomous council would have legislative or only executive powers; and what internal-security arrangements would be established. By May 1980, when the deadline set for an autonomy agreement arrived, it was evident that the gap between Israel and Egypt would be difficult to overcome. Tense relations caused by these disagreements were further exacerbated when the Knesset passed a law on July 30 reaffirming a 1967 decision to make Jerusalem, "complete and united," the eternal capital of Israel.

The Jerusalem law, approved by a vote of sixty-nine to fifteen, did nothing to change the status of Arab or East Jerusalem, which Israel had annexed thirteen years earlier. It did set off a chain of international protests, including censure by the UN, criticism by the United States, and a request by Sadat for suspension of the autonomy talks. Thirteen countries with embassies in the city responded by moving them to Tel-Aviv.

Relations with Egypt

Despite the slowdown of normalization caused by disagreements over the West Bank and Gaza, there was a remarkable opening in relationships between Egypt and Israel. For the first time Israel had full diplomatic relations with an Arab state: ambassadors were exchanged; Egypt opened an embassy in Tel-Aviv and Israel opened one in Cairo. The borders between the two countries were opened to tourists, commerce, and trade and direct air travel began with El-Al flights from Ben-Gurion Airport to Cairo. Telephone and telecommunication links were established. There were exchanges of artists, academicians, trade missions, and the like. Although the traffic was much heavier from Israel to Egypt and many Israelis would have liked to see greater interest by Egyptians in these contacts, Israelis were well received and experienced few difficulties in their visits to Cairo.

In addition to disagreements over autonomy, other events and policies of Begin's government retarded the process of normalization. In June 1981 Egypt found it difficult to accept Israel's air attack on Iraq's nuclear reactor at Osirak near Baghdad. The surprise attack on June 7 was necessary, stated Begin, to prevent production before the end of the year of atomic bombs similar to those dropped on Hiroshima. Within a short time the reactor would have begun operations and become "hot." A later attack "would have caused a huge wave of radioactivity over the city of Baghdad, and its innocent citizens would have been harmed," according to the Israeli government.[44] The attack was condemned unanimously by the UN Security Council as a "clear violation of the United Nations Charter and the norms of international conduct." It was called "a serious threat to the entire IAEA [International Atomic Energy Association] safeguards regime which is the foundation of the NPT [Non Proliferation Treaty]." The United States expressed displeasure over the attack by suspending delivery to Israel of sixteen fighter planes for ten weeks.[45]

Actions in Lebanon

Israel's policies in Lebanon also caused difficulties in relations with Egypt and the United States, to say nothing of other countries. Since the invasion of Lebanon in 1978, the establishment of a UN force there, and a new border relationship between Lebanon and Israel, hostilities had continued against the PLO and Lebanese leftists. Israel charged that the PLO was continuing to build up its forces in Lebanon and was using Lebanon as a base from which to operate numerous international terrorist activities. Periodically the PLO fired across the border into Jewish settlements in northern Israel. Israel's retaliation was usually swift and heavy, and in July 1981 an Israeli air strike at PLO offices in a heavily populated district of Beirut killed more than 300 people and wounded some 800, mostly civilians. The intensity of the air attack was strongly criticized by the United States and resulted in new condemnations by the UN and the international community.

Events in Lebanon were exacerbated by hostilities between Israel and its Phalangist allies on the one hand and Syrian forces on the other. The Syrians, who intervened in Lebanon during the civil war of 1975–1976, kept their forces in that country, receiving an *ex post facto* imprimatur as an Arab League "peace keeping" force. During altercations between the Syrians and Phalangists, Israeli jets shot down two Syrian helicopters; Damascus responded by installing several units of SAM-6 antiaircraft missiles, which Begin threatened to destroy on the grounds that they undermined Israel's security. This missile crisis and the raid on Beirut became the occasion to renew the peace-keeping mission of U.S. envoy Philip Habib, and by the end of July 1981 he negotiated a cease-fire between Israeli and PLO forces along the Lebanese frontier. Israel maintained that it reached the accord with the United States, while the PLO insisted that it halted fighting after agreement with the UN.

The missile crisis and Begin's activist policies in Lebanon caused more disagreement with the Labor opposition. In an interview with the *Jerusalem Post*, former Prime Minister Yitzhak Rabin stated that the Syrian presence in Lebanon had been agreed to during his term of office, but as part of the tacit agreement, Syria was not to move in SAMs.[46] Ex-Foreign Minister Yigal Allon and ex-Secretary of State Henry Kissinger had negotiated terms of Syrian entry acceptable to Israel in an "agreement" contained in the minutes of a conversation between Rabin, Kissinger, and ex-President Ford during June 1976. Although Syria had never signed the terms or formally accepted them, there was a tacit understanding that the Syrians observed for five years. On the basis of the agreement, Israel stayed put when Syrian troops entered Lebanon, "and did not have second thoughts about accepting the Syrian presence," according to Rabin.[47]

He observed that "the Christians publicly welcomed the Syrian troops [in 1976] and with their help overcame the Muslim-Leftist-PLO troops at Tel El-Zaatar, for example." Some Maronite leaders were apprehensive about the Syrian presence and secretly appealed to Israel for military assistance. Rabin agreed to help the Phalangists "to help themselves" with Israeli weapons.[48]

He charged that Maronite "extremists" stepped up their efforts to involve Israel in a war with Syria after Begin became prime minister. Although "we warned them against it," Phalangist leader Bashir Gemayel tried to push the Syrians by blocking the main road between Beirut and Damascus. This, according to Rabin, triggered the whole incident leading to the 1981 "missile crisis."[49]

Although Begin's escalation of the Israeli commitment to the Phalangists was not the most significant issue in the 1981 election, it was one point attacked by Labor. The chairman of the alignment charged that Begin had "virtually contracted a unilateral treaty with the Christian leadership in Northern Lebanon and given it the power to determine when, where, and how the Israel Defense Forces should intervene in Lebanon." A few weeks before the election, the alignment stated in a campaign advertisement:

> The undeniable fact is that Menahem Begin, without authority, in an unprecedented move, committed Israel militarily. This was done in an irresponsible manner. Without prior consultation or reflection, without relying on any process of decision making, he committed the Israeli Air Force to support the Christian forces in Northern Lebanon. He thus placed a Syrian or Phalangist finger on the trigger of the Israeli Defense Forces. This man cannot be relied upon to bear the responsbility for the conduct of Israel's defense forces.[50]

The cease-fire negotiated by Philip Habib held firm for over ten months, although there were occasional incidents, which each side perceived as violations. In March 1982, after an Israeli soldier was killed by a mine in Lebanon, Israel retaliated with heavy air attacks on Palestinian outposts. The PLO then refrained from any counter-action, and the truce was preserved. In June the truce collapsed after Israel's ambassador to London, Shlomo Argov, was seriously wounded by Arab terrorists. Although the PLO disclaimed responsibility, and British intelligence officials asserted that the terrorists also intended to attack the PLO in England, Israeli jets again struck PLO positions in Lebanon. On June 6, soon after the Palestinians responded by shelling Jewish settlements in northern Israel, the sixth Arab-Israeli war began.

Initially, the government stated that its objective was to push PLO forces twenty-five miles north of the border, out of artillery range of Israeli settlements. The operation, called "Peace for Galilee," quickly drove the Palestinians north of the twenty-five-mile zone and soon reached the environs of Beirut. As the war expanded, fighting also broke out between Israelis and Syrians, and Israel extended its objectives to remove all Palestinian and Syrian forces from Lebanon.

Both Syrian and Palestinian losses were heavy. Between 7,000 and 9,000 prisoners were taken by Israel, most of them accused of being PLO terrorists. Syria lost between sixty (Syrian estimates) and eighty (Israeli estimates) war planes, nearly all its antiaircraft missiles in the Bekaa Valley, and scores of tanks. In addition, Israel captured from the Palestinians large quantities of military material, including enough heavy equipment—it stated—to equip several divisions.

By the end of June, Israel held most of the territory south of the road between Beirut and the Syrian border, except for Syrian outposts in the Bekaa. Both PLO and Syrian forces in West Beirut were beseiged. The eastern part of the city was controlled by Israel's Phalangist allies who, to Israel's dismay, played a very minimal role in the war despite previous Israeli aid. Nonetheless, Israeli forces moved freely through East Beirut. Intense negotiations through the United States and several new UN Security Council and General Assembly resolutions calling on Israel to withdraw failed to break the siege until the end of August. Agreement was finally reached on a cease-fire to include total withdrawal of Syrian and PLO forces from Beirut under the supervision of a new international force composed of military forces from the United States, France, and Italy. By September 1, nearly all the 15,000 PLO guerrillas and several hundred Syrians were evacuated by sea and land to other Arab countries. The truce included a tacit understanding that Israel would not enter West Beirut.

The Israeli invasion, which destroyed the PLO state-within-a-state in Lebanon, also changed the balance of political forces in the country in favor of the Maronites. Thus Maronite leader Bashir Gemayel was elected president by the Lebanese parliament, with Israeli troops not far from the election site. Following departure of the PLO from Beirut, Gemayel and more than a score of his colleagues were killed in an explosion at Phalangist headquarters.

Immediately after the explosion, Israeli troops occupied West Beirut, extending their authority to all the capital, with the stated purpose of preventing chaos. Maintaining that many PLO fighters were hidden in West Beirut, Israel authorized Phalangist troops to enter Palestinian refugee camps there, to "cleanse" them of remaining guerrillas. The Phalangist operation would save the lives of Israeli soldiers, according to Defense Minister Ariel Sharon.

During the next two and a half days, the Phalangists massacred several hundred Palestinian men, women, and children trapped in the camps, before being halted by the Israelis. When news of the massacre spread, it raised a storm of protest in Israel and had wide repercussions on internal politics. It focused attention on rising criticism of the war in Lebanon that had been brewing within the government and among the public. "Peace for Galilee" was the first large-scale military operation to arouse active protest, especially during the period of combat. Because of his proclivity to initiate major military operations without cabinet approval, Sharon was the target of attack by members of the government, by many Israeli newspapers, and segments of the public. The massacre was followed by a demonstration against many of Begin's policies, the largest demonstration ever held in Israel. An estimated 400,000 Israelis (over 10 percent of the population) of most political persuasions participated.

Initially the cabinet labeled accusations of the government's indirect responsibility for the massacre as a "blood libel" and refused to appoint a full independent judicial investigation.[51] But after the resignation of one cabinet member and several other high officials, Israel's Supreme Court president was asked by Begin to establish an independent commission to conduct an investigation and to make recommendations.[52] The court's president headed the inquiry; he appointed another Supreme Court member and a retired major-general to assist him in an official inquiry that was expected to last several months.

In October Prime Minister Begin announced that the war in Lebanon had established, "for the first time," a state of security on all of Israel's borders. However, the price was high. In addition to the economic costs, the casualties were higher than anticipated. By October, the number of Israeli dead reached 369, with nearly 2,400 wounded. The number of Lebanese, Syrian, and Palestinian casualties was still unknown, but total deaths were expected to be several thousand, with tens of thousands wounded, homeless, or in a new refugee status.[53]

Although PLO military strength and its capacity to strike across Israel's northern frontiers seemed to have been destroyed, the organization appeared, at least initially, to have maintained its political influence among Palestinians, in the Arab world, and on the international scene. Soon after the departure from Beirut, PLO leader Yasir Arafat was received by the prime ministers of Greece and Italy and by the Pope in Rome, an event that stirred deep anger in the Israeli government and among many of its supporters abroad.[54]

Departure of the PLO was also the occasion for several new peace proposals, from the United States, from the Arab League, and from Jordan. U.S. President Ronald Reagan's plan proposed full autonomy for the Palestinians in the West Bank and Gaza giving "due consideration . . . to the principle of self-government." The United States, he stated, would support neither "the establishment of an independent Palestinian state in the West Bank and Gaza" nor "annexation or permanent control by Israel." It was the "firm view of the United States that self-government by the Palestinians . . . in association with Jordan offers the best chance for a durable, just and lasting peace." He also called for "the immediate adoption of a settlement freeze by Israel" as a way, "more than any other action," to "create the confidence needed for wider participation" in the peace talks. Jerusalem "must remain undivided, but its final status should be decided through negotiations."[55]

Israel's cabinet unanimously rejected Reagan's plan, calling it a "serious danger" to national security. Furthermore, stated Begin, the plan was a serious deviation from the Camp David agreement; therefore, the Israeli government "resolved that . . . it will not enter into any negotiations with any party" on the basis of the plan.[56] Government rejection of the plan out of hand and refusal even to discuss it was again the subject of intense internal dispute. Many in the Labor opposition viewed the plan as a step forward and called for a debate on its contents. However, the Knesset supported the government's position by a vote of fifty to thirty-six.

By the end of 1982 it seemed that the momentum toward peace was again slowed. Egypt had withdrawn its ambassador from Tel-Aviv in protest against Israel's invasion, and President Mubarak stated that the diplomat would not return until Israel left Lebanon. The autonomy talks were suspended, and, if not dead, they would remain in limbo for the indefinite future. Relations with the United States were tense. Although Israel was still receiving extensive American military and economic aid (and the United States clearly profited by learning of the weaknesses of Soviet weaponry), the war in Lebanon had sparked the first overt criticism of Begin by U.S. politicians who had been regarded as defenders of Israeli interests. Growing disenchantment with Israeli policies among American Jewry and in the U.S. Jewish establishment was becoming serious enough to warrant a visit by Begin in November of 1982. Although Israel's military security was now assured, it remained to be seen whether the government's response to the new flurry of diplomatic activity would be flexible enough to finally terminate the war and bring peace to the country.

Notes

1. See Asher Arian, "The Electorate: Israel 1977," in Howard R. Penniman (ed.), *Israel at the Polls: The Knesset Elections of 1977* (Washington, D.C.: American Enterprise Institute, 1978), pp. 59–84.

2. *Jerusalem Post* (*JP*), June 12, 1981.

3. See series of articles on the campaign by Aharon Bakhar, *Yediot Ahronot,* June 5, 12, and 19, 1981.

4. The other ethnic or Sephardi lists were *Ihud* (Unity), *Oded, Ohalim* (Tents), and *Amcha.*

5. S. F. Landau, "Future Time Perspective of Delinquents and Non-delinquents: the Effect of Institutionalization," *Criminal Justice and Behavior,* 1975; cited in Simha F. Landau and Benjamin Beit-Hallahmi, "Aggression in Israel A Psycho-Historical Perspective," unpublished paper.

6. *Jerusalem Post International Edition* (*JPI*) 1123, May 9–15, 1982.

7. According to a poll conducted by Dahaf Research Institute and published in *Monitin* in June 1980, the Labor Alignment would have won sixty-three seats to Likud's twenty-five; see Don Peretz and Sammy Smooha, "Israel's Tenth Knesset Elections—Ethnic Upsurgence and Decline of Ideology," *Middle East Journal,* vol. 35, no. 4 (August 1981), pp. 506–526. For an analysis of these domestic problems, see Ira Sharkansky and Alex Radian, "Changing Domestic Policy 1977–1981," in Robert O. Freedman (ed.), *Israel in the Begin Era* (New York: Praeger, 1982), pp. 56–75.

8. Peretz and Smooha, "Israel's Tenth Knesset Elections," p. 506.

9. In December 1980, the value of the shekel was 7.55 per U.S. dollar; by mid-November 1982, the value of the shekel was 31.12 per U.S. dollar, the equivalent of 311 former Israeli pounds per dollar.

10. *JPI* 1063, March 5–21, 1981.

11. *JPI* 1075, June 7–13, 1981, and 1056, January 25–31, 1981.

12. Israel's oil-import bill in 1980 reached $2 billion; debt financing over $900 million per year.

13. *The Military Balance 1982–1983* (London: the International Institute for Strategic Studies, 1982), p. 124.

14. An article by Macabee Dean in *JPI* 1055, January 18–24, 1981, placed Israel as "the least productive among the world's eleven most productive countries," with an output of $14,300 per worker compared to $24,200 for the U.S. worker.

15. *New York Times,* October 26, 1982.

16. *JPI* 1067, April 12–18, 1981.

17. *JPI* 1073, May 24–30, 1981; *JP,* June 23, 1981.

18. In 1980 Israel received economic assistance in loans of $261 million and grants of $525 million; military assistance in credit sales of $500 million and grants of $500 million; and other assistance of $301.4 million. Total U.S. loans and grants to Israel between 1946 and 1980 totaled economic aid of $5,585.8 million, military aid of $12,904.2 million, and other aid of $901.3 million. *The Middle East,* Fifth Edition (Washington, D.C.: Congressional Quarterly, 1981), p. 53.

19. *JPI* 1145, October 10–16, 1982.

20. *Political Handbook of the World, 1980,* p. 22. For an analysis of the political infighting during this period, see David Pollock, "Likud in Power: Divided We Stand," in Freedman (ed.), *Israel in the Begin Era,* pp. 28–57.

21. Ezer Weizman, *The Battle for Peace* (New York: Bantam Books, 1981), pp. 250–251.

22. *JPI* 1079, July 5–11, 1981. For an analysis of the Labor Party's political campaign, see Myron J. Aronoff, "The Labor Party in Opposition," in Freedman (ed.), *Israel in the Begin Era*, pp. 76–101.

23. The political dynamics of Israel's religious parties are discussed in Daniel Elazar, "Religious Parties and Politics in the Begin Era," in Freedman (ed.), *Israel in the Begin Era*, pp. 102–120.

24. Based on results of a Dahaf survey conducted by Dr. Mina Tzemak, reported in *Monitin*, February 1981.

25. Eliahu Haseen, "Israeli Democracy—The Beginning of the End?" ibid.

26. *JPI* 1139, August 29–September 4, 1982.

27. *JPI* 1127, June 6–12, 1982.

28. *JPI* 1079, July 5–11, 1981. For a recent analysis of Israel's Arabs, see Ian Lustick, "Israel's Arab Minority in the Begin Era," in Freedman (ed.), *Israel in the Begin Era*, pp. 121–150.

29. See Don Peretz and Sammy Smooha, "The Arabs in Israel," *Journal of Conflict Resolution*, vol. 26, no. 3 (September 1982), pp. 451–484.

30. *JPI* 1131, July 4–10, 1982.

31. Peretz and Smooha, "The Arabs in Israel," pp. 455, 457.

32. Ibid, pp. 459, 463.

33. *JPI* 1133, July 18–24, 1982.

34. *JPI* 1143, September 26–October 2, 1982.

35. See extensive interview on the West Bank with Meron Benvenisti, former deputy mayor of Jerusalem, "Creating Facts on the West Bank," in *JPI* 1143, September 19–25, 1982.

36. Ibid.

37. Ibid.

38. Although Israel's evacuation was completed by April 1982 in accord with the peace treaty, Taba—a tiny area of beachfront in Sinai adjoining Eilat, about 750 yards long—remained in dispute. Egypt contested Israel's right to construct a tourist hotel there, and at the time of Israel's final departure from Sinai the two countries had agreed to negotiate their differences over Taba.

39. See *The Camp David Summit September 1978*, U.S. Department of State publication 8954, September 1978, and *The Egyptian-Israeli Peace Treaty March 26, 1979*, U.S. Department of State publication 8976, April 1979.

40. Aryeh Shalev, Brig. Gen. (Ret.), *The Autonomy Problems and Possible Solutions*, Paper no. 8, chapter 11, "Israel's Position" (Tel-Aviv: Center for Strategic Studies, Tel-Aviv University, 1980).

41. Ibid.

42. Ibid, p. 54.

43. Ibid.

44. See *Israeli Attack on Iraqi Nuclear Facilities*, hearings before U.S. House of Representatives subcommittees on International Security and Scientific Affairs, Europe and the Middle East, International Economic Policy and Trade,

and Committee on Foreign Affairs, 97th Congress, 1st session, June 17 and 25, 1981 (Washington, D.C.: U.S. Government Printing Office); and *Documents and Statements on Middle East Peace, 1979–82,* Report for House Subcommittee on Europe and the Middle East, June 1982 (Washington, D.C.: U.S. Government Printing Office).

45. *Documents and Statements.*

46. *JP,* May 19, 1981.

47. Ibid.

48. Ibid.

49. Ibid.

50. *JP,* June 1, 1981.

51. In a Knesset debate on the massacre on September 22, 1982, the Labor opposition proposed establishment of a judicial commission of inquiry under a 1968 Inquiry Law. The Labor proposal was defeated by a vote of 48 to 42.

52. The Inquiry Commission resembled the body created after the 1973 war to examine the country's setbacks during the war and military shortcomings.

53. The annual report of the United Nations Relief Works Administration (UNRWA) commissioner-general to the UN General Assembly stated that "detailed surveys in all areas except Beirut" show that by the end of August there were 81,500 Palestinian refugees "homeless and destitute," and 114,500 who required emergency relief. In West Beirut: "Thousands of persons were made homeless, living in shops, schools, garages and cinemas, etc. Many hospitals were repeatedly damaged in the air, land and sea bombardments to which West Beirut was subjected. Among the homeless were an estimated 64,000 Palestine refugees, displaced either from other parts of Beirut or from outside Beirut." General Assembly Official Records; Thirty-Seventh session, Supplement No. 13 (A/37/13). Interestingly enough, however, the UN report did not note the fact that many of the destroyed buildings were being used as a cover for PLO forces.

54. See Chapter 8 by Aaron Miller.

55. "A New Opportunity for Peace in the Middle East," U.S. Department of State, Current Policy No. 417, September 1, 1982.

56. *New York Times,* September 3, 1982.

7
Egyptian Policy

Louis J. Cantori

Dear brothers and sisters, the Middle East is witnessing extremely grave events that will leave their imprint on the future of all of us. We cannot adopt the stand of a spectator or observer with regard to these events. Our position must always remain in the forefront because immortal Egypt shoulders a special responsibility in defending security and peace in the area. Egypt is the basic factor in establishing stability and balance.

—President Husni Mubarak
Speech to the Egyptian Parliament
October 3, 1982

Passenger: *Egypt is among the most beautiful of countries and its people among the most hospitable and generous.*
Taxi Driver: *Yes sir, Egypt is the mother of the world (Aywa ya Basha, Misr umn al-dunya).*

The Hegemonial Role of Egypt

At the very beginning of his revolution, President Gamal Nasser spoke of a role in search of a hero. The role was that of leadership of the Arab nation. The hero was to be Egypt.[1] Nasser was an ambitious charismatic visionary, but in this case the vision was not his alone but rather one widely held in Egypt itself.

Behind the self-assurance of statements by a president and a taxi driver in contemporary Egypt lie objective factors of geography and history to support them. Throughout recorded history the Nile River appears to have given the people of the Nile Valley the wealth and size of population to sustain both high levels of cultural advancement and the military strength to defend and at times extend that growth. Thus from Pharaonic times until the present, Egypt has had a hegemonial relationship with the Eastern Mediterranean area comprising present-day Syria, Lebanon, Jordan, and Israel[2] as well as with the area containing present-day Sudan and Ethiopia. With the founding of Islam in the seventh century A.D., Egypt also came to play a dominant role in the Hegaz, present-day western Saudi Arabia.

In more modern times this hegemonial role has been exerted twice. The first time was under Muhammad Ali (r. 1805–1848), the great modernizer of Egypt. By 1822 his military reach had been extended south into present-day Sudan, where his troops founded the present capital of Khartoum, and southeast into the Hegaz (1811–1823). In 1833, his army was in the north in mid-Anatolia at Konya, with the conquest of the Ottoman Empire as a near possibility. The British and French at the London Conference of 1840 put a final end to the Egyptian urge to dominate the empire that they were anxious to preserve as a buffer against expansion of Russian influence in the Eastern Mediterranean.[3]

This constraining role of the earlier great powers was to have its equivalent with the superpowers in the present period. Against the background of U.S. pressures to join a British-dominated anti-Soviet alliance (Baghdad Pact of 1955), Nasser nationalized the Suez Canal from its British and French private owners in July 1956. In the next decade Nasser went on to claim Egypt's heroic leadership role, including leadership of the United Arab Republic (1958–1961) with Syria. The disastrous defeat of June 1967 by Israel, with the loss of Sinai and the closing of the Suez Canal, temporarily diminished Egypt's modern hegemonial role.

Sadat: The Road to Peace

Anwar Sadat assumed the presidency in a constitutional manner following Nasser's death by illness. From the beginning Sadat's foreign policy was to be governed by the decisions of the defeated Arab states at the Khartoum Conference of August 1967. It was decided that the official Arab policy henceforth was to be first the recovery of the territories occupied by Israel and only secondarily the defeat of Israel itself. The first objective in reference to occupied Sinai almost immediately became Sadat's first concern as a new president. Sadat, in the period from his accession to power in September 1970 until the abortive coup against him in May 1971, was known popularly as "Sayid Naʿam Naʿam" (Mr. Yes-Yes), because he alone among the revolutionary free officers of 1952 was still near the pinnacle of power. It is possible that the first major inkling to those around him of his decisiveness, courage, and vision came in his positive response to the peacemaking initiative of February 1971 by UN mediator Gunnar Jarring, when both publicly and secretly Sadat stated that in exchange for an adjustment on Sinai and the Suez Canal he was prepared to recognize Israel.[4]

The diplomatic opportunity was lost, perhaps because on the one hand the Israelis felt strong because of their recent massive military armament by the United States and on the other hand the United States was too distracted by the Vietnam War. Likewise, when in July 1972 the Egyptians expelled over 10,000 Soviet advisers, Washington's view was one of appreciation of a cost-free loss for the USSR, but the appreciation apparently did not extend to a U.S. peace initiative.[5]

Sadat reasonably seems to have concluded that in light of a failure of Israel and the United States to respond positively to these events, something dramatic needed to be undertaken to get diplomatic attention. Thus began the planning of the October 1973 war in which, from the beginning, the Egyptian objective was diplomatic and not territorial.[6] Following the war's outcome in which Egypt secured its diplomatic objective with its territorial gains in Sinai and Israel penetrated to the west of the Suez Canal, both sides felt that they had "won" and therefore could talk to one another.

The calculated character of Egyptian policy, with its shrewd utilization of military means to political ends and its successful outcome, succeeded in causing Henry Kissinger to redefine American policy from an exclusive reliance upon Israel to a use of Egypt as a cornerstone of policy. Thus from the beginning, as in later years, Egyptian and U.S. policy found itself in a working relationship.[7] The consequence was the step-by-step shuttle diplomacy that led to the agreements of the Egyptians and Israelis in the Sinai I agreement. This agreement between the Egyptians and the Israelis provided for the withdrawal of Israeli forces from the Suez Canal.

The conclusion of the Sinai II (September 1975) agreement with Israel brought the further benefits of Israeli withdrawal east of the militarily important Mitla and Giddi Pass areas of central Sinai and the return of the northern Red Sea oil fields of Abu Rudeis. The Israelis in return were able to negotiate the demilitarization of Sinai and the right to free passage of their cargoes through the Suez Canal.

Egypt emerged from the U.S. "shuttle diplomacy" with only part of her foreign-policy objectives attained. There was a peace of sorts, a lessening dependence upon the Soviets, and an alternative American arms supply of sorts. These issues were related to domestic support, especially in the case of the army. "Peace of sorts" related to the ambiguity of the question of whether or not Egypt possessed military security. An "arms supply of sorts" raised the real and objective question of whether—if called upon—the military could in fact ensure Egypt's security. Both questions related to the question of whether or not Sadat could rely politically upon the army.

In addition, there remained the question of redeeming the promise of economic prosperity following upon peace. Even if the economy could perform well, there was the question of whether or not a partial peace could deliver a peacetime prosperity. As long as a more complete peace eluded Sadat, he would face unfulfilled economic expectations. And these expectations were not simply hypothetical. First in January 1975 and then more seriously in January 1977 (when over seventy persons were killed), these unrealized expectations erupted in political violence directed against the regime.

Sadat appears to have felt the lack of U.S. and Israeli policy initiatives in 1977 occasioned by domestic preoccupations with elections and new administrations in both countries, and he therefore began a personal decision-making process that led him to state in late October 1977 that if invited, he would visit Israel and appear before its parliament.[8] His visit in November appears to have been a reaction against the new Carter administration's efforts to launch a new diplomatic effort in the Middle East.[9] The end result was President Carter's invitation for both Sadat and Begin to meet with him at Camp David in September 1978.

The outcome of the Camp David meeting was two accords intended to be the framework for future negotiations. Significantly, in view of the importance of the Palestinian issue from the Egyptian and U.S. point of view and in view of its later relegation to a secondary status, the framework for negotiations appears first in the official release at the end of the conference and the framework for bilateral negotiations between Israel and Egypt appears second. Also contrary to the Egyptian point of view, if not the American as well, the two issues are treated as structurally distinct and internally make no reference to one another. The separate and unrelated character of the two frameworks appears to represent a concession to Begin and Israel in order to gain the latter's acquiescence.[10] This separate and unrelated character may have been the price that the Egyptians, and possibly the Americans, had to pay in order to get at least the partial outcome of peace between Egypt and Israel. This structural flaw has since proven to be the most central explanation of the later abortive "autonomy" talks on the West Bank and the major criticism directed against the validity of the idea that Camp David continues to provide the basis for a regional peace process. Sadat was determined from the beginning that his pursuit of the narrower Egyptian interest in the return of Sinai and peace with Israel should go hand-in-hand with progress towards Palestinian self-determination. The Camp David accords represented the fracturing and frustration of this desired interconnection. The accords also had a second major flaw, which followed from the different perceptions of the principal participants. From the beginning, Sadat spoke regularly of self-determination and a separate nation-state status for the Palestinians.[11] The Israelis on the other hand, employed the term "autonomy" for the Palestinians. This is the term that found its way into the Camp David accords. What the Israeli's intended specifically at the time was that the Palestinians would eventually have authority over administrative municipal functions (e.g., education, sewerage, and perhaps police) but not significant political authority.[12] As it has later developed, in fact, they appear to have intended to maintain de facto, if not de jure, control of "Judea" and "Samaria."

The subsequent history of Camp David has shown the evidence of these two flaws. Although Camp David had begun with at least an Egyptian and U.S. vision of a comprehensive Middle Eastern peace, the peace treaty that emerged in March 1979 focused nearly entirely upon a bilateral Egyptian-Israeli peace. For example, the Palestinian issue is not mentioned by name in the treaty. Instead, the Camp David framework is simply reaffirmed as a "basis for peace" with other Arab states.[13]

The consequence of the separate treatment of the Palestinian issue and that of peace between Israel and Egypt in the Camp David framework and the near absence of mention of the Palestinian issue in the March 1979 peace treaty was that Sadat immediately became subjected to criticism from within and without Egypt. The criticism from within was expressed both politically and intellectually. On the political side, two things occurred. First there was the resignation of important personalities, such as Foreign Minister Ismail Fahmy and others.[14] Second, the Camp David accords and the later peace treaty were opposed by all the opposition political parties. Such opposition ranged from the "Left" and the National Union Progressivists who referred to the abandonment of the Palestinian Arab cause, to the far-right illegal religious opposition groups who referred to the abandonment of Islamic Palestine. Intellectually, important numbers of the most well informed journalists, academics, and professionals vocally opposed Sadat's commitment to Camp David. Such domestic opposition should be put into the perspective, however, of the fact that Sadat's diplomacy received the majority support of the population.[15]

Arab diplomatic criticism was, however, more serious. This criticism mounted in a predictable fashion after Sadat's November 1977 visit to Jerusalem. In December the radical states of Syria, Libya, Algeria, and South Yemen met in Tripoli, Libya, and formed a new front of resistance to Egypt (Steadfastness Front: *Jabhat al-Samud*), whereupon Egypt severed diplomatic relations with them. After Camp David, an Arab summit meeting in Baghdad on November 5, 1978, called for a political boycott of Egypt in the event of a treaty with Israel. Finally, in March 1979, upon conclusion of the treaty, eighteen members of the Arab League, plus the PLO, severed diplomatic relations with Cairo and called for an economic boycott.[16] Such a severance contributed to domestic Egyptian pressure upon Sadat.

The treaty itself consisted of phased territorial adjustments, demilitarization procedures, and economic compensations—especially for Israel in exchange for its returning territory to Egypt. While the Israelis needed supplementary reassurances from the United States regarding Israeli security and guarantees of oil deliveries if the treaty broke down, they did adhere rigorously to the treaty's territorial provisions. Thus, two months after its formal inauguration (April 25, 1979), al-Arish, the administrative capital of Sinai, was returned. By November 25, 1979, the Alma oil fields had been returned and by January 25, 1980, two-thirds of Sinai. On the latter date the land borders with Israel were opened. Finally, on April 25, 1982, the remainder of Sinai was turned back to the Egyptians; with the establishment of the demilitarized zones, territorial peace was in place and operating.

Autonomy Talks

If there was steady and relatively conflict-free progress toward the implementation of the March 1979 peace treaty, this was not the case with efforts to implement the Camp David "Framework for Peace in the Middle East." The centerpiece of this broader framework for a comprehensive peace was the question of Palestinian autonomy. While the Golan Heights and Jerusalem figured in the framework, its geopolitical center was the West Bank and Gaza. The major conceptual impediment to the implementation of the framework, as already noted, has had to do with the definition of autonomy. But there was a more specific disagreement having to do with Israeli settlement of the West Bank. Sadat had claimed, and he was backed up in this by President Carter, that it was understood that further such settlements would not be undertaken while discussions of the implementation of the framework were underway. Begin, however, claimed that his understanding was for three months only.[17] In fact, on April 22, 1979— less than a month after the signing of the treaty on March 26 and three days before its implementation on April 25—the Israeli cabinet gave approval for two more settlements on the West Bank, and on June 7 actual work began near Nablus.[18] A few days later Begin stated publicly that Israel would pursue both settlements and the autonomy plan.[19] Subsequently, in February 1981, Israel announced that it would expand the number of settlers on the West Bank by 40 percent in that year alone. In fact, from 1979 until 1982, the number of Israeli settlers increased from 10,000 to an estimated 23,000.[20]

The issue of the settlements began almost immediately to complicate the autonomy talks called for by Camp David. These began with Begin, Sadat, and U.S. Secretary of State Vance in attendance in Beersheba on May 25, 1979, the day al-Arish was returned to the Egyptians. Just how interfering the settlement factor was to become was evidenced by the fact that even Israeli Defense Minister Ezer Weizman departed from the Israeli negotiating team because of his opposition to continued settlements.[21] Several meetings were held through 1979 and 1980, with some agreement as to procedures (e.g., electoral procedures), but no agreement on substance (e.g., what would be the powers of the elected Palestinian representatives). One thing agreed to was that the May 26, 1980, deadline set in the Camp David accords was a target date and not a mandatory one.[22] In May 1980, Sadat indefinitely suspended the talks. Under U.S. pressure, they resumed once more, only to be suspended once again by Sadat in protest against the July 30 Knesset action laying claim to all Jerusalem and against continued settlements.[23] Resumed once more in October, the talks were suspended once again in December in order to await the appointment of President-elect Reagan's representative.

On June 4, 1981, a meeting of Sadat and Begin was held at Sharm el-Sheik in order to ease strains between the two countries and facilitate the progress under the bilateral peace treaty.[24] Three days later, much to the anger and consternation of Sadat—who, from the point of view of Arab opinion, looked like an accomplice in the act—Israeli war planes bombed an Iraqi nuclear reactor. Meanwhile, the continuing pattern of attacks among Israelis, Palestinians, and Syrians in southern Lebanon created a crisis atmosphere that U.S. envoy Philip Habib was finally able to solve on July 24, after the bombing of Beirut by the Israelis on July 17.[25] In this crisis atmosphere, it was only after a further meeting between Begin and Sadat in Alexandria on August 26 that the autonomy talks were agreed to once again on September 23.[26] With the assassination of Sadat on October 6, the talks were once again suspended.

The autonomy talks were, of course, mandated in the Camp David accords. Given the divergence of Egyptian and Israeli views on what constituted autonomy, one has to look to underlying factors as to why so many repeated efforts were made to sustain them. The fact is, both parties had elements of self-interest at stake in their continuance.

At least until the election of President Reagan, U.S. policy was to go beyond the narrowness of the March 1979 peace treaty in an attempt to achieve a comprehensive peace. Egyptian interests were also significantly linked to this objective, in order to redeem Egyptian diplomacy in the eyes of brother Arab states. Egyptian interests were also committed in a narrowly defined way to the process in order not to deeply offend the Israelis and thus impede the phased execution of the Israeli withdrawal from Sinai. The Israelis also had to defer to the urgency of the later U.S. peace effort, but in addition—as the bilateral peace process unfolded—the Israelis did not want to destabilize Sadat domestically by embarrassing him with failure. The Israelis were especially intent upon achieving the normalization of relations with Egypt, an issue about which Egypt felt significantly less enthusiastic. Thus, the autonomy talks not only have dealt with the substantive issue of autonomy for the Palestinians, but they have also become an expression of other issues and concerns.

Arab Relations

Sadat's decision to visit Jerusalem in November 1977 and to carry on subsequent diplomatic negotiations with Israel undoubtedly was a calculated one in terms of balancing Egyptian national interests versus Arab and Palestinian concerns. It was Sadat's position that Egypt, having borne the heavy burdens of life and treasure in the 1948–1949, 1956, 1967, and 1973 wars and the skirmishes and military preparations in between, was to be excused if it was to be more accommodationist in its approach. In fact, however, whether in front of the Knesset itself in November 1977 or later at Camp David or afterwards, Sadat always insisted that what he was embarked upon was simply a different approach than that of the other Arab states to the same end of self-determination for the Palestinians.[27] Put into perspective, it might be argued that in fact his policy was simply more honest. Like the other Arab states, whether radical (Syria or Iraq) or moderate (Saudi Arabia), Egypt simply was putting its national interest before that of the Palestinians without, however, abandoning the latter. The question that remains unanswered is whether or not Sadat's own diplomatic approach to the solution of the Palestinian problem will have been any more successful than the more militant one of the other Arab states.

The distinction between the more militant or more moderate Arab states has been one that dates at least from what Kerr has called the Arab cold war of the 1960s.[28] It has perhaps never been so clear as it has been in relation to Egypt and the recent peace process. It was the militant states (Syria, Iraq, Libya, Algeria, and South Yemen) with whom Egypt broke off diplomatic relations in December 1977 following the Steadfastness Front summit in Tripoli, Libya. Again it was the same grouping that then broke off political and economic ties on September 24, 1978, after Camp David. In early November, at a summit meeting in Baghdad, the moderate Arab states took a position not of action against Camp David itself (although it was soundly condemned verbally) but of a threat of political and economic boycott if a treaty was signed. Even the latter position was weakened, however, by the absence of several of the moderate states.[29] The fact that a delegation of this summit group then attempted to meet with Sadat indicates their preference for persuasion rather than confrontation. After their rebuff by Sadat, the peace treaty itself became the ultimate provocation. At a second summit meeting in Baghdad on March 31, 1979, eighteen members of the Arab League voted to sever diplomatic and economic relations and move the headquarters of the Arab League from Cairo (where it had been located since its founding in 1945) to Tunis.[30] The teeth in the threat of an economic boycott against Egypt took on substance when, in May, Saudi Arabia announced that the Saudi-led grouping of Gulf Arab states was ending its financing of an Egyptian-based Arab arms-manufacturing consoritum.[31]

Sadat is reported to have replied, when asked about the effect of this political boycott, that it was not Egypt that was isolated as a result of it, but rather it was the Arab states that were isolated from Egypt. While largely a statement of bravado, the Arab states were isolated from Egypt in terms strictly of leadership and political power. The conclusion of the peace treaty conferred upon Israel the very major benefit of neutralizing her one really important potential adversary in the region. With her southern and western flanks secured, Israel has been permitted to concentrate her forces to the north and east against the PLO and Syria in Lebanon. Even on the very day that Sadat said to the Egyptian parliament that he was prepared to appear before the Israeli parliament, Israeli jets were bombing PLO positions in southern Lebanon.[32] Interference in Lebanon continued with impunity and although it stopped for much of 1981, it resumed again with the Israeli invasion of June 6, 1982. The Arab states have been deprived of a possible countermilitary role by the Egyptians as a consequence of the treaty. Israeli military action in south Lebanon in 1981 and 1982 was accompanied by a sharply increased settlement program on the West Bank, which was highly provocative to the Egyptians. The inability of the Egyptians to bring about even a freezing of this latter policy, to say nothing of not achieving the Camp David objective of autonomy for the Palestinians, has illustrated both the weakness of the Arabs without the military might of Egypt and the ineffectiveness thus far of Egypt's own policy.

But if the Arabs have been weakened by Egypt's absence from their ranks, they have not been able to impose their will upon the Egyptians either. In strictly political terms it has been evident that the Arabs need Egypt perhaps more than Egypt needs them. Contributing to the disunity of the Arab ranks have been their inability to present an effective military/diplomatic alternative to Egyptian policy and the proliferation of diversionary international and domestic factors. The long-standing Syrian-Iraqi conflict has found its most recent expression in Syrian support for Iran after Iraq invaded that country in the summer of 1980. Syria has had as its major preoccupation the involvement of 30,000 of its troops in Lebanon since 1976 and rising internal political opposition. The rise of the revolutionary regime of the Islamic Republic of Iran has created a crisis focus for all the Arab states rimming the Gulf. Saudi Arabia is especially concerned with the international-security dimensions of the Iranian threat as well as the possible domestic appeal of the Iranians in the aftermath of the seizure of the mosque in Mecca by 300 individuals in November 1979.

An additional factor contributing to Egypt's ability to withstand Arab political pressure is the country's sustained political relationships with four Arab states (Sudan, Oman, Morocco, and Somalia). And although the Arab economic boycott has had the effect of depriving Egypt of about $1 billion in annual economic assistance from Saudi Arabia and the Gulf states, this has been offset by continued U.S. economic assistance in excess of $1.2 billion annually, as well as increased revenues from tourism. Moreover, while there has been an Arab-government economic boycott, Arab private banking and investment activity in Egypt has even increased since the declaration of the November 1979 boycott. In addition, there has been no decline in numbers of the 400,000 migrant workers in the Gulf states and Libya. Their remittances of about $1 billion dollars a year remain important to the Egyptian economy.[33] Finally, even at the government level, there is evidence that not only have the thousands of Egyptian-government employees who were seconded to other Arab governments continued to serve, but that recently the number may even have increased.[34]

Domestic Constraints

Anwar Sadat's leadership of Egypt was characterized by a primacy of concern with foreign policy. He had inherited a situation in which the foreign power of Israel occupied a significant portion of his country and in so doing prevented Egypt from having access to economically and commercially important oil reserves in Sinai and the Red Sea. This occupation not only had kept the Suez Canal from operating and deprived Egypt of its toll revenues but also had displaced hundreds of thousands from the cities along its banks. For these reasons, as well as those of national pride, Sadat's war and peace policies received widespread popular support. As evidence of his basic commitment to democracy and as part of a "de-nasserification" process, Sadat had introduced economic and political liberalization from 1974 onward, starting with a process in 1975 in which groups representing roughly the socialist, center, and capitalistic points of view were permitted to organize themselves within the parliament and within the mass-line single-party structure of the Arab Socialist Union. These groups from then until now, in a "guided" democracy fashion of a mixture of paternalism and repression, have evolved into a modified multiparty or perhaps what is best described as a single-party dominant-party structure with the National Democratic party representing Sadat (or Mubarak) and the regime. At first, it was only the National Union Progressivists (democratic-socialists) who were opposed to the overture to Israel. With the increasing pace of Israeli settlements as well as the annexation of Golan and especially Jerusalem, the illegal religious right has expressed its opposition to the peace treaty.[35]

After the Peace Treaty: Mubarak

Husni Mubarak's accession to the presidency of Egypt was a testimony to that nation's essential political stability. The accession was conducted in the same constitutional manner as Sadat's had been upon the death of Nasser in 1970. From the point of view of the peace process, the transition in leadership also answered the question frequently asked in Israel: had peace been made with a man or with a nation? Mubarak was quick to restate Egypt's commitment to the peace treaty.[36] He also, of course, has been concerned to politically consolidate his own new accession to power by asserting the essential continuity of policy. In addition, however, he was constrained by the imperative of national self-interest in regaining—by terms of the peace treaty—the final portion of Sinai in April 1982. This was perhaps no more dramatically evident than in the fact that when an initial group of about sixty of the politically most prominent persons arrested by Sadat was released by Mubarak in December 1981, he called them to his office for discussions. It subsequently became clear that they agreed with Mubarak that there would be a moratorium upon opposition politics until the Israeli evacuation in April 1982.[37]

If there was continuity with Sadat's policies, however, Mubarak has felt it necessary also to disassociate himself from some aspects of Sadat's policy and to adopt in rhetoric—if not in fact—the concepts of Nasser, both in domestic and foreign policy. Thus, for example, Mubarak has stressed nonalignment and positive neutralism, while in domestic policy he has given more stress to the public sector.

Autonomy Talks

Whether because of the impending April 1982 withdrawal and the necessity to continue to go through the motions of diplomacy or whether because he really thought that the autonomy talks could achieve something, Mubarak kept Egypt committed to the talks. When after April 1982, Israel began to insist that the talks be held alternately in Egypt and in Jerusalem, Egypt became significantly less supportive of them. An increasing Egyptian skepticism was reenforced by the provocations of Israeli policy in annexing Jerusalem and the Golan Heights as well as accelerating the rate of settlement of the West Bank. The final evacuation of the 6,000 settlers from Yamit in April 1982 was acutely traumatic for Begin and his ministers. Accused of having begun a policy of the evacuation of the occupied territories that might carry over into the West Bank, they appear to have reacted with a strong compensatory settlement on the West Bank. The result has been a heightening of the original divergence of Egyptian-Israeli views on what constitutes autonomy for the Palestinians. As far as the talks themselves are concerned, having faltered significantly during the winter and spring of 1982, they became moot with the Israeli invasion of Lebanon on June 6, 1982. That invasion, arguably launched precisely in order to eliminate the PLO as a force in the West Bank and as a diversion from the continued policy of West Bank settlement, has created a crisis atmosphere possibly calling for new diplomatic initiatives in order to reenergize the autonomy talks.

Arab Relations

President Sadat had always vigorously argued that Egypt remained united with the Arab states in a commitment to Palestinian independence. In this respect, he stated that they only differed in the means to achieve this and once the fruitfulness of this approach became evident, there would be a reconciliation of the Arab states with Egypt. Until the time of his death, however, there was little formal effort at such a reconciliation. Perhaps contributing significantly to this lack of movement was the effect of Sadat's at times overbearing self-confidence in the pursuit of his objectives. In any case, the estrangement of Egypt from the Arab state system has been so unusual and artificial that the tendency towards reconciliation perhaps has been inevitable.

The death of Sadat had the obvious effect of removing his personality as an obstructionist factor in relations with other Arab regimes. Perhaps the clearest evidence of the possible positive effect of his removal was the absence of vitriolic outpouring against Egypt both in the period leading to the first Fez summit conference of November 25, 1981, and at the second conference on September 7, 1982. In fact, the absence of his personality may have combined with what might be argued to be evidence of his success in bringing at least the moderate Arab states to his point of view. Reference is made here to the peace plan put forward by Prince Fahd in August 1981 calling for the peaceful existence of all states of the region (including, by implication, Israel). This plan did not gain acceptance at the first conference at Fez, and in fact the conference broke up in disagreement about committing the Arab states to it. It did, however, succeed in modified form at the second Fez conference in September 1982.[38]

What has emerged since Mubarak's coming to power is in fact a more active policy of rapprochement with the Arab states. Egypt, for example, has been an important supplier of Soviet-made military spare parts to Iraq in its war with Iran.[39] Mubarak has stated that Egypt stands prepared to assist brother states in the defense of the Gulf.[40] In early April 1982, even prior to the evacuation of the Israelis and at a time when, on another level, Egypt was reassuring emergent Israeli anxieties on the subject, Egypt sent a delegation to the meeting of a planning committee of the nonaligned states in Baghdad. The delegation was headed by Esdmet Abd al-Magid, the Egyptian ambassador to the UN. What was noteworthy about the meeting was the Egyptian delegation's presence in the capital of the organizer of the Baghdad conferences, Iraq, and what the delegation said publicly. Basically, it reaffirmed Egypt's commitment to the Palestinian cause, but it also said that the way to peace and the realization of the Palestinian cause was through negotiations with Israel. The absence of an attack upon this statement either within the conference itself or by the Iraqi press was noteworthy.[41]

Further to this point of specific evidence of relaxation of tensions was the fact that Morocco and Jordan congratulated Egypt upon regaining Sinai at the end of April. Even more dramatic was the visit of Mubarak to Saudi Arabia in June to pay condolences to the new King Fahd upon the death of King Khalid.[42]

Reenforcing the factual pattern of increasing interaction with the Arab states has been the evidence of an increasing willingness on the part of the Arab states to in effect commit themselves to a diplomatic, rather than military, approach to the Palestinian problem. Thus, at a renewed meeting at Fez, even the PLO and the Syrians committed themselves to an admittedly watered-down version of the original Fahd proposal.[43]

Israel

It might reasonably be argued that Mubarak's own initial embracing of the peace treaty was simply tactical in nature in order not to (1) disrupt the process of consolidating himself in power and (2) disrupt the process of the return of the final portion of Sinai. This would be an inadequate understanding of the depth of his commitment to the treaty, however, in view of the fact that even the extreme provocation of the invasion of Lebanon by the Israelis did not lead directly to the recall of the Egyptian ambassador. Mubarak has been quite explicit about the nature of Israeli-Egyptian relations. He has characterized them as being "normal" but not "special," i.e., the peace treaty with Israel is a legal commitment similar to any such agreement with any other sovereign state. Other political, commercial, and cultural relations are to be of a similar nature.[44]

Prior to the June 1982 invasion of Lebanon, Egypt continued the autonomy talks, even if with diminishing enthusiasm. Since the invasion, however, it appears the roles have been reversed. Pessimistic about Israeli intentions and desirous of signaling to the Arab world that its relations with Israel do not mean an uncritical stance vis-à-vis that country, Egypt has been reluctant to engage in talks while Jerusalem and Golan remain annexed, the annexation of the West Bank appears underway, and Israeli troops remain in Lebanon.

Superpowers

If Egypt's alienation from the Arab-states system is forced and unnatural, so too are her relationships with the superpowers. For reasons having to do with a perception of Soviet heavy-handedness and for tactical ones having to do with Sadat's sense that the United States held the most cards in the Middle East situation, Sadat aligned himself with the Americans. Mubarak has continued his commitments to the United States, but he has reasserted the Nasser doctrine of neutralism and nonalignment.[45] The result has been a certain public prickliness regarding U.S. concerns with military bases in Egypt and an effort to specify the nature of the relationship. In addition, the steady decline in Egyptian-USSR relations under Sadat has been arrested or even slightly improved. Mubarak has stated that normal relations with the Soviet Union would be desirable.[46] In fact, he has reinvited Soviet technicians to come and assist in repairs to the Soviet-built turbine tunnels at the Aswan High Dam, to work in the same capacity in the Helwan steel mills, and to assist in agricultural irrigation projects. It would seem that only the timing might be a question as to when the diplomatic missions in each country will be enlarged and ambassadors exchanged once again.

A factor that has symbolic importance, at least, is the procuring of weapons systems in some degree disassociated from the increasing preponderance of U.S. weapons. Thus, Egypt has purchased twenty French Mystere 2000 jets at a price of $1 billion, which includes the cost of factory production capabilities for future spares and even aircraft production. In addition, Egypt appears to be buying British ships for its Navy.[47]

Domestic Constraints

Mubarak, as did Sadat, has had to face certain domestic constraints in pursuing his foreign policy. Unlike Sadat, especially in his later years, Mubarak has done so far less repressively. As already noted, he forged an apparent agreement with the political opposition not to engage in undue criticism of Israel until at least the April 25, 1982, withdrawal from Sinai. After that date, the Egyptian press and political leaders became increasingly vocal in their criticism of Israeli settlement policies on the West Bank.

The increasing tempo of these settlements, the increase in violent Palestinian resistance on the West Bank, and especially the Israeli bombing attack upon PLO positions in Lebanon in April 1982, just before the final evacuation of the Sinai, all provided a backdrop to the reaction to the Israeli invasion of Lebanon on June 6. This reaction found all members of the secular opposition united in condemnation of the Israelis and a call for the breaking off of diplomatic relations.

The Invasion of Lebanon and the New U.S. Peace Initiative

For the Egyptians, the invasion was a supreme test. Would it, for example, lead to a break in relations with Israel? The invasion elicited three responses from the Egyptians. The first was a degree of verbal criticism equal to or stronger than that of most other Arab states. The second was action "permitted" within the treaty itself, namely— in the words of Foreign Minister Kamal Hasan Ali—that the "nor-malization" much sought after by the Israelis was put in a "deep freeze." The third reaction was a continuation of one already begun by the Egyptians, an opening to Europe. In this case, as the international maneuvering to contain the conflict began, Egypt as an albeit-ostracized

Arab state joined with France—as the former League of Nations mandatory power in Lebanon—to call for a cease-fire and an Israeli withdrawal.[48]

It is difficult to gauge any significant discernible impact of all this upon the Israelis, but it did have the effect of evidencing anew Egypt's Arab credentials to its Arab brothers. Thus, the invasion seems to have had the effect of drawing Egypt closer to the Arab-state system. Sadat had begun this process, Mubarak had already developed it further, and the invasion only intensified it. A major reason for this appears to be that if Egypt had been roundly condemned for having abandoned the Arab cause, no Arab state, including Syria, really put the Palestinian cause and that of Lebanon before its own. The result was a high degree of inaction and a high degree of guilt on the part of those who did little in the face of thousands of Palestinian and Lebanese deaths. As the Arab states dallied, they discovered that Egypt had a value as a potential mediator, or at least communicator, with Israel itself or with the United States.

A potential role for the Egyptians came when the PLO evacuation from Beirut was negotiated. All of the Arab states felt the need to voice the pieties that they would be "glad" to accept evacuated fighters (but not, tragically as it turned out, their families). All the Arab states felt, as they always had, that the Palestinian resistance was a potentially disturbing force for them domestically. Perhaps because Sadat's political liberalization had gone so far and therefore provided greater opportunities for public discussion, the presence of hundreds or thousands of Palestinians in Egypt could have had the potential of creating domestic unrest over Egyptian foreign policy.[49] For this reason Mubarak decided not to take any of the PLO evacuees.

If from the Egyptian point of view the Israelis had aggravated the Lebanese situation so much by entering West Beirut on September 16, 1982, their implication in the Shatilla and Sabra massacres was an ultimate provocation. Its impact upon the Egyptians was that the Egyptian ambassador to Tel-Aviv was withdrawn for consultations on September 20 and Egyptian-Israeli relations slipped to a new low and a minimal "correctness."

It was in this context that the Reagan plan was put forward as an attempt to retrieve a diplomatic situation that, from the U.S. point of view, was deteriorating. The plan is an effort to reenergize the Camp David momentum and spirit.[50] The essence of the plan is the manner in which it faces up to the irreconcilable elements in the original Camp David accords regarding the political future of the West Bank, which lay at the heart of the three-year impasse in the autonomy talks. The plan addresses itself to the question of the future of the West Bank after the five-year transition period, and it answers the question by denying the sovereignty Israel assumed it would acquire, while providing the Palestinians not with an independent state but with an affiliation with Jordan. It was the denial of Israeli sovereignty and the call for a freeze in settlements that caused an immediate Begin government rejection.[51] This denial of Israeli ambitions and the promise of genuine political power for the Palestinians during the transition period are presumably inducements for the Jordanians to play a role as the representative of the Palestinians in renewed autonomy talks.[52]

The Egyptians and the Jordanians (and perhaps behind the latter, the Palestinians) have for their part made it clear that the pursuance of the proposals by them is contingent upon the withdrawal of the Israelis from Lebanon and the stopping of the settlement process on the West Bank. The expectation is substantive as an objective precondition for negotiations, but it is also symbolic as a test of the degree of U.S. commitment and will. In the fall of 1982 and the winter of 1983 the negotiations between the Israelis and Lebanese for withdrawal had difficulty in even setting an agenda of issues to be discussed. Hence the "high road" of autonomy talks has become a hostage to the "low road" of withdrawal talks. Not unexpectedly, it is Israel that has slowed the talks as it has attempted to provide concrete accomplishments for its invasion such as insistence on peace and/or nonbelligerancy with Lebanon, "normalization," and other things of a provocative (from the point of view of Lebanese relations with Arab states) nature.[53]

With the increasing evidence of the U.S. inability to influence the Israelis (if anything, Israel seemed encouraged in its resistance to American policy by such things as the fiscal 1984 congressional *increase* in economic and military support for Israel), a situation has developed of increasing frustration and potentially destabilizing proportions for the Mubarak regime. This regime has sought to establish itself politically in the aftermath of the Sadat assassination by a judicious combination of emphasis upon the continuities of some of Sadat's foreign policies (principally the peace treaty with Israel) and domestic policies and a repudiation of others, with even a throwback to those of Nasser. Almost two years after the assassination, a continued tenuousness of the regime can be seen in that Mubarak has yet to appoint a vice-president. This suggests an uncertainty as to whether the military or civilian elements or some faction of them should be rewarded. The inability of the Americans to act to bring about an Israeli withdrawal from Lebanon and to energize a comprehensive peace-negotiating process would only call into question Mubarak's continued commitment to Sadat's reliance upon U.S. influence to seek a solution to the Palestinian question. With the decline of American diplomatic vigor, Mubarak's options might appear somewhat limited. They include the continued fostering of Saudi Arabian relations, which might lead to increasing economic assistance to lessen Egyptian dependence upon the Americans; continued efforts to foster relations with the Arab states; a continued diversification of weapons systems; and a normalization of relations with the Soviet Union by elevating diplomatic representatives to the ambassadorial level. It could be argued that even if these measures may have limited foreign-policy impact, they may be necessary and, more pessimistically, even inadequate to maintain Mubarak in power.

Notes

1. Gamal Abd al-Nasser, *The Philosophy of the Revolution* (Buffalo, N.Y.: Smith, Keynes and Marshall, 1959).

2. P. M. Holt, *Egypt and the Fertile Crescent: 1516–1922* (London: Longmans, Green, 1966).

3. P. J. Vatikiotis, *The History of Egypt*, Second Edition (Baltimore, Md.: Johns Hopkins Press, 1980), pp. 64–67.

4. George Lenczowski, *The Middle East in World Affairs*, Fourth Edition (Ithaca, N.Y.: Cornell University Press, 1980), p. 451, and William Quandt, *Decade of Decisions* (Berkeley, Calif.: University of California Press, 1977), pp. 135–136.

5. Quandt, *Decade of Decisions*, p. 152.

6. Anwar el-Sadat, *In Search of Identity* (New York: Harper, 1978), p. 289.

7. Quandt, *Decade of Decisions*, pp. 210–211.

8. el-Sadat, *In Search of Identity*, p. 305 ff.

9. In fact it was Carter's determination to convene a Geneva conference at which all parties to the Middle East conflict, including the USSR, would be present that helped motivate Sadat to make his Jerusalem visit.

10. The texts appear in Congressional Quarterly, *The Middle East*, Fifth Edition (Washington, D.C.: Congressional Quarterly, 1981), p. 253 ff.

11. See for example the major emphasis he placed upon a just settlement including statehood for the Palestinians in his speech before the Israeli Knesset on the occasion of his historic visit on November 20, 1977. Text in el-Sadat, *In Search of Identity*, pp. 330–343. See also the remarks of former President Carter in excerpts from his memoirs as published in *Time*, October 1982, p. 43.

12. *Time*, October 1982, p. 44. See Ezer Weizman, *The Battle for Peace* (New York: Bantam Books, 1981), p. 309, for the former Israeli defense minister's realization that this granting of administrative autonomy would result at the end of the five-year transition period (provided for in the Camp David accords) in the denial of Israeli sovereignty over the West Bank. In

fact, former Foreign Minister Dayan suggests that the major reason Begin agreed to any concept of autonomy for the Palestinians was that he felt he had to make a gesture in response to Sadat's peace initiative. Moshe Dayan, *Breakthrough* (New York: Alfred Knopf, 1981), p. 101.

13. This reference to the Camp David accords and their linkage to other Arab states, but not explicitly the Palestinians, appears in the preamble to the treaty. See the text in Congressional Quarterly, *The Middle East*, p. 253. According to then Foreign Minister Moshe Dayan, this separating of the issues represented a success for the Israeli position. Dayan, *Breakthrough*, p. 176.

14. See interview with Ismail Fahmy, "Sadat's Tragic Mistake," *Worldview* (September 1979), pp. 19–25. Fahmy had resigned on the eve of Sadat's trip to Jerusalem. He was replaced by Muhammad Ibrahim Kamel as foreign minister, who himself resigned along with his aide Nabil-al-Arabion on September 16, 1978, in protest against concessions made to Israel in the Camp David accords.

15. See Louis J. Cantori, "Egypt at Peace," *Current History* (January 1980), p. 26 ff., for a general discussion of this opposition, and Louis J. Cantori, "Religion and Politics in Egypt," in Michael Curtis, ed., *Religion and Politics in the Middle East* (Boulder, Colo.: Westview Press, 1981), pp. 77–95 for references to religious opposition to the peace treaty.

16. See Alan Taylor, *The Arab Balance of Power* (Syracuse, N.Y.: Syracuse University Press, 1982), pp. 73–81, for a general discussion of these developments in the Egyptian estrangement from the Arab-state system. Even as this alienation was occurring, however, there is evidence that Sadat was working to reformulate and restate Egypt's Arab policy. See Anwar el-Sadat, "Egypt and the New Arab Reality," published in English in the *Egyptian Gazette*, April 16–18, 1980, and republished in U.S. Government *Foreign Broadcast Information Service: Middle East and Africa*, May 27, 1980, pp. D9–D47 (hereafter cited as *FBIS*). Interestingly enough, however, the article was not reprinted in Egypt's Arabic-language press.

17. See *Time*, October 1982, p. 59 for former president Carter's insistence that the freeze was for the five-year transition period leading to a plebiscite by the Palestinians to determine their political future. Dayan, on the other hand, strenuously upholds Begin's position that the agreement was for three months. Dayan, *Breakthrough*, pp. 181–188.

18. *New York Times*, April 23, 1979, and June 8, 1979.

19. *New York Times*, June 12, 1979.

20. At the time of Begin's election in May 1977 there were 3,200 Israeli settlers on the West Bank as a result of Labor Party policy. By the time of his reelection in June 1981 there were 18,000. American Friends Service Committee, *A Compassionate Peace* (New York: Hill and Wang, 1982), p. 21. Present plans call for an increase to 100,000 by 1985.

21. Weizman, *The Battle for Peace*, p. 383 ff.

22. *New York Times*, March 28, 1980.

23. Ibid., August 10, 1980.

24. Ibid., June 5, 1981.

25. Ibid., July 25, 1981.

26. Ibid., September 24, 1981.

27. Speech before the Egyptian Parliament, May 14, 1980, *FBIS*, May 15, 1980, pp. D30–D31.

28. Malcolm Kerr, *The Arab Cold War*, Third Edition (New York: Oxford University Press, 1971).

29. Taylor, *The Arab Balance of Power*, pp. 76–77.

30. The communique is found in *FBIS*, April 2, 1979, pp. A1–A5.

31. *New York Times*, May 15, 1979.

32. *New York Times*, November 10, 1977, for reports of both events.

33. *Middle East Economic Digest*, September 3, 1981, pp. 9–10 for a general profile of the Egyptian economy.

34. From notes of presentation by Tagi Sagafi-Nejad entitled "Technology Exports from LDC's: The Case of Egypt," The Middle East Studies Association, November 5, 1982, Philadelphia, Pa.

35. See Cantori, "Egypt at Peace," and more generally Raymond Baker, *Egypt's Uncertain Revolution Under Nasser and Sadat* (Cambridge, Mass.: Harvard University Press, 1978).

36. *New York Times*, October 15, 1981.

37. This theme of Mubarak's perhaps returning to some themes of Nasser's domestic and foreign policy is found in Habib Boulares, "Et si Moubarak succédait à Nasser?" *Jeune Afrique*, February 3, 1982.

38. The text of Prince Fahd's plan can be found in American Friends Service Committee, *A Compassionate Peace*, p. 226. Article seven stated: "Affirming the right of all countries of the region to live in peace." It is this article that has been interpreted as implying Israel's right to exist from Saudi Arabia's point of view. On the breaking up of the November 25, 1981, conference in disagreement over accepting the plan, see Taylor, *The Arab Balance of Power*, p. 112. Note, however, the acceptance of the Fahd plan a year later at Fez. In fact article seven reappears in the Fez proposals modified to the extent that the U.N. Security Council guarantees peace among all states of the region. On the Fez conference of September 9, 1982, see Leonard Binder, "U.S. Policy in the Middle East: Exploiting New Opportunities," *Current History* (January 1983), p. 40 and p. 33, for the text of the Fez proposals.

39. *New York Times*, April 5, 1982.

40. In this he has continued Sadat's policy, although the latter had linked such assistance to providing military "facilities" for the United States to play the key role. Speech, *FBIS*, May 15, 1980, p. D32. Saddam Hussein has been quoted as saying that he would welcome Egyptian troops in Iraq's struggle with Iran. Quoted in *al-Siyasa* (Kuwait), as reported in the *New York Times*, May 25, 1982. In addition, there have been Saudi press discussions and unofficial reports of a desire for Egyptian–Gulf Cooperation Council coordination so that Egypt could play a security role in the Gulf. *New York Times*, April 26, 1982.

41. Text of ʿAbd al-Magid's speech in *FBIS*, April 8, 1982, pp. C3–C5.

42. Not only was this presence itself significant but whereas other heads of state remained only a few hours, Mubarak remained several days. *New York Times*, June 20, 1982.

43. See footnote 38 above. Mubarak in fact described himself as midway between the Fez plan and its call for a Palestinian state and the Reagan plan with its Jordanian option for the Palestinians, but greater likelihood of being implemented. *New York Times*, September 12, 1982.

44. This was elaborated upon in an important article by the Minister of State for Foreign Affairs Butrus Butrus Ghali, "The Foreign Policy of Egypt in the Post-Sadat Era," *Foreign Affairs* 60 (Spring 1982), p. 777.

45. Ibid., p. 785.

46. Ibid., p. 786.

47. John Merriam, "Egypt Under Mubarak," *Current History* (January 1983), p. 26.

48. *New York Times*, July 3, 1982.

49. For the record, however, the Egyptians said that if the Palestinians came to Cairo their organization should be reconstituted as a provisional government. This request seemed to be related to the diplomatic initiatives that the Egyptians were engaged in at the time in attempting to diplomatically thread the eye of the needle formed by the Fez plan on the one hand and the Reagan plan on the other. *New York Times*, July 3, 16, and 17, 1982.

50. Former U.S. Ambassador to Cairo Herman Eilts, in an article on the plan, endorses it and states that he understands it to be consistent with the Camp David accords, and he quotes former President Carter to the same effect. "Reagan's Middle East Initiative," *American-Arab Affairs*, no. 2 (Fall 1982), p. 2.

51. *New York Times*, September 2, 1982, and September 3, 1982.

52. The official text of President Reagan's speech is contained in U.S. Department of State, Current Policy No. 417, "A New Opportunity for Peace in the Middle East," September 1, 1982, and Secretary Shultz's more detailed statement is in U.S. Department of State, Current Policy No. 418, "President Reagan's Middle East Peace Initiative," September 10, 1982.

53. An additional motivation may be to prolong the Lebanese negotiations in order to both obtain greater concessions to Israeli security concerns in Lebanon and to divert American attention from the West Bank, especially with the 1984 presidential election campaign looming on the horizon.

8
The PLO

Aaron David Miller

The Israeli invasion of Lebanon and the forced evacuation of the Palestine Liberation Organization (PLO) from West Beirut will profoundly influence the future of the Palestinian national movement. For the moment the PLO is faring remarkably well. It has survived its military defeat in Lebanon and picked up important political gains in the process. The Israeli invasion has generated increasing support for the Palestinian cause and closely identified the PLO with a solution to the Palestinian problem. Moreover, Yasir Arafat has emerged as the movement's unchallenged leader and retained considerable room to maneuver within the Arab world. Syrian leverage over the PLO is at its lowest point in over a decade, and recent talks between Arafat and Jordan's King Hussein suggest that both realize the importance of finding some *modus vivendi*. The Reagan peace initiative of September 1982, although ruling out the possibility of an independent Palestinian state, comes closer to meeting Palestinian and Arab demands than any other previous U.S. initiative.

Nonetheless, the PLO's new opportunities should not obscure the hard realities that it will confront in the wake of the Israeli invasion. The loss of Lebanon as a base of operations will pose enormous problems for an organization already too dependent on its friends and highly vulnerable to its enemies. The morale of dispersed Palestinian fighters is already declining, and the physical separation between those PLO groups based in Damascus and Arafat's organization headquartered in Tunis will reinforce existing political divisions. Unless Arafat can turn the support and sympathy resulting from the

---

The views expressed in this chapter are those of the author and do not necessarily reflect the views of the Department of State or the U.S. government.

Lebanese war into concrete political gains toward a Palestinian state, the road from West Beirut will become increasingly hazardous. The longer the PLO remains in limbo—without a coherent political strategy or viable military option—the more vulnerable it will become to its own internal division and to the partisan interests of its Arab supporters.

The fact that the PLO may turn military defeat in Lebanon into a significant political victory should not mask the precarious position it occupied on the eve of the Israeli attack. Events in Lebanon raise important questions about effectiveness of PLO tactics and strategy and about the strengths and weaknesses of the Palestinian national movement. Why was the PLO so vulnerable in June 1982? Why, despite its increasing prestige abroad, has the PLO's position within the Arab world and vis-à-vis Israel remained so precarious? Indeed, why after eighteen years does the PLO—the accepted institutional embodiment of Palestinian nationalism—seem no closer to regaining an inch of Palestine than when it was created in 1964?

The answers to these questions go well beyond the immediate events leading to the Israeli invasion of Lebanon. Analyzing the PLO's development since the Egyptian-Israeli peace treaty offers a partial explanation. To understand the PLO's past behavior, make sense of its position in 1982, and analyze its future also requires a look at the nature of the organization and the environment in which it has operated since the 1960s.

The PLO's perennial problems have resulted primarily from its unique structure and its highly vulnerable position in a volatile Middle East. Although the Palestinian resistance movement has been remarkably independent, given the constraints under which it operates, it is really a prisoner of events and circumstances over which it has little control. The PLO has no secure base of operations and no independent and reliable source of financial and military support. Moreover, it is physically separated from a majority of its constituents and the territory it seeks to liberate.

Since the 1960s the PLO has increasingly made its own opportunities and committed its own mistakes. It has frequently acted as a catalyst to set into motion important developments in the Arab-Israeli conflict. Palestinian raids into Israel played an important role in exacerbating tensions in the months before the 1956 and the 1967 Arab-Israeli wars. Nonetheless, the Palestinians played little role in deciding how the major battles and diplomatic initiatives of those conflicts would be waged. Rather they were forced to react to major developments and to adjust their tactics and strategy accordingly. It is no coincidence that the PLO's most dramatic policy reassessments occurred in the wake of the 1967 and 1973 wars—conflicts in which they played a very small role. Palestinians were equally taken aback by Nasser's acceptance of the Rogers plan in July 1970 and Sadat's diplomatic initiatives following the October 1973 war.

Thus in order to explain the PLO's successes and setbacks, it is necessary to determine those factors and constraints that influence its behavior. These constraints fall into two broad categories and focus on two central dilemmas that have plagued the Palestinian national movement since its inception. The first set of constraints is external or environmental. How does the PLO's dependency on Arab states and its vulnerability to Israel shape its tactics and strategy? The second is internal or organizational in nature: How can a national movement composed of various groups—often with competing ideologies, personalities, and patrons—formulate a coherent and unified strategy to achieve its goals?

These external and internal factors shape the PLO's approach to regional and international developments. Its leaders and institutions are heavily influenced by these Palestinian and inter-Arab constraints. They are particularly important in analyzing Fatah's efforts to control PLO decision making and maneuvering through the maze of Arab alliances and rivalries. Although these factors frequently serve as a system of checks and balances, they have historically weakened the PLO leadership's ability to articulate and implement a coherent political strategy and have undermined its ability to pursue a strategy independent of Arab interest and concerns. Nowhere is the interaction between these external and internal constraints better illustrated than in the period from the Egyptian-Israeli peace treaty to the Israeli invasion of Lebanon—a period that witnessed a steady rise in the PLO's prestige abroad but a sharp decline in its ability to maneuver within the Arab world vis-à-vis Israel. Whether the Israeli invasion and the PLO's exodus from West Beirut will reinforce or weaken these constraints is not yet clear. One thing is certain, however. Unless the Palestinian national movement can better manage the constraints, there is little chance it will be able to realize any of its goals.

External Constraints:
The PLO in the Inter-Arab System

The PLO was created in 1964 partly as an Egyptian effort to control the Palestinian movement and to break Syrian trusteeship over the Fedayeen. Today it remains locked in the complex and perilous world of inter-Arab rivalries in which it was born. Since 1967 the PLO has, to be sure, broadened its sources of support and acquired a remarkable degree of independence, particularly in the international arena. Nonetheless it is still heavily dependent on the Arab world. Arab states provide the majority of the PLO's financial resources, host most of its important constituencies, plead its case in world capitals, and either provide directly or facilitate transfer of a majority of its military equipment.

Moveover, two of the PLO's subgroups—Saiqa and the Arab Liberation Front (ALF)—are wholly controlled subsidiaries of the Syrian and Iraqi regimes. Created to protect Arab interests in the Palestinian resistance movement, these groups further tie the PLO to Arab politics. Other subgroups like the Popular Front for the Liberation of Palestine (PFLP) and the Democratic Front for the Liberation of Palestine (DFLP), while nominally independent, derive the majority of their support from Arab states and cannot afford to ignore totally their patrons' concerns. Even Fatah, which has tried hard to maintain its independence and neutrality, cannot avoid taking sides in inter-Arab disputes and getting caught in bitter rivalries.

The PLO's dilemma is clear. Palestinian strength depends upon Arab power.[1] And some Arab states not only are determined to subordinate Palestinian goals to their own national interests but to do it forcefully if necessary. Indeed, in two instances, appropriately cast by Palestinians themselves in the "darkest" terms—Black September (1970) and Black June (1976)—the Jordanian and Syrian regimes engaged in major military conflicts with the Palestinian resistance.

It is not surprising then that the PLO has fared particularly poorly when the Arab world is badly divided. Although inter-Arab tensions have periodically increased the PLO's room to maneuver, they have more often narrowed its options.[2] Regional rivalries or disputes over strategies on accommodation or conflict with Israel are inevitably played out within the Palestinian movement. Some Arab states such as Syria, Iraq, and Libya seek to use their Palestinian surrogates to protect their interests. Others, like Saudi Arabia—with no direct control over PLO subgroups, hope that their political and financial resources will influence PLO actions. The PLO is invariably caught in the middle. Chronic cold wars between Egypt and Syria and deteriorating relations between Syria on the one hand and Iraq or Jordan on the other force Arafat into the difficult position of trying to balance relations with some of his most important supporters. The present disarray in the Arab world, as we shall later see, has created serious problems for the PLO leadership.

Over the years Palestinian groups have developed important relationships—cooperative and competitive—with Arab states. Algeria had a significant influence on Fatah's concepts of nationalism and armed struggle; Iraq and Libya have provided financial and military aid and helped to support the maximalist goals of the more radical PLO groups; Jordan, by virtue of its large Palestinian population and role in the West Bank, has enjoyed a special—albeit stormy—role in the PLO's history and strategy. Saudi Arabia has also played a key role in using its financial and political resources to support Fatah and thus to validate its pan-Arab and anti-Zionist credentials. Kuwait's large Palestinian population has pushed it into active support for PLO goals.

Nevertheless, two states—Egypt and Syria—traditionally have had the greatest impact on the PLO and have competed for influence over the Palestinian national movement. During the 1950s, Egypt emerged to play a leading role. Palestinian activists, many of whom spent considerable time in Egypt, were influenced by Nasser's pan-Arabism and nationalism and also by the Islamic values of the Muslim Brotherhood in Egypt and Saudi Arabia. By the early 1960s, however, Fatah (created in 1957) was increasingly influenced by the ideas of the Algerian and Syrian nationalist left, which provided organizational and military support.[3] It was no coincidence that Fatah's first military operation in January 1965—an attack against Israel's national water-carrier project—was launched with Syrian support.[4]

Throughout the 1970s the Syrians continued to play the dominant Arab role in Palestinian resistance politics, emerging as the PLO's staunchest defender and paradoxically as a potentially powerful adversary. In 1968, Damascus created its own Palestinian group, Saiqa—a result of Ba'athi political rivalry and a desire to protect Syrian influence in the Palestinian national movement. Armed and financed by Damascus, Saiqa has emerged as the second most powerful group in the PLO—cooperating with Fatah on many issues but manipulated by Syria to serve its interests in Lebanon and keep a close watch on Arafat.

Moreover, after the Fedayeen were ejected from Jordan in 1970–1971 and shifted their major base of operation to Lebanon, Syrian influence increased dramatically. Finally, as Egypt moved cloer to the United States and into negotiations with Israel, the PLO began to lose a valuable ally and counterweight to Damascus. Sadat's trip to Jerusalem and the March 1979 peace treaty further enhanced Syria's image as the only "confrontation state" ready to defend Palestinian interests. The convening of the 1979 and 1981 Palestine National Council (PNC) meetings in Damascus (rather than Cairo) attested to Syria's increasing influence.

Before the Israeli invasion of Lebanon in 1982, Syria's position in Lebanon, its assets within the PLO, and its claim to defend the

Palestinian national cause gave it formidable leverage over the PLO. Although Palestinian spokesmen consistently praised Syria as a "strategic ally" and conceded only "minor problems" in the relationship, PLO-Syrian ties were characterized by suspicion and mutual distrust.[5] Several PLO leaders, including Arafat and Habash, have been imprisoned in Damascus. Both are painfully aware of Syria's intervention against the Palestinian resistance and its Lebanese allies in June 1976 during Lebanon's civil war.

Then Syria switched sides and provided the PLO with invaluable support in Lebanon, facilitating supplies of weapons and at times defending PLO interests against its Lebanese rivals. Syrian support came at an enormous price, however. For Damascus, determined to play a preeminent role in Arab politics yet increasingly isolated, influence over the PLO is one way to insure a voice in inter-Arab decisions and to prevent other Arab states from coordinating a response to Arab-Israeli issues that ignores Syrian interests. Assad's pressure on the PLO at the last two Arab summits underscores his determination to keep Arafat on a short leash and to insure that Syria plays a key role in formulating any strategy for "confrontation or coexistence" with Israel.

Syria has formidable resources at its disposal. Damascus dominated the PLO's primary base of operations, controlling overland arms channels and supply routes. Syria's control over Saiqa, the PLO's second largest subgroup, and its influence with smaller groups like the Popular Front for the Liberation of Palestine–General Command (PFLP-GC) and Popular Struggle Front (PSF) gave it leverage from within. The Syrians also were said to be using anti-Arafat splinter groups, such as Black June, to intimidate and embarrass Arafat and to strike at his Fatah colleagues.[6] Finally, through its National Movement and Shia allies, the Syrians were able to heat up local tensions and embroil the PLO in costly factional fighting.

Although Syria could not control Arafat and did not want to appear to be dictating to the PLO, Damascus blocked major initiatives it believed would seriously damage its interests. At the Amman summit in November 1980, Syria pressured the PLO to boycott the meeting; at the Fez summit in November 1981, Syria leaned on Arafat to oppose the Saudi eight-point peace plan. Neither Egypt—locked into treaty commitments with Israel and preoccupied with economic recovery, Iraq—embroiled in its war with Iran, nor Saudi Arabia—reluctant to break with Damascus over this issue, was able to counter Syrian influence. As long as the PLO sat in the shadow of Damascus, it was forced to take Syrian interests into consideration. Syrian tutelage has made it very difficult for Arafat to emerge as an independent negotiator in any serious solution of the Arab-Israeli conflict. The Israeli invasion of Lebanon has temporarily relieved Syrian leverage, but, as we shall see later, by no means eliminated Damascus's influence.

The internal constraints of dealing within the inter-Arab system are compounded by the PLO's position vis-à-vis Israel. Despite the PLO's success in mobilizing Arab and international support for its cause and isolating Israel, the Palestinians are no closer to recovering "Palestine" or even part of Palestine than they were twenty years ago. Israel is still implacably hostile to the PLO, intensely suspicious of Arafat's efforts to cultivate a moderate image, and opposed to a negotiated settlement that could lead to a Palestinian state on the West Bank and Gaza.

In some respects, the PLO has managed to exploit Israel's hostility for it to the organization's advantage. The PLO leadership has used Israeli policies to unify Palestinian ranks, increase material support from the PLO's allies, and help enhance the PLO image abroad. Indeed, the Israeli bombing of Beirut in July 1981 and its blockade of Beirut in 1982 may have marked a turning point in the PLO's public-relations campaign to portray Israel as the "aggressor" and the PLO as "victim."

Moreover, PLO-Israeli enmity has allowed the PLO to avoid many issues that could have a divisive impact on the movement. Sensitive issues such as changing the Palestine National Covenant, the nature of a Palestinian state, and coexistence with Israel are frequently shelved on the grounds that Israel is not prepared to make meaningful concessions or recognize the PLO. Arafat's flirtation with the Fahd plan generated serious opposition from other PLO groups and revealed how divisive discussion of recognizing Israel's right to exist could be.

Nonetheless, Palestinians have rarely dealt with Zionism and Israel from a position of strength. Divided within its own ranks, exploited by the Arab states, lacking reliable great-power support, and physically separated from the overwhelming majority of their supporters in the West Bank, Gaza, and the Arab world, the PLO is at a considerable disadvantage.

Since 1977 the PLO's situation has become increasingly more precarious. Even though PLO spokesmen claim that the policies of the Begin government have contributed to Israel's isolation, complicated relations with the United States, and handed the Palestinians a major public-relations windfall, they also recognize how determined Israel has become to weaken, if not destroy, the PLO. On the West Bank, Israel has taken steps to root out PLO influence, banning the National Guidance Council, dismissing mayors, and attempting through Village Leagues to create an alternative leadership that will support the government's interpretation of autonomy. Moreover, the Begin government has stepped up its efforts to link the territories conceptually and institutionally to Israel, raising fears that Israel may ultimately move to annex the territories.

Finally, more than any of its predecessors, the Begin government has demonstrated its determination to weaken, if not to destroy, PLO capabilities in Lebanon. From the Litani operation in March 1978, to the policy of "preemptive strikes" in 1979, to the June 1982 invasion, the Begin government has seemed to suggest that there may indeed be a "military solution" to dealing with the PLO.

Internal Constraints: The Palestinian Dimension

Although the PLO's dependence on Arab power accounts for much of its stormy history, organizational constraints have contributed to its perennial ups and downs. Personal and ideological rivalries and transgroup loyalties have made the PLO a difficult organization to manage. Without an appreciation of this internal dimension of Palestinian resistance politics and its relationship to external factors, it is impossible to understand the PLO's behavior. Moreover, these internal constraints become particularly relevant in trying to evaluate the extent to which Arafat's Fatah organization can control the PLO and shape its policies.

From the inside the PLO has conventionally been described as an umbrella organization housing eight different groups, six of which are represented on the PLO's Executive Committee (PLO/EC)—its most important decision-making body. Although the PLO has tried to develop viable institutions and a sophisticated network of medical, social, and political services, designed to bind the organization together, power resides not in an overarching structure but in the various subgroups. Unlike other movements of "national liberation," the PLO has not been particularly successful in subordinating subgroup influence and loyalties to a centralized structure or in forging widely accepted bonds between each group and the movement as a whole.[7]

By 1969 (the year Arafat assumed chairmanship of the PLO/EC and Fatah moved to unite the PLO) the corporate identities of the various groups were already becoming established.[8] Groups like the PFLP and DFLP emerged as independent organizations with revolutionary/internationalist outlooks in contrast to Fatah's more conservative nationalism. Not only were they determined to resist integration into a highly centralized structure, but they were eager to develop tightly knit organizations with detailed programs for political action, further reinforcing group loyalties. Other groups like Saiqa and the ALF were wholly controlled subsidiaries of Syria and Iraq. All presented obstacles to Fatah's efforts to unify and dominate the PLO and to shape its policies.

The umbrella image requires some adjustment, if only to take into account the varying degrees of influence and power of the various subgroups. Fatah is the PLO's dominant group or, for our purposes, the center shaft of the umbrella structure. Indeed Fatah characterized its own strategy of unification as a "backbone" principle from which it would emerge as the preeminent resistance group. Despite splits within Arafat's organization, Fatah has had a more stable leadership, a broader Palestinian, Arab, and international constituency, more money, and more fighters under arms than any other Palestinian group. With the support of the "independents," Fatah has had considerable success in controlling the PLO's most important decision-making bodies.

If Fatah represents the umbrella's center shaft, then the various subgroups constitute the connecting rods that help to support the entire organization. The smaller groups are important for several reasons. First, they help to demonstrate the PLO's claim that the resistance movement is a heterogeneous one encompassing broad currents of the Palestinian community. Establishing the "democratic" nature of the PLO is an important element in maintaining the image of a representative and legitimate movement. This is particularly important given the fact that the PLO is physically isolated from most of its constituents.

Second, because of the principle of parity in the PLO/EC—one vote for one group regardless of its size—the smaller groups theoretically have an equal voice with Fatah in the PLO's most important decision-making body. This gives even the smallest group considerable power and serves as a balancing mechanism to prevent any one group from totally enforcing its will on the others.[9] Groups such as the PFLP and DFLP with radical ideologies and charismatic leaders cannot compete with Fatah for control over the PLO's day-to-day operations, but they are capable of setting limits beyond which the "mainstream leadership" cannot go. Indeed these groups, often backed by hard-line Arab states, set themselves up as the guardians of the PLO's maximalist goals and protectors of the purity of the "Palestinian revolution."

Third, those subgroups, created by Arab states to protect their interests in the PLO, reinforce linkages between the Arab world and the Palestinian national movement. These linkages and transgroup loyalties make the PLO a microcosm of the Arab world, invariably reflecting chronic cold wars and regional rivalries.[10] Moreover, Arab states have used Palestinian surrogates to attack each other, Israel, and unfriendly Western governments. Using the Palestinian movement in this way creates dissension and makes it impossible to develop a cohesive, tightly knit organization. As long as these subgroups have independent sources of financial and military support and can use the threat of their patrons' coming to their defense, no single group will be able to enforce its will on the others.

Finally, some of the smaller groups have emerged as powers in their own right. Some, like the PFLP-GC, have acquired reputations for military skill. Others, like the DFLP, have subordinated "armed struggle" to political action and gained reputations for political organization. The PFLP, with its charismatic leadership and sensational terrorist operations, has exercised an influence far out of proportion to its size. Indeed, the PFLP has tried to present itself as a major alternative to Fatah's leadership of the PLO.[11]

The relationship between subgroups (backed by their respective Arab patrons) has made the PLO a dynamic organization that is difficult to control. The process of "fission and fusion" that has characterized the organizational development of most of these groups has increased divisive tendencies and prevented the forging of strong bonds between subgroups and loyalty to an overarching structure.[12] Arab states have been quick to exploit these differences for their own ends.

Nonetheless the internal and external constraints oddly enough may work as a system of checks and balances to preserve a semblance of unity and cohesion. Until the PLO can achieve its interim or final goals, its main objective is to preserve a unified structure and to retain its influence with its Palestinian and Arab supporters. Fragmentation would destroy its credibility, end its claim to be the sole legitimate representative of the Palestinian people, and create opportunities for others to lay claim to the West Bank and Gaza or to increase their influence with Palestinian constituencies. Thus, the heterogeneous nature of the PLO, the need to accommodate diverse ideologies, and the emphasis on "parity" work as a safety valve to minimize the chance that a single group could force a crisis and risk splitting the movement by enforcing its views on another. Similarly Fatah, in order to limit controversy and splits within the movement, has avoided drawing up clear blueprints on long-term strategy or on the nature of a Palestinian state. It is presumably for much the same reason that the PLO has been reluctant to declare a "government-in-exile" or to risk changing the Palestine National Covenant—amended only once in 1968.

Although Fatah has emerged as the dominant PLO subgroup and Arafat as the organization's preeminent leader, these structural problems have impaired its ability to impose its views on the PLO as a whole and limited his independence. Nor has Fatah succeeded in creating strong new bonds to replace previous or existing loyalties or group ties to independent ideologies or Arab patrons.[13] Even if Fatah could somehow impose its will on the PLO, it would still have to contend with Syria's determination to insure that Palestinian goals remain subordinate to its national interests.

Arafat's immediate goal is to maintain control of the PLO and to preserve as unified a structure as possible. To accomplish this and to accommodate and manage the diverse trends within the organization requires an enormous amount of consensus politics, compromising, and back pedaling. Arafat has tried to pursue policies that will attract as broad a constituency as possible and not risk irreversibly alienating any faction. Thus, he has tried to cultivate ties with both East and West, maintain relations with conservative and radical Arab states, and toy with the possibility of a negotiated settlement while advocating "armed struggle." This balancing act is designed to maintain his credibility at home while cultivating a moderate image abroad.

The problem of accommodating the heterogeneous elements within the Palestinian resistance is most acute when the PLO and Arab regimes are debating prospects of negotiated settlements—primarily reacting to U.S., European, and Arab peace proposals. While Arafat and many of his Fatah colleagues may view a negotiated settlement with Israel as a tactical imperative at this stage of the struggle they have to deal with elements within Fatah, other PLO groups, and Arab regimes who are committed to more militant tactics and maximalist goals and who have their own national or group agendas.

Arafat doubtless uses this "radical-moderate" image to gain sympathy in the West and to avoid confronting potentially divisive issues such as changing the PLO covenant or recognizing Israel or Resolution 242. But he is still under real pressure. Although there is probably general agreement on strategy, there are serious divisions over tactics. Arafat has been criticized for his European and Jordanian initiatives and for his efforts to take Fatah and the PLO out of international terrorism. Moreover, other groups are suspicious of Arafat's efforts to cultivate a moderate image abroad and his hints to Western media about PLO readiness to recognize and coexist with Israel.

Indeed Arafat is in a tactical dilemma. He appears to want to enhance the PLO's respectability and moderate image abroad and yet maintain his revolutionary credentials at home. This predicament accounts for what amounts to a carefully orchestrated campaign of calculated ambiguity and Arafat's vacillation and inconsistency on key issues. Abroad he talks about a West Bank/Gaza state—at home about the notion of "full return." This approach, however, invariably arouses the suspicions of his more radical colleagues. It also raises serious questions abroad about his credibility as a responsible interlocutor.

From the Peace Treaty to the Iran-Iraq War: Rising Fortunes

Sadat's trip to Jerusalem in November 1977 and the Camp David Accords that followed a year later struck a severe blow against the PLO's regional and international position. The formal separation of Egypt from the "confrontation line," a development that PLO strategists had feared since the 1974–1975 disengagement agreements, denied the PLO an important ally. It also raised PLO fears that Egypt, Israel, and the United States, perhaps with Jordan's help, might succeed in hammering out an autonomy arrangement on the West Bank and Gaza. The PLO's position was further complicated by Israel's move into Lebanon in March 1978 and by an internecine war between Fatah and Iraq. The stormy session of the PNC in January 1979 indicated serious splits between Fatah and the rejectionists and seemed to suggest that Arafat was having serious trouble within his own oganization.

It was ironic, then, that the formal conclusion of a peace treaty between Israel and Egypt should have initiated an upward swing in the PLO's position at home and abroad. Arafat seemed aware of the disastrous implications of the peace agreement on the PLO, but he was also attuned to the opportunities it could create. The treaty seemed to offer a chance to close PLO ranks, mend its fences in the Arab world, create international opposition to the Camp David Accords, and highlight the necessity of including the PLO in any settlement.

The first development favorable to the PLO actually preceded the treaty signing. By early 1979, PLO spokesmen were hailing the Iranian revolution as a major windfall.[14] The Khomeini regime's decision to break ties with Israel and stop oil deliveries and the collapse of the U.S.-Iranian alliance were quickly followed by statements attacking Camp David and Egypt. Although close identification with an Islamic fundamentalist regime risked displeasing secular groups within the PLO, and perhaps angering Iraq, Fatah probably saw important advantages in promoting ties with Iran. Teheran could provide an additional source of funds, be used to counter Iraqi influence, and possibly be recruited somehow in the struggle against Israel.

Arafat quickly moved to take advantage of the new situation. He arrived in Teheran in mid-February 1979, the first foreign leader to be received formally by Khomeini. In a symbolic gesture, the Iranians converted the Israeli Trade Mission into an embassy for the PLO. Arafat, well aware of the importance of the Iranian connection, sent one of his most trusted advisers, Hani al-Hasan, to handle PLO interests in Teheran. "I told His Eminence Ayatollah Khomeyni," Arafat stated in a press conference, "that I really saw the walls of Jerusalem when I heard about the victory of the Iranian revolution."[15]

The PLO's response to the signing of the Egyptian-Israeli treaty a month later was predictably harsh. Speaking at the Sabra refugee camp outside of Beirut hours before the treaty signing, Arafat reportedly threatened to "chop off" the hands of the treaty signers.[16] Two days later at the Baghdad summit, the PLO, Libya, and Syria walked out of the meeting in protest against Saudi unwillingness to adopt more extreme measures against Egypt.[17] Similarly, between April and June the PLO stepped up terrorist operations in Israel, the West Bank, Gaza, and Europe. Early in June the PLO claimed responsibility for the murder of the Imam of Gaza, apparently in retaliation for his strong support of the peace treaty.[18]

The treaty also challenged Arafat to consider practical ways of furthering Palestinian goals in a new environment. The PLO's primary objective was to mobilize opposition to the Camp David Accords on all levels—within the Palestinian movement, on the West Bank, in the Arab world, and abroad. Indeed, the treaty accelerated Arafat's efforts to mend ties with Jordan and coordinate opposition to the Camp David Accords with other Arab states.

It was on the international front, however, that the PLO made its greatest gains. By the summer of 1979 the PLO had initiated a major campaign to gain increased recognition abroad. PLO strategy, which focused primarily on Europe, was designed to build a broad consensus against the Camp David Accords and to convince the Europeans that the PLO was a vital ingredient to any solution. Moreover, in keeping with Arafat's desire to cultivate an image of respectability abroad, he intensified efforts to underscore the PLO's "flexibility" and highlight Israel's "intransigence." Arafat may even have calculated that Europe provided a vehicle to help change the U.S. attitude toward the Palestinian problem and open a dialogue with the PLO.

The opening shot in Arafat's strategy was his July meeting with Austrian Chancellor Kreisky, the first time Arafat was formally received by a European head of government on the continent. The meeting, which coincided with the fourth round of the autonomy talks in Alexandria, was a great political success. The joint communique expressed "extreme concern" over Israeli settlement policy and designated the Palestinian issue as the "central problem" of the Middle East conflict.[19] The PLO doubtless saw the meeting as a form of recognition by Austria and may have believed that it would become a stepping-stone to European community recognition. Amidst criticism from Israel over the meeting, Kreisky stated that it was "absolutely ridiculous" to believe the PLO was out to destroy Israel.[20]

Throughout the summer PLO diplomacy continued. In August the PLO's Central Committee adopted a resolution authorizing Arafat to continue his European initiatives. In an interview with the *Washington Star* Arafat stated that the PLO had begun a campaign to erase its terrorist image and achieve legitimacy in the eyes of the world.[21] Within a week Arafat was in Bucharest meeting with President Ceausescu. In a joint communique, Romania confirmed its support for the "Palestinian people under the PLO leadership."[22] The PLO's image was given a further boost by the controversy surrounding the resignation of UN Ambassador Andrew Young for his meeting with a PLO representative. Voice of Palestine hailed the affair as a "turning point" in Palestinian efforts to explain the "true story" of the Palestinians to the United States. The Young affair also accelerated the PLO's efforts to broaden its ties with the American Black community.[23] Finally, upon returning from the Non-Aligned Movement Conference in Havana, Arafat visited Spain in September, meeting with both the prime minister and foreign minister.

Although the PLO enjoyed rising success in the international arena, its opposition in the Arab world was more complicated. The anti-Sadat consensus that had been forged at Arab summits in 1978 and 1979 was beginning to show signs of strain as traditional Arab rivalries rose to the surface. The Arab boycott of Egypt was not being applied uniformly, and by the summer of 1979 the Iraqi-Syrian rapprochement had begun to sour.[24]

For Arafat the new situation provided risks and opportunities. Tension between Damascus and Baghdad raised the risk that the PLO would again be caught in the middle, but it also broke up an anti-Fatah front within the PLO and gave Arafat additional maneuvering room to pursue other options.[25] Although PLO-Libyan ties were strained and South Lebanon continued to complicate Palestinian-Lebanese relations, Arafat renewed his efforts to effect a rapprochement with Jordan and generally succeeded in keeping on good terms with his most important supporters.

Despite deep-seated tensions between Jordan and the Palestinian resistance, by the mid 1970s Arafat and many of his Fatah colleagues had begun to realize the importance of developing closer relations with King Hussein. The assessment was based on a number of inescapable realities. The presence of a million Palestinians in Jordan (one-quarter of the total Palestinian population) and Jordan's traditional access and ties to the West Bank were reason enough to cultivate relations with Hussein. By 1978, Arafat's fear that Jordan might be drawn into the Camp David negotiations and his long-standing belief that King Hussein had designs on the West Bank accelerated his efforts to continue the dialogue that had been broken off in 1977. Arafat's primary objective in renewing a dialogue was to prevent Hussein from taking any action that might undercut the PLO's influence in the occupied territories or its role in an eventual settlement. Since Camp David, Arafat had met Hussein at least twice. The week before the treaty signing, the two met again at Mafraq near Amman.[26]

Palestinian resistance to a dialogue with Jordan had not made Arafat's task any easier. The PFLP and DFLP, embittered by Hussein's actions against the Fedayeen in 1970–1971, wary of his ties to Saudi Arabia and the United States, and suspicious of Arafat's motives, insisted that any dialogue be based on a quid pro quo. Not only did they push for release of Palestinians in Jordanian prisons, but they sought a greater freedom to organize politically in Jordan and to launch operations against Israel—something Hussein refused to allow.

Nonetheless, Arab determination to oppose the Camp David Accords and to keep Hussein out of any negotiations facilitated Arafat's Jordanian initiative. Under the cover of the PLO-Jordanian joint committee established to coordinate opposition to the Camp David Accords and channel funds promised by the Baghdad Summit to West Bank municipalities, Arafat and Hussein entered into a closer dialogue. The relationship was tactical at best, but it became a vital part of PLO strategy after 1978. In September 1979, Arafat visited Amman briefly for the first time in nine years.[27]

Throughout 1980 the PLO continued its campaign to gain increasing recognition abroad and to maintain its maneuverability in inter-Arab politics. Arafat had followed up his visits to Austria and Spain with high-level talks in Turkey, Portugal, and the Soviet Union. Moreover, the PLO enjoyed a steady stream of successes at the UN, cooperating on a series of anti-Israeli resolutions passed by Arab and Third World countries. Indeed on March 1, the United States, although later retracting its vote, joined with other Security Council members to pass a resolution condemning Israeli settlement activity.

It was in Europe, however, that the PLO made most of its gains. During March, French President Giscard d'Estaing on a six-nation tour of the Middle East, called for a greater regard for Palestinians' rights and stressed the importance of including the PLO in the peace negotiations.[28] Arafat personally hailed the declaration as the first time a large Western European country had called on the PLO to join the negotiations.[29] There were even rumors that Giscard d'Estaing had invited Arafat to visit France.[30] Similarly, in April the European Parliament called on Israel to recognize the PLO as the representative of the Palestinian people, and the EEC declaration in June acknowledged that the PLO would have to be "associated" with the peace negotiations.[31] Although PLO spokesmen publicly criticized these statements and complained that they did not go far enough, they were apparently pleased that the Europeans had at least begun to focus on the Palestinian issue.

Although the PLO's position in the region was invariably complicated as inter-Arab rivalries intensified, Arafat continued his efforts to maintain his ties with both conservative and radical regimes. In April, at the Fourth Conference of the Arab Front for Steadfastness and Confrontation, Arafat sought to mend his fences with Libya and at least give the appearance of coordinating closely with the Steadfastness Front. At the same time, he tried to maintain his ties with Jordan and Saudi Arabia.[32]

Moreover, as Israeli-Egyptian talks sputtered, stalled, and temporarily broke down in the summer of 1980, the PLO's position was further strengthened. Pro-PLO nationalist sentiment in the West Bank and Gaza also seemed to be increasing. Fatah's May terrorist attack against Yeshiva students in Hebron and the success of the attackers in eluding capture seemed to suggest increased support for the PLO and its network in the occupied territories. The assassination attempts against West Bank mayors Khalaf and Shaka in June and the subsequent deportations of mayors Milhem and Qawasma increased pro-PLO sentiment and further alienated and radicalized West Bankers.

By the summer of 1980, however, there were signs that PLO fortunes had begun to turn. Fatah's Fourth Congress in Damascus produced a militant set of resolutions calling for the "complete liberation of Palestine" and the liquidation of the Zionist entity— rhetoric that was sure to please hard-line Arab states, but that caused some difficulty for Arafat's campaign to cultivate a more "moderate" image abroad. In subsequent interviews with the Western press, Arafat sought to soften and even disclaim the resolutions.[33] Nonetheless, they demonstrated that there were constraints—even from within Arafat's own organization—on efforts to transform the PLO's image.

By August Israel had also stepped up its policy of "preemptive strikes" against Palestinian targets in Lebanon—a policy that had actually been enunciated in April 1979 after a PLO raid near Nahariyya. The Israeli raids were designed to disrupt training routines, keep

PLO guerrillas off balance, and strike at concentrations of supplies and forces. On August 18–19, Israel launched the largest incursion into South Lebanon since the 1978 Litani operation, attacking nineteen targets and using air power for the first time in months.[34]

Finally, inter-Arab rivalries, particularly between Iraq and Syria, began to intensify. Traditional tensions were exacerbated by Iraqi claims that Syria was actively backing Iran and by Syrian accusations that Baghdad was supporting a Muslim Brotherhood campaign to overthrow Assad. Although Palestinian spokesmen publicly insisted that the PLO maintained good relations with Iran, Iraq, and Syria and retained "sufficient room for maneuver," it was clear there was trouble ahead.[35]

The Iran-Iraq War, The Amman Summit, and the Syrian-Jordanian Cold War: The Slippery Slope

With the eruption of the Iran-Iraq war, PLO fortunes seemed to decline as rapidly as they had risen. The war widened existing differences in the Arab world, pushed the Palestinian issue off center stage, and exacerbated tensions within the PLO. Arafat, who had long sought to maintain neutrality in inter-Arab rivalries, was forced into the precarious position of trying to balance his relations with several key supporters.

First, the PLO tried to maintain relations with Iran, which it had actively courted since the revolution and which it hoped to use as a counter to growing Syrian influence over the PLO. Arafat was also reluctant to cross Baghdad, which had supported Palestinian splinter groups in their war against Fatah and could easily do so again. Second, the PLO was caught in a deepening rift between Syria, which had thrown its support to Iran, and an emerging Jordanian-Iraqi alliance supported by Saudi Arabia and the Gulf states. Arafat could not risk alienating Damascus but did not want to jeopardize the PLO's rap-prochement with Jordan or its ties to Saudi Arabia and Iraq. This split between the "moderates" and "radicals," however, went far beyond the war itself and would come to include a range of issues including alternative views on how best to proceed with a settlement of the Arab-Israeli conflict. Finally, these regional rivalries were reflected in increased factional tension between Syrian and Iraqi groups in the PLO and between pro-Iranian and pro-Iraqi elements within Lebanon.

The main legacy of the war for the PLO, however, was new complications in relations with Syria. Damascus's support for Tehe-ran—primarily an anti-Iraqi measure—left Syria increasingly isolated in the Arab world. As the Jordanian-Iraqi alliance crystallized, Syrian suspicions reached new levels. Pressed at home by the Muslim Brotherhood, the Assad regime came to believe that the Iraqis, perhaps with Jordanian help, were aiding internal opposition. Moreover, the new "Sunni consensus" seemed to threaten Syria's bid for influence in the Arab world and prejudice its interests in Arab-Israeli issues.

As the Syrians became more isolated they moved to increase their control over the PLO—a key bargaining card in protecting Syrian interests and prestige in the region. Damascus possessed formidable assets in this campaign, both in Lebanon and within the Palestinian resistance movement. And Assad sought to use them to prevent Arafat from moving too close to the "moderates" and too far from its lead in determining strategy and tactics on Arab-Israeli issues. Syria's efforts would restrict Arafat's room to maneuver and complicate the PLO's regional and international strategies.

Arafat's immediate problem, however, was to maintain the PLO's neutrality, keep the PLO and Palestinian issue on center stage, and help to mediate the conflict. Toward these ends, he began the first of a series of unsuccessful mediation efforts.[36] By October 1980 the PLO had reportedly called for an Arab summit and presented a four-stage plan to end the war.[37] Arafat's mediation efforts succeeded only in antagonizing the major combatants. In fact, there were rumors that Syrian army officers, concerned that Arafat's efforts would be to Iraq's advantage, were pressing Assad to adopt sanctions against the PLO. Apparently aware of the risk of high-visibility mediation, the PLO sought to tone down its role. By late October, the PLO reportedly denied that it was engaged in efforts to settle the conflict.[38]

As the eleventh Arab summit approached (scheduled for Amman in late November), the PLO was headed into an inter-Arab squeeze. Syrian suspicion of Iraqi and Jordanian collusion mounted as Damascus became more isolated at home and abroad. Syria's decision in October to sign a Treaty of Friendship and Cooperation with the Soviet Union and its public accusations of Iraqi and Jordanian support for Muslim Brotherhood elements indicated how besieged Damascus was feeling. Indeed, by mid-November the Syrian government had launched its campaign to postpone the upcoming summit. Assad had no intention of going to Amman to sit with his arch rival, Saddam Hussein, only to be criticized by his Arab brothers for his support of Iran.

Syria's isolation inevitably restricted the PLO's maneuvering room. Already suspicious of Arafat's independence, the Assad regime suspected that the PLO might be cooperating with his rivals. Damascus seemed concerned about Saudi and European efforts to moderate the PLO's position and encourage it to consider a settlement. These fears were exacerbated by talk of a "Jordanian option." Given Washington's previous efforts to court King Hussein and the prospects that a Labor government, long interested in some form of territorial compromise with Jordan, might replace the present Likud government in the next Israeli elections, Assad was determined not to lose his influence over the PLO. If Assad was not going to attend the Amman summit, neither was Arafat. After what must have been a week of intensive negotiating, the PLO's Executive Committee announced the day before the summit opened that the PLO would not attend.[39]

Although PLO spokesmen denied that Syria had pressured the PLO to boycott the summit, it was obvious that Damascus was the primary influence on Arafat's decision.[40] Given the PLO's vacillating position on the summit (five days before the summit opened there were reports that the PLO would attend), Arafat probably tried initially to bargain with Assad.[41] He then visited Saudi Arabia, possibly in an effort to persuade the Saudis to postpone the summit or to help him change Assad's mind.[42] However, when it became clear that Assad was determined to boycott the summit, Arafat had no choice but to comply. Nor could he have pushed a decision through the PLO/EC without risking an open split within the PLO. As one observer wryly noted, the Saudis were offering Arafat *nuqud* (cash) and the Syrians were offering him *wujud* (existence). He chose the latter.[43]

The PLO's boycott of the Amman summit—the first the organization missed since it was created in 1964—was a temporary, but serious, setback for Arafat. Arafat revealed his dependence on Damascus and probably irritated the Saudis and Jordanians in the process. The summit under more ideal circumstances would have provided a forum to focus attention on the Palestinian issue, collect subsidies, and promote "Arab unity." Instead Arafat watched from the sidelines as the Arabs discussed the Palestinian question. Although the final communique of the summit reaffirmed support for the PLO as the sole and legitimate representative of the Palestinian people, Arafat could not help but notice that King Hussein, as conference host, did not mention the PLO in his address. Indeed, Arafat was already suspicious that Hussein, despite his assurances to the contrary, was trying to chip away at the Rabat decision of 1974 in which the Arab states acknowledged the PLO as the only representative of the Palestinian people.

The summit also exacerbated tensions between Syria and Jordan. The issues at stake varied—Assad's suspicion that Jordan and Iraq were supporting the Muslim Brotherhood, the Iran-Iraq war, and different perceptions of possible solutions to the Arab-Israeli conflict. But the message Assad sent by mobilizing his troops on the Jordanian-Syrian border during the summit was clear enough: Syria would not allow its Arab brothers to ignore or undermine its prestige and interests in the region.

The Syrian-Jordanian cold war had serious consequences for the PLO. The PLO's campaign to maintain its "dialogue" with Jordan was an early casualty. By late November 1980, both Saiqa and the PFLP-GC, presumably at Syrian urging, had announced their intention to withdraw from the PLO-Jordanian joint committee.[44] Other PLO groups, such as the PFLP and DFLP, now redoubled their efforts to sink the relationship. Days after the summit there were reports that a "group of radicals" was insisting on severing all PLO ties with Jordan.[45] Early in December, a high-ranking PFLP official accused King Hussein of pushing "vicious methods" to undercut the PLO's role as sole representative of the Palestinian people.[46]

As relations between Syria and Jordan deteriorated in early 1981, Arafat had to adjust to increasingly limited maneuverability. The kidnapping of the Jordanian chargé in Beirut, reportedly by a Syrian-backed group, further strained relations. The joint committee continued to meet, but Arafat's Jordanian initiative came under attack from pro-Syrian groups. In fact early in April, Farouq Qaddumi, head of the PLO's Political Department, stated that the "dialogue" had been discontinued, although the joint committee would continue to meet.[47] It remained to be seen how strains in Syrian-PLO relations would influence the fifteenth meeting of the Palestinian National Council—scheduled for mid-April in Damascus.

From the PNC Meeting to the Israeli Invasion of Lebanon: New Opportunities and Risks

With Arafat's successful handling of the PNC meeting, PLO fortunes gradually began to improve. There were setbacks such as the debacle at the Fez summit and risks as Israel sought to root out PLO influence on the West Bank and hold it hostage militarily in Lebanon. But Arafat also exploited new opportunities, making important political gains through his role in the cease-fire that ended the July fighting with Israel and enhancing the PLO's status abroad. Moreover, Sadat's death, deadlocked autonomy talks, Israel's return of Sinai, and prospects of Egypt's improved ties with the Arab world seemed to hold out new possibilities.

The PNC meeting opened in Damascus amidst speculation that Syria might try, through its supporters in the PLO and influence in Lebanon, to increase its influence within the organization. Assad left little doubt that he hoped Arafat would closely coordinate PLO policy with Damascus. "The convening of the PNC once again in Damascus,"

Assad announced in his opening address, "is a new assertion of the ties of brotherhood . . . that combine the sons of Syria and those of Palestine."[48] Nonetheless, Arafat skillfully managed the PNC meeting to serve his interests. Arafat was, not surprisingly, reelected chairman of the PLO/EC. He picked up an additional seat for Fatah on the committee and resisted the efforts of two smaller groups to gain representation on the PLO/EC. The final political statement reaffirmed support, although in less than glowing terms, for Arafat's two key policies—the European and Jordanian initiatives.[49]

While Arafat was scoring important gains at the PNC session, the Lebanese situation presented new risks. By mid-April, 1981, Syria and its Lebanese allies were engaged with the Phalangist-dominated Lebanese Front in the most serious fighting in three years. Moreover, on April 26 Israeli aircraft downed two Syrian helicopters in the Bekaa Valley as a warning to Damascus not to press its offensive against the Phalange. Syria responded by placing surface-to-air missiles in the area, setting the stage for further escalation.

For Arafat and the PLO the Lebanese imbroglio created immediate dangers. Well aware of the disastrous consequences of Palestinian involvement in the 1975–1976 civil war, Arafat seemed determined to avoid being drawn into the Lebanese fray. Throughout May, Arafat shuttled around the Gulf and through North Africa in an effort to discuss the Syrian-Israeli crisis, among other things, and perhaps to arrange a foreign-ministers' conference.[50] "The last place the [Palestinian] resistance wants to fight is in Lebanon," said a Palestinian official of the Institute of Palestine Studies.[51]

This was easier said than done, however. The Syrians were already making use of their Saiqa allies and Palestine Liberation Army (PLA) units along Beirut's confrontation line, and it was obvious that if the situation deteriorated, Fatah might be drawn in. Not only was there bitter enmity between the Phalange and the PLO, but Damascus and its Lebanese allies might look to Arafat and Fatah for support. Moreover, the situation in South Lebanon was beginning to boil. Israel had stepped up its preemptive strikes against PLO positions. Early in June, Israeli aircraft hit the Damur area (twelve miles south of Beirut) and naval vessels shelled Palestinian positions north of Tripoli—the deepest raid into Lebanon in over two years. War with Israel, PNC Chairman Khalid al-Fahum stated is "very likely."[52]

Indeed, it was South Lebanon that provided the scene of major fighting between Israel and the PLO. The July mini-war (July 14–24) witnessed the heaviest cross-border bombardments and Israeli air strikes since Israel's Litani operation of 1978. Although the military consequences of the July fighting were important, particularly for

Israeli strategy in the future, the political implications for the PLO carried more immediate impact.

Arafat made important tactical concessions in agreeing to the UN-U.S.–brokered cease-fire of July 24, 1981. Had the fighting continued, Israel would almost certainly have launched a large-scale attack into South Lebanon designed to push PLO guns and rockets beyond the range of its northern towns. Nonetheless, the intensive PLO bombardment of northern Israel had placed the Israeli government in the difficult position of concluding a cease-fire or launching a large-scale attack that carried the risk of serious casualties and international complications. Khalil al-Wazir, the PLO's deputy military commander, conceded that PLO firepower was no match for the Israelis, but added that PLO shelling succeeded because of the "sensitive positions we held."[53] PLO rockets were mobile and well camouflaged. Conceding the effectiveness of PLO tactics, Hirsch Goodman, the *Jerusalem Post*'s military correspondent, wrote that although Israel could destroy bridges and depots and even attack PLO headquarters, it would always be possible to "sneak a katyusha into Southern Lebanon and even a 130 mm. gun."[54]

Arafat also clearly hoped to use the cease-fire to achieve important political gains. For one thing, PLO spokesmen apparently believed that international opinion was on their side. PLO officials sought to use the Israeli bombing of Beirut, heavy civilian casualties, and the image of the PLO as the underdog—fighting against the might of the Israeli army—to portray the Israelis as the aggressors. Similarly, Arafat probably hoped that the cease-fire would provide the beginning of a dialogue with the United States. Indeed, the day after the cease-fire, Arafat stated that while the conflict with Israel would not produce a sudden change in U.S. attitudes toward the PLO, it might constitute a "turning point."[55] Other Palestinian officials noted with satisfaction that U.S. coverage of the Beirut bombing had talked about "Israeli aggression" and "Palestinian retaliation."[56]

Finally, Arafat sought to profit from the cease-fire to enhance the PLO's international image. Despite the Begin government's insistence that the cease-fire had been concluded between Israel and Lebanon, Arafat advanced the claim that the PLO had been recognized as a legitimate party to the negotiations. Moreover, by adhering to the cease-fire the PLO leader probably calculated that he could demonstrate that the PLO was a responsible interlocutor and that he was capable of maintaining discipline within his own ranks. "Our adherence to the cease-fire," Arafat noted in August, reflects the "authority of the PLO."[57] Reports that Arafat stopped the PFLP-GC from violating the agreement doubtless helped in this regard.[58]

Arafat's agreement to the cease-fire, however, quickly created new problems, particularly with the Syrians. Damascus failed to support the PLO in its confrontation with Israel. Some Palestinians seemed to believe that Damascus viewed a periodic Israeli drubbing of the PLO as a good way to keep it in line. According to an Arafat aide, "Syria would love to see Israel wipe out the PLO. If only the political shell of the PLO remains, they will be able to fill it with their own men."[59]

The Syrians, long suspicious of Arafat's independence, were reportedly disturbed by his decision to agree to the cease-fire without their prior approval.[60] Although Damascus clearly wanted to avoid a major Israeli move into Lebanon and was doubtless happy that the situation had not escalated, the PLO's creditable showing and elevated status seemed to indicate that Arafat was prepared to take major decisions without consulting Damascus. The PLO-Israeli fighting had upstaged the Syrian "missile crisis," embarrassed Damascus, and opened new opportunities for Arafat on the diplomatic front. On July 28, four days after the cease-fire was concluded, Arafat met with Assad in Damascus. The Voice of Palestine announced after the meeting that "coordination and joint action" between Syria and Palestinian resistance would be continued.[61] That same day there were reports that Arafat and Ahmad Jabril, leader of the pro-Syrian PFLP-GC (which was said to be intent on violating the cease-fire), agreed to "reaffirm" the Palestinian-Lebanese joint command decision to uphold the cease-fire.[62]

Apparently determined to prevent Arafat from straying too far, Syria set out to emphasize his dependence on Damascus. One of the tools at Damascus's disposal was support of anti-Arafat Palestinian splinter groups, such as Black June.[63] This group, led by a Fatah renegade Sabri al-Banna (Abu Nidal), had originally worked for Iraq against Syria but was now said to be aligned with Damascus. Black June had claimed responsibility for the murder of the PLO representative in Brussels in June. In a speech delivered at Naim Khadir's funeral, Salah Khalaf hinted about whom the PLO thought was to blame. "Our hands are tied because we do not intend to start battles with any Arab regime, particularly those we consider as being strategically aligned with us. I tell those regimes which harbor the groups of the rancorous Sabri al-Banna to get rid of this agent."[64]

In late August, Black June struck again—this time targeting a synagogue in Vienna. The attack, for which PLO officials vehemently denied responsibility, occurred the day before Arafat was to meet with French Foreign Minister Cheysson in Beirut and was clearly intended to embarrass Arafat.[65] It was no coincidence that the incident took place in Austria, where Kreisky had bent over backwards to push the PLO's "moderation." In the aftermath of the incident, press reports began to quote PLO sources who placed primary responsibility on the Syrian-backed Abu Nidal organization. "In Damascus nobody operates on his own," a PLO official maintained.[66]

Despite strains with Damascus, PLO fortunes continued to rise. PLO officials expressed satisfaction over Sadat's assassination early in October 1981. Hundreds of Palestinians and Lebanese gunmen, firing weapons and carrying pictures of former Egyptian President Nasser, took to the streets of Beirut. "We clasp the hand that fired the shots," Salah Khalaf exclaimed. Arafat's reaction was hardly less restrained: "Didn't I say that Egypt's might will not be long and that if the deluge comes it will wash away all the renegades and agents."[67]

While PLO spokesmen publicly speculated that Mubarak would likely follow Sadat's "treasonous course," they probably hoped that the assassination would herald a major political change in the area.[68] The Palestinians did not expect Egypt to break its treaty commitments with Israel even after the return of Sinai. But they must have reasoned that Mubarak, free of the personal investment in Sadat's initiative and the bitter quarreling with the other Arabs, might be able to mend ties with other Arab states and return at least to the political battlefield. Similarly, Egypt's "return to the Arab world" could ultimately be used as a possible counterweight to Syrian efforts to dominate the PLO.

The PLO's diplomatic initiatives also continued to gain ground. In October Arafat visited the Far East and the Soviet Union. The tour was designed to increase the PLO's recognition abroad and maintain its ties with both "East and West." In Viet Nam, China, and North Korea, Arafat's rhetoric was strident. In Tokyo, the PLO leader took a more moderate line, dropping hints about peaceful relations with Israel and endorsing the Saudi eight-point peace plan.[69]

Arafat's trip to Japan—his first to a major pro-Western industrial power—was viewed in Palestinian circles as a great success. Although the PLO leader was not received as an official guest of the Japanese government, he met with the prime minister and foreign minister. Enthusiastic over his reception, Arafat reportedly remarked: "If this is not an official visit, I wonder what an official visit is."[70] Arafat's major objective in Japan, as in all his European initiatives, was to persuade the international community to recognize the PLO as an indispensible part of a solution to the Arab-Israeli conflict.

Arafat's Far Eastern trip was followed by an official visit to the Soviet Union. Here Arafat was received formally by Brezhnev amidst prominent media coverage. Moscow granted the PLO full diplomatic status that appeared to give it the authority to deal directly with the Soviet government rather than through the Afro-Asian Solidarity Committee to which the PLO had been accredited.[71] The Soviets were clearly attempting, in the wake of Sadat's assassination, to reassert their influence with the PLO, although they had probably long considered the idea of upgrading their relations. Commenting on the Soviet decision, Salah Khalaf noted that it "signified recognition of a Palestine state before its birth."[72]

Soon after the Moscow visit, the new Greek Prime Minister Andreas Papandreou invited Arafat to Athens to discuss the upgrading of relations. The invitation laid the foundation for Arafat's visit to Greece in mid-December, a trip that would result in the upgrading of the PLO's information office in Athens to the level of a diplomatic mission with all the rights enjoyed by other diplomatic representatives.[73]

Despite Arafat's diplomatic success, the PLO's position in the region continued to be plagued by inter-Arab rivalries. The divisions that had been exacerbated by the Iran-Iraq war and fanned by the Amman summit continued. The Syrian missile crisis had helped temporarily to ease Syrian isolation in the region, but Damascus's relations with both Jordan and Iraq were severely strained. By the fall of 1981 a new and troublesome ingredient had been added to the inter-Arab mix—the Saudi eight-point peace plan. For Arafat, this initiative seemed to hold both risks and opportunities as he sought to guide the PLO through the hazardous world of inter-Arab politics.

When Crown Prince Fahd first surfaced the Saudi proposals in August 1981, the PLO reaction was mixed. While the PFLP and DFLP immediately attacked the plan, Fatah officials reacted cautiously. Khalil al-Wazir called the proposals "positive" and applauded the Saudi decision to reject the U.S. approach to the Middle Eastern problem.[74]

Fatah's cautiously favorable reaction to the Saudi initiative was not surprising. Although the eight points did not specifically mention the PLO, they outlined a solution based on a West Bank/Gaza state with East Jerusalem as its capital, a solution compatible with the PLO's interim objectives. Eager to avoid a split within the PLO and to see how the Saudi initiative would be received elsewhere, the PLO/EC deferred a formal reaction.[75]

The exact motivation behind the Saudi plan was unclear. It may have been an effort to facilitate the sale of AWACS by demonstrating Saudi willingness to recognize Israel or a Saudi effort to test the waters by floating an alternative to Camp David. Whatever the reason, by October 1981 the plan had received considerable notice. The Sadat assassination, the lack of progress in the autonomy negotiations, and concern about the future of the peace process after the anticipated return of Sinai to Egypt in April 1982 focused attention on alternative frameworks. Early in November, the Saudis—in an effort to broaden support for their initiative—raised it again in more detail. The Egyptians, Jordanians, British, and even the Americans reacted favorably to certain elements of the plan, particularly point seven regarding the right of all states in the area to live in peace, interpreted by many as Saudi recognition of Israel.[76]

Arafat, buoyed by the prospects of an Arab initiative centered on a Palestinian state, reacted positively but cautiously. He could not afford to ignore the opportunity to support what appeared to be an alternative to the Camp David Accords pushed by the PLO's primary financial benefactor. Moreover, he may have calculated that Sadat's death and the Fahd proposals had created a unique opportunity to create a new framework in which the PLO might be able to play a key role. Had not two former U.S. presidents, Ford and Carter, called for a U.S. dialogue with the PLO only weeks before? The Saudi proposals provide "a positive step, a very important starting point for the settlement of the Middle East issue," Arafat announced before Japanese television.[77]

Nonetheless, Arafat's reaction was cautious. The plan did not specifically mention the PLO. Nor did Arafat and Fatah seem prepared to play their "recognition card" without guarantees that Israel and the United States would reciprocate. Arafat doubtless anticipated the opposition the Fahd plan would generate from within the PLO and from the Syrians. The Saudi proposals contained a veiled reference to recognition and perhaps coexistence with Israel—a concession that groups such as PFLP and DFLP were not likely to accept. Nor were these elements eager to endorse a plan initiated by Saudi Arabia, a state they considered to be reactionary and a client of the West. Moreover, Arafat clearly anticipated tough opposition from the Syrians. In fact, the day after his Tokyo statement, three pro-Syrian PLO groups condemned the plan.[78]

With the approach of the twelfth Arab summit at Fez (scheduled for late November 1981), differences over the Fahd plan began to sharpen. Damascus had serious doubts about a "peace initiative" that had been drafted without its approval and already endorsed by the Jordanians. Badly isolated in the Arab world and involved in bitter feuds with the Iraqis and Jordanians, Syria could not negotiate from a position of influence. The Syrians did not want to confront the Saudis openly and risk losing Riyadh's financial support, but they could not afford to sit back and wait. Damascus chose to air its criticism through a former Syrian government official and senior

Ba'ath party leader. In an interview with the leftist daily *as-Safir,* Muhammed Haidar stated that it was a mistake to present such a plan. "The timing was wrong, the content was wrong, and the unilateral presentation of it was also wrong."[79]

In an effort to gain support for the plan and above all to prevent disagreements at Fez, Arafat embarked on some traditional presummit shuttling, visiting Syria, Saudi Arabia and the Gulf, and North Africa. Although Arafat was evidently not yet prepared to give up hope on the Saudi plan, he continued to hedge his bets. "If it is presented at the Fez summit," he told an interviewer, "it will be discussed."[80] Early in November the DFLP organ *al-Hurriyah* carried statements by three PLO groups attacking the plan, including one by Salah Khalaf. One week before the summit opened Farouq Qaddumi announced that current conditions were not suitable for presenting peace proposals.[81]

By the opening of the summit on November 25, the stage was set for what Beirut's *Monday Morning* called the "fiasco at Fez." Assad, apparently not eager to confront the Saudis but determined to sack the Fahd plan, joined Libya's Kaddafi and Iraq's Saddam Hussein in staying away from Fez, sending Foreign Minister Khaddam instead. Assad's absence sent clear signals to Arafat, already under mounting criticism from the PLO.[82] Five PLO groups, four of which were represented on the PLO/EC, had already condemned the plan. In a closed-door session, Arafat reportedly informed Fahd that while the plan was "generally positive," he had never concealed his "reservations" and "anxieties" over some of its points. According to another press report Arafat recommended that the controversial point seven be taken out of the plan.[83]

The abrupt breakup of the Fez summit hours after it had begun was a clear setback for Arafat and an indication of the external and internal constraints under which he operated. The PLO was again caught in the middle of bitter Arab rivalries that exacerbated splits within the organization and prevented formulation of a united Arab position on even the most general of proposals for a negotiated settlement. Such a consensus would have provided an opportunity to isolate Israel further and score points with the Europeans and the United States. Instead Fez revealed the deep divisions between those Arab states (Jordan and Saudi Arabia) who saw a need for a negotiated settlement and those states (such as Syria, Iraq, and Libya) who were either opposed to or in no particular hurry for a negotiated settlement. Indeed, the controversy over point seven—recognition of Israel—created the impression that Arab attitudes toward Israel had not fundamentally changed in thirty years.

Whether Arafat believed he could convince Damascus not to oppose the plan or whether he was depending on Saudi Arabia to do so is not clear. Arafat's cautious endorsement of the Fahd plan in the weeks before the summit suggests that he expected opposition but underestimated how intense it would be. Moreover, it is not clear how seriously Arafat regarded the Saudi initiative. The Fahd plan may have provided a way to test the waters—European, Arab, and U.S.—for an alternative to the Camp David framework after April 1982. Moreover, if the Saudis were committed to the plan and asked for his support, he could not afford to ignore their request.

In any event, when confronted with the disarray at Fez, Syrian pressure, and opposition from within the PLO, Arafat quickly moved to oppose or at least postpone a decision on the Saudi initiative. Although Arafat probably angered the Saudis and damaged his credibility in the process, his first priority was to preserve his domestic constituency and avoid a serious conflict with the Syrians. To support the plan would have forced a split within the PLO over the controversial issue of accepting Israel's right to exist—a concession Arafat could not have made without support of the major PLO groups and Syria. Some PLO groups viewed this as a final negotiating card to be traded only for dramatic Israeli or U.S. concessions; others were implacably opposed to making such a move under any circumstances. According to Salah Khalaf, the PLO opposed the Fahd plan because it "implied the prior recognition" of Israel.[84] With this in mind one wonders whether Arafat actually expected endorsement of the plan from within his own ranks.

Although Arafat's performance at Fez exacerbated tension within the PLO, angered Syria, and irritated the Saudis, it did not seriously undermine his prestige or influence over the PLO. There were rumors of serious splits within Fatah over the plan, but Arafat managed to outmaneuver or coopt his opposition. Arafat succeeded in maintaining support for his major policies—European initiative, dialogue with Jordan, and support for the cease-fire.[85] Moreover, in several interviews with the Arab and international press, Arafat continued to espouse cautious support for the plan, presumably to keep the Fahd plan alive as an alternative framework after April.[86]

Arafat's hopes that the Camp David era was rapidly fading were buoyed by the lack of progress in the Egyptian-Israeli autonomy negotiations, which seemed to drag on interminably with no signs of real breakthroughs. The upcoming return of Sinai to Egypt, despite the PLO's criticism of Mubarak's policies, seemed to signal the beginning of Cairo's ultimate reintegration into Arab ranks. Remarks by several Egyptian officials concerning the importance of including the PLO in the negotiations and the need for the United States to start a dialogue with the Palestinians also encouraged PLO officials.[87] Moreover, Mubarak's decision not to visit Jeusalem and his criticism of Israeli policies on the West Bank seemed to suggest to the Palestinians that relations between Israel and Egypt would become much more complicated after April. In any event, PLO spokesmen seemed prepared to give Mubarak a chance to change his policy.

Although PLO fortunes had improved since the fall of 1980, Arafat had little cause for real optimism. The PLO continued to make gains abroad, but its position in the region was very uncertain. External and internal pressure continued to limit Arafat's independence. Relations with Syria remained strained. In the wake of the Hama uprising, the Assad regime evinced even more suspicion of Iraqi-Jordanian plotting and seemed more determined to keep an eye on the PLO. The March PLO-Syrian meetings in Damascus to develop a "basis for Syrian-Palestinian strategy" were a clear sign that Assad was determined to insure that PLO policies remained closely aligned with Syrain interests.[88]

Moreover, despite Arafat's success in gaining European support, the Europeans had not yet formulated a joint initiative acceptable to the PLO. Nor had the European campaign proved to be an effective way of influencing U.S. attitudes toward the PLO. France's efforts to improve relations with Israel and Mitterand's visit to Israel in March (the first by a French president) seemed to end hope for a unified "anti-Israel" European consensus. Despite Mitterand's call for a Palestinian state, PLO leaders bitterly criticized the visit and his statements calling on the PLO to recognize Israel.[89]

Developments on the West Bank also seemed particularly worrisome. Israel's banning of the National Guidance Committee, dismissal of three pro-PLO mayors, and Village League strategy indicated that the Begin government was determined to root out PLO influence in the occupied territories and create an alternative leadership more amenable to its interests. The PLO was doubtless encouraged by the West Bank response, the most violent demonstrations since 1976. But the Beirut leadership appeared fearful that Israel was laying the groundwork for eventual annexation of the territories.

Moreover, the PLO seemed unable to respond effectively to Israeli actions. Physically isolated from the West Bank and unable to promote an organized resistance, Arafat had little choice but to watch from the sidelines. The PLO moved to mobilize Arab and international opinion and issued a stream of "solidarity" communiques, but it could do little to challenge the Israelis. Fearful of giving the Israelis an excuse to move against PLO forces in Lebanon, Arafat even seemed reluctant to initiate military operations on the West Bank.

The PLO's credibility problem on the West Bank was highlighted by Jordan's efforts to increase its visibility. Apparently acting on its own, Jordan issued a decree on March 9, 1982, giving West Bankers one month to withdraw from the Village Leagues or be subject to prosecution for treason. The move, apparently designed to keep Hussein's hand in the West Bank pot, caught the PLO by surprise. Five days later a PLO official in Amman issued a short statement indicating that the Jordanian ultimatum was having a "positive" effect. Although the PLO and Jordan would coordinate their response to Israeli policies on the West Bank through the joint committee, Arafat was doubtless suspicious of King Hussein's motives. Nor could Arafat be happy with increasing activity of Islamic fundamentalists and communists in the territories, both potential threats to the PLO bid for leadership.

Finally, the PLO was facing the possibility of a large-scale Israeli attack into Lebanon. Throughout early 1982 the Israelis continued to warn of the consequences of a breakdown of the cease-fire in southern Lebanon—now nine months old. Indeed, Israel attempted to broaden the definition of what constituted a cease-fire violation and to lower the threshold for a military response. According to the new Israeli ambassador to the United States, Moshe Arens, if the Israelis were provoked and moved into Lebanon, "this might be the end of the PLO."[90]

The PLO Beyond West Beirut

The Israeli invasion of Lebanon appears to have temporarily weakened the internal and external constraints discussed above. Arafat remains the preeminent PLO leader and Fatah the dominant group. No other PLO group, including the PFLP, now has the resources or authority to seriously challenge his control. The creditability of those groups sponsored by or closely associated with Damascus has been weakened. The DFLP has once again decided that a tactical alliance with Fatah would probably best serve its interests. In the event Arafat finds a way to move the PLO into the negotiating process, the leverage of the smaller and more radical groups would be further reduced.

Moreover, although the PLO remains more dependent than ever on Arab support, it retains considerable room to maneuver. Syrian leverage is at its lowest point in almost a decade. Arafat is exploring the prospects of establishing a *modus vivendi* with King Hussein and cautiously calculating the benefits of pursuing improved ties with Egypt and perhaps even the United States. Arab moderates, concerned about the dangers of a more radicalized PLO, are lobbying the United States more intensely than ever to include the PLO in the negotiating process and to press Israel for concessions.

Nonetheless, the Israeli invasion has created new problems for the PLO that could easily threaten its newfound gains. Whether Arafat can effectively cope with the harsh realities created by the dispersal of PLO fighters and leaders from West Beirut will depend on his ability to manage the traditional Palestinian and Arab constraints and make concrete progress toward the establishment of a Palestinian state. All of this will hinge on the PLO's capacity to get into a negotiating process and to secure the support of the United States.

First, the loss of Lebanon as the PLO's primary base of operations will have a profound impact on the organization's tactics and strategy. The PLO's position in Lebanon was never really secure. Israeli and Syrian intervention and the cauldron of Lebanese factionalism were persistent threats. Nonetheless, in Lebanon the PLO developed an infrastructure and political/military organization that could never have evolved in any other Arab state. No Arab government will permit its new Palestinian guests to develop a military capability. This is particularly true the closer one gets to the confrontation line with Israel. All—the Egyptians, Jordanians, Syrians, and Lebanese—know the dangers of Israeli retaliation. Similarly, these states, particularly Syria, will work to insure that Palestinian political goals remain closely attuned to their respective national interests. Although out of Lebanon Arafat may have more independence from Damascus, he needs the Syrians to retain access to the 400,000 Palestinians in Lebanon (assuming the new Lebanese government allows them to remain) and maintain influence with the hard-line PLO groups based in Damascus. Moreover, Syria is still the only Arab state willing to risk military confrontation with Israel.

Second, the dispersal of PLO fighters and leaders throughout the Arab world will place tremendous strain on an organization already plagued by a lack of cohesion and unity. Even if PLO fighters now located in several Arab countries relocate, coordinating PLO policy and resources will be a major problem. Lacking a central base and an infrastructure it will be difficult for Arafat's Fatah organization— the largest and most powerful of the Palestinian groups—to use its direct control over financial and military resources to influence the other groups. Now more than ever, key Arab states, particularly the Syrians, will be able to maintain greater leverage over Palestinian elements residing in their countries. Similarly, Jordan's leverage with Arafat has now increased. The centrality of Jordan's role in U.S.

diplomacy as revealed in the Reagan peace initiative leaves Arafat no choice but to establish closer ties with King Hussein. The king needs Arafat as well, but the PLO may be forced to lower its expectations on an independent state and accept a confederal arrangement for the time being.

Third, if Arafat succeeds in getting the PLO into a negotiating framework and compromising on historic Palestinian demands, there is a good chance that the PLO could fragment. The largest groups will likely form around Arafat and those Fatah elements pushing political/diplomatic tactics; a second bloc of "independents" like the PFLP will continue to espouse armed struggle and maximalist goals and gravitate toward Syria; and a third group composed of elements like the Arab Liberation Front and Saiqa—wholly controlled subsidiaries of the Iraqi and Syrian regimes respectively—will follow the lines of their patrons. New Arab-sponsored Palestinian groups will likely emerge.

For now the PLO leadership will try to maintain unity and order in the ranks. Arafat's prestige within the Palestinian community is as high as ever. He is perceived as having resisted the might of the Israeli army and negotiated honorable terms for the pullout from West Beirut. Indeed, no other PLO leader or group appeared ready to assume the enormous responsibility for the Beirut siege and the survival of the PLO. Once the United States committed its resources to finding a negotiated settlement to the crisis, the PLO's politicians rather than its fighters took center stage. Only Arafat had the prestige and authority to become the PLO's chief negotiator.

Although developments at the September 1982 Fez summit appear to have strengthened Arafat's position within the movement and with regard to Syria, the road from Fez will not be easy. Arafat's continued authority will depend on whether he can translate the sympathy, prestige, and support generated by the Israeli attack into concrete gains, such as U.S. recognition and support. This, however, would require major Palestinian concessions. The post-Lebanon era may not be conducive to such changes. Now that the media coverage of the two-month-old siege of Beirut—and the subsequent massacre of Palestinians by Lebanese Christians—is fading and the PLO is on the road, the organization may well find itself embroiled in the recriminations and leadership crisis of the "who lost Lebanon debate." Indeed, without real progress toward a Palestinian state, the debate may ultimately focus on the wisdom of Arafat's approach to gaining a Palestinian state.

PLO hardliners, supported by Arab radicals, will be watching closely, eager to fill the gap should Arafat stumble. Their arguments will be strengthened considerably by the realities of a permanent Palestinian diaspora. Thus a new and uglier Palestinian phoenix—devoted to terrorism and the subversion of conservative Arab regimes—could ultimately emerge from the flames of West Beirut.

Notes

1. Gabriel Ben Dor, "Nationalism Without Sovereignty and Nationalism with Multiple Sovereignties: The Palestinians and Inter-Arab Relations," in Gabriel Ben Dor, ed., *The Palestinians and the Middle East Conflict* (Ramat Gan, Israel: Turtle Dove Publishing, 1978), pp. 143–163.

2. Malcolm H. Kerr, *The Arab Cold War, Gamal 'Abd al-Nassir and His Rivals, 1958–1970,* Third Edition (New York: Oxford University Press, 1971), pp. 133–153.

3. John W. Amos II, *Palestinian Resistance: Organization of a Nationalist Movement* (New York: Pergamon Press, 1980), pp. 99–110.

4. William B. Quandt, Fuad Jabber, and Ann Mosely Lesch, *The Politics of Palestinian Nationalism* (Berkeley: University of California Press, 1973), pp. 160–161.

5. See interview with Salah Khalaf, *Monday Morning,* October 5–11, 1981, vol. 10, no. 485, p. 30. Also interview with Yasir Arafat, *al-Hawadith,* January 8, 1982 (quoted in Foreign Broadcast Information Service, Middle East and Africa Daily Report, January 11, 1982—hereafter cited as *FBIS* and date).

6. *The Middle East,* no. 86 (December 1981), pp. 8–11. Also interview with Salah Khalaf, *The Middle East,* no. 87 (January 1982), pp. 27–28.

7. Michael Hudson, "The Palestinian Resistance Movement Since 1967," in Willard A. Beling, ed., *The Middle East: Quest for an American Policy* (Albany: State University of New York Press, 1973), pp. 101–125.

8. Bruce Stanley, "Fragmentation and National Liberation Movement: The PLO," in *Orbis* (Winter 1979), pp. 1033–1055.

9. Matti Steinberg, "The PLO and the Mini-Settlement," *The Jerusalem Quarterly,* no. 21 (Fall 1981), pp. 129–144. In April 1981 Fatah received an additional vote on the PLO/EC.

10. Michael Hudson, "The Palestinians: Retrospects and Prospect," *Current History* (January 1980), pp. 22–48.

11. Amos, *Palestinian Resistance,* p. 71.

12. Stanley, "Fragmentation and National Liberation Movement," pp. 1050–1055.

13. Ibid.

14. *New York Times,* February 19, 1979, p. 1. See also Arafat message to Khomeini, January 26, 1979, *Journal of Palestine Studies* (Spring 1979), pp. 169–170.

15. Voice of Palestine, February 22, 1979—quoted in *FBIS,* February 22, 1979.

16. *New York Times,* March 27, 1979, p. 1.

17. Tamar Yegnes, "Saudi Arabia and the Peace Process," *Jerusalem Quarterly*, no. 18 (Winter 1981), p. 118.

18. Voice of Palestine, June 2, 1979—quoted in *FBIS*, June 4, 1979.

19. *New York Times*, July 9, 1979. See also Kreisky and Arafat Joint Statement, July 8, 1979, *Journal of Palestine Studies*, August 1979, pp. 189–190.

20. *New York Times*, July 10, 1979.

21. *Washington Star*, August 12, 1979.

22. Joint Palestinian-Romanian Communique, August 26, 1979, *Journal of Palestine Studies* (Winter 1980), p. 165.

23. Voice of Palestine, August 19, 1979—quoted in *FBIS*, August 20, 1979.

24. *Middle East Intelligence Survey (MIS)*, August 16–31, 1979, vol. 7, no. 10.

25. *The Middle East*, no. 59 (September 1979), p. 11.

26. Amman Domestic Service, Arafat and Hussein Joint Statement, March 17, 1979—quoted in *FBIS*, March 19, 1979.

27. Amman Domestic Service, September 19, 1979—quoted in *FBIS*, September 20, 1979.

28. Joint Jordanian-French Communique, Amman Domestic Service, March 10, 1980—quoted in *FBIS*, March 11, 1980.

29. *MIS*, March 1–15, 1980, vol. 7, no. 23, pp. 181–182. See also Voice of Palestine, March 13, 1980; Arafat interview with *LeMonde* (March 9–10); *LeMatin* (March 11, 1980)—quoted in *FBIS*, March 14, 1980.

30. Kuwait KUNA, March 10, 1980—quoted in *FBIS*, March 12, 1980.

31. *New York Times*, June 14, 1980.

32. Joint PLO-Syrian Declaration, June 17, 1980, *Journal of Palestine Studies*, no. 37 (Autumn 1980), pp. 195–196. See also excerpts from Final Communique of the Special Session of the Arab Economic and Social Council, Amman, July 6–9, 1980, ibid., pp. 196–198.

33. See interviews with Arafat, *International Herald Tribune*, July 31, 1980, and *The Middle East*, no. 72 (October 1980), pp. 14–16.

34. *Jerusalem Post*, International Edition, August 24–30, 1980, p. 3. See also interview with Deputy Defense Minister Mordechai Zipori, ibid., September 14–20, 1980, p. 10.

35. Interview with Farouq Qaddumi, *The Middle East*, no. 71 (September 1980), pp. 16–17. See also *MIS*, August 16–31, 1980, vol. 8, no. 10.

36. Voice of Palestine, September 25, 1980—quoted in *FBIS*, September 26, 1980.

37. Tunis, TAP, October 20, 1980—quoted in *FBIS*, October 21, 1980. See also interview with Salah Khalaf, Kuwait *al-Watan*, October 14, 1980—quoted in *FBIS*, October 21, 1980.

38. *Jerusalem Post*, October 24, 1980. See also Kuwait KUNA, October 26, 1980—quoted in *FBIS*, October 27, 1980.

39. Voice of Palestine, November 24, 1980—quoted in *FBIS*, November 25, 1980.

40. Interview with Khalil al-Wazir, *The Middle East*, no. 75 (January 1981), p. 15. See also *New York Times*, November 25, 1980; *Washington Post*, November 25, 1980.

41. Voice of Palestine, November 14, 1980 and Amman *Ar-Ray*, November 14—quoted in *FBIS*, November 14, 1980.

42. Riyadh Domestic Service, November 18, 1980, and Riyadh SPA, November 17, 1980—quoted in *FBIS*, November 18, 1980.

43. Amman Domestic Service, November 25, 1980—quoted in *FBIS*, November 16, 1980. See also Final Statement, Amman Petra JNA, November 27, 1980—quoted in *FBIS*, November 28, 1980.

44. *Middle East Reporter*, November 22, 1980.

45. Kuwait KUNA, December 1, 1980—quoted in *FBIS*, December 2, 1980.

46. Damascus Domestic Service, December 4, 1980—quoted in *FBIS*, December 5, 1980.

47. Qaddumi interview, *Monday Morning*, vol. 10, no. 459 (6–12 April, 1981), p. 53.

48. Damascus Domestic Service, April 12, 1981—quoted in *FBIS*, April 13, 1981.

49. Final Political Statement, Voice of Palestine, April 21, 1981—quoted in *FBIS*, April 22, 1981.

50. *Monday Morning*, vol. 10, no. 465 (May 18–24, 1981), p. 16.

51. *Christian Science Monitor*, June 2, 1981.

52. Al-Fahum interview, London *al-Majallah*, May 30–June 5, 1981—quoted in *FBIS*, June 5, 1981.

53. Voice of Palestine, June 28, 1981—quoted in *FBIS*, July 29, 1981.

54. *Jerusalem Post*, July 20, 1981.

55. Arafat interview, *as-Safir* (Beirut), July 25, 1981—quoted in *FBIS*, July 29, 1981.

56. *The Middle East*, no. 83 (September 1981), pp. 11–13.

57. Ibid., p. 14–15.

58. *London Times*, August 7, 1981; *as-Safir* (Beirut), July 26, 1981—quoted in *FBIS*, July 28, 1981. See also *London Times*, July 28, 1981.

59. *Christian Science Monitor*, August 5, 1981.

60. *Washington Post*, September 13, 1981; *New York Times*, September 13, 1981.

61. Voice of Palestine, July 28, 1981—quoted in *FBIS*, July 29, 1981.

62. Voice of Palestine, July 28, 1981—quoted in *FBIS*, July 29, 1981.

63. *Christian Science Monitor*, August 5, 1981; *Washington Post*, September 13, 1981; *New York Times*, September 13, 1981; *The Middle East*, no. 81 (July 1981), p. 15.

64. *The Middle East*, no. 80 (June 1981), p. 115.

65. Voice of Palestine, August 30, 1981—quoted in *FBIS*, August 31, 1981; Monte Carlo Radio, September 10, 1981—quoted in *FBIS*, September 11, 1981.

66. *Washington Post*, September 13, 1981; *Monday Morning*, vol. 10, no. 481 (September 7–13, 1981), pp. 42–44.

67. *Monday Morning*, vol. 10, no. 486 (October 12–18, 1981), p. 19; Voice of Palestine, October 6, 1981—quoted in *FBIS*, October 7, 1981; PLO statement issued on behalf of Arafat, October 6, 1981—quoted in *FBIS*, October 7, 1981.

68. Voice of Palestine, October 12, 1981—quoted in *FBIS*, October 13, 1981.

69. Arafat's meetings with Japanese parliamentarians, business leaders, prime minister, and foreign minister, Tokyo KYODO, October 13, 1981—quoted in *FBIS*, Asia and Pacific Daily Report, October 19, 1981.

70. *Monday Morning*, vol. 10, no. 487 (October 19–25, 1981), p. 67.

71. Galia Golan, *The Soviet Union and the Palestine Liberation Organization: An Uneasy Alliance* (New York: Praeger, 1980), pp. 9–14.

72. Voice of Palestine, October 21, 1981—quoted in *FBIS*, October 22, 1981; *Monday Morning*, vol. 10, no. 488 (October 26–November 1, 1981), pp. 30–33.

73. Voice of Palestine, October 24, 1981—quoted in *FBIS*, October 26, 1981; Athens Domestic Service, December 16, 1981—quoted in *FBIS*, December 17, 1981; *FBIS* Daily Report Western Europe, December 17, 1981; *Monday Morning*, vol. 10, no. 496 (December 21–27, 1981), pp. 38–39.

74. Monte Carlo Radio, August 8, 1981—quoted in *FBIS*, August 11, 1981.

75. Cairo MENA, August 13, 1981—quoted in *FBIS*, August 14, 1981.

76. See George Rentz, "The Fahd Peace Plan," *Middle East Insight*, vol. 2, no. 2 (Jan./Feb. 1981), pp. 21–24.

77. Tokyo NHK Television Network, October 12, 1981—quoted in *FBIS*, October 14, 1981.

78. *as-Safir* (Beirut), October 15, 1981.

79. *Monday Morning*, vol. 10, no. 487 (October 19–25, 1981), p. 41.

80. Arafat interview, *an-Nahar* (Beirut), October 31, 1981—quoted in *FBIS*, November 3, 1981.

81. *al-Hurriyah* (Beirut), November 9, 1981. See also Beirut Domestic Service, November 15, 1981—quoted in *FBIS*, November 16, 1981.

82. *New York Times*, November 26, 1981, November 27, 1981; *The Middle East*, no. 85 (November 1981), pp. 9–10.

83. *LeMonde* (Paris), November 27, 1981; Kuwait KUNA, November 27, 1981—quoted in *FBIS*, November 30, 1981.

84. Khalaf interview, Paris *Le Matin*, March 9, 1981—quoted in *FBIS*, March 15, 1982; *The Middle East*, no. 87 (January 1982), pp. 13–15.

85. *Sunday Times* (London), January 24, 1982.

86. Arafat interview, *Time Magazine*, February 8, 1982; *al-Hawadith* (London) January 8, 1982—quoted in *FBIS*, January 11, 1982; Budapest Domestic Television Service, February 7, 1982—quoted in *FBIS*, February 11, 1982.

87. Kamal Hasan Ali interview, Jerusalem Domestic Service, January 23, 1982—quoted in *FBIS*, January 25, 1982; see also Mubarak questions and

answers before National Press Club, Cairo, MENA, February 5, 1982—quoted in *FBIS*, February 8, 1962.

88. Voice of Palestine, March 1, 1982—quoted in *FBIS*, March 2, 1982; *as-Safir* (Beirut), March 3, 1982—quoted in *FBIS*, March 9, 1982.

89. Voice of Palestine, Statements of Salah Khalaf (March 5), Abu Mayzar (March 7)—quoted in *FBIS*, March 8, 1981.

90. Tel-Aviv *Yediot Aharonot*, February 25, 1982; Jerusalem Domestic Service, February 24, 1982—quoted in *FBIS*, February 25, 1982.

Focus Lebanon: The Middle East, January–October 1983

Robert O. Freedman

By January 1983, the initial shock of the Israeli invasion of Lebanon had worn off and the nations and peoples of the Middle East were seeking ways to adjust to the new realities caused by the invasion. To be sure, some things had not changed very much. The Iran-Iraq war continued to rage through 1983, and the oil spill created by the war threatened to cause lasting damage to the Gulf.[1] While Iran remained on the offensive, Iraq threatened to use newly acquired French planes to destroy Iranian oil installations, a threat that brought a counter-threat from Iran that it would close the Straits of Hormuz in retaliation. The Iranian threat, in turn, brought a warning from the United States that it would act to keep the Straits open if Iran tried to close them. The series of threats and counter-threats reflected growing frustration, especially on the Iraqi side, as the war continued with no end in sight. Despite the tension over Iran's threats to close the Gulf, there was a marginal improvement in Iranian-U.S. relations in 1983 as trade increased[2] and more U.S. banks reached settlements with Iran. Meanwhile, Soviet-Iranian relations deteriorated as the Iranian government cracked down on the pro-Soviet Iranian Communist party, the Tudeh, extracting from its leader, Nuredin Kianouri, a public confession of treason, while also expelling eighteen Soviet diplomats.[3]

On the other side of the Middle East, tension rose again in North Africa. Despite meetings between King Hassan of Morocco and the leaders of Algeria and Libya, Moroccan forces again engaged the Polisario guerrillas in major battles, and a peace settlement in that long-standing conflict over the former Spanish Sahara seemed as far off as ever. In addition, there was a recurrence of tension between Libya and the United States. In February, the United States dispatched

AWACS aircraft to the Sudan in response to an alleged Libyan-supported plot to overthrow the Sudanese government. During the summer a major airlift of U.S. military equipment was undertaken to Chad, an action joined by France, which supplied not only equipment but also French troops to help the regime of Hassan Habré in its battles against the Libyan-supported forces of Habré's old enemy Goukouni Oueddi, which had seized the northern section of the country by the end of August.

Although the conflicts in North Africa and the Gulf long predated the Israeli invasion of Lebanon, it was the aftermath of the invasion that dominated Middle Eastern events from January to October 1983. The first major impact of the invasion was felt in Israel. On February 8, 1983, the Kahan Commission—which had come into being as a result of intense public pressure on the Begin government to investigate Israel's involvement in the Sabra and Shatilla massacres—issued its report. The report concluded that direct responsibility for the acts of slaughter rested with the Christian Phalange (Maronite) Lebanese troops who "were steeped in hatred for the Palestinians in the wake of the atrocities and severe injuries done to the Christians during the civil war in Lebanon by the Palestinians and those who fought alongside them and these feelings were compounded by a longing for revenge in the wake of the assassination of the Phalangist's admired leader Bashir [Gemayel] and the killing of several dozen Phalangists two days before their entry into the camps."[4] While the Kahan Commission found the Christian Phalange directly responsible for the massacres, it found that Israeli officers were indirectly responsible for (1) allowing the Phalange into the camps without seriously considering the possibility of a massacre taking place; (2) improperly supervising the Phalange whose purpose was supposed to be the uncovering and identifying of PLO terrorists hiding in the camps; and (3) not reacting quickly to stop the massacres when the first reports of the atrocities began to arrive. Primary indirect responsibility was given to Defense Minister Ariel Sharon, and the commission recommended that he be removed as defense minister. Israeli Chief of Staff Rafael Eitan also received a major share of the indirect blame for the massacres, but the commission did not recommend his removal from office since he was due to retire two months after the issuance of the report. The commission did recommend the removal from office of two other officers: the chief of military intelligence, Major General Yehoshua Saguy, and the commander of Israeli forces in the Beirut area, Brigadier General Amos Yaron. It also found Foreign Minister Yitzhak Shamir at fault for not paying sufficient attention to a report from a fellow cabinet minister that a massacre was taking place; Israeli Prime Minister

Begin was also criticized for not being sufficiently interested in Phalangist activities in the camps.

Following the release of the report, the Israeli cabinet met in continuous session as pro-Sharon forces harassed an anti-Sharon protest march organized by Israel's Peace Now movement. Indeed the clashes grew so violent that an anti-Sharon demonstrator, Emil Grunzweig of Peace Now, was killed and eight other Peace Now demonstrators (including the son of Israeli Interior Minister Yosef Burg) were wounded by a hand grenade. The next day the cabinet voted 16-1 to accept the Kahan Commission recommendation that Sharon and the two generals be removed from their posts. Sharon was replaced as defense minister by Moshe Arens, although Begin was to keep the ex-defense minister in the cabinet as minister without portfolio. While Begin's retention of Sharon was bitterly attacked by opposition parties, the prime minister was able to win three no-confidence votes in the Knesset by votes of 64-56. Nonetheless, Sharon's influence in the government diminished rapidly and in mid-July, following the cabinet's defeat of his call for an inquiry into the government's conduct of the Lebanese war, there were rumors in the Israeli press that he was considering resigning from the cabinet.

As Israel was adjusting politically to the Kahan Commission's report, the PLO was beset by conflict. Yasser Arafat, who had been meeting with King Hussein and flirting with the Reagan plan, was now under attack from opponents within the PLO, and both Syria and Libya actively sought to undermine Arafat's position. The efforts of the anti-Arafat forces were to prove successful as the Palestine National Council, which after a number of postponements finally convened in mid-February in Algiers, formally stated its refusal to consider the Reagan plan "as a sound basis for a just and lasting solution to the Palestine problem and the Arab-Israeli conflict."[5] The Soviet Union was also pleased with this development; *Pravda* correspondent Yuri Valdimirov praised the council's policy document as a reaffirmation of the organization's determination to continue the struggle against imperialism and Zionism.[6]

As sentiment within the PLO hardened against the Reagan plan, King Hussein of Jordan, who on January 10 had stated that he would make his decision about joining peace talks with Israel by March 1, began to back away. Indeed, on March 19, after delaying any official statement, the king indicated during a visit to London, that unless the United States succeeded in getting all of the foreign troops out of Lebanon and got Israel to stop building settlements on the West Bank, the talks could not get started.[7] Under these circumstances, the United States stepped up its efforts to keep the Reagan plan alive.

Thus President Reagan tied the sale to Israel of seventy-five F-16 fighter bombers to an Israeli agreement to withdraw from Lebanon and promised King Hussein that if Jordan joined the Middle East peace talks, the United States would try to bring about a halt to the building of Israeli settlements on the West Bank.[8]

Despite these U.S. actions, by the end of March it appeared that the Reagan plan was in deep trouble. On March 30, Arafat himself rejected the Reagan plan at a Palestinian rally in Damascus.[9] The Arafat rejection cast a predictable pall on the final round of Arafat-Hussein talks in Jordan and it was not surprising that on April 10 King Hussein, claiming that Arafat had reneged on an earlier agreement, stated that Jordan would not enter into the peace negotiations.[10] Hussein's statement was greeted with great relief by Soviet leaders, who had long feared that Jordan would be attracted to the Reagan plan, which they saw as an extension of Camp David.[11]

Meanwhile, as the Reagan plan was faltering—a development that weakened U.S. influence in the Middle East—Moscow was seeking to improve its position in the region by issuing a public warning to Israel not to attack Syria. The Soviet warning, issued on March 30 after a series of Syrian warnings, was limited in nature: Moscow warned that Israel was "playing with fire" by preparing to attack Syria, but it made no mention of the Soviet-Syrian treaty. Indeed, in listing those on Syria's side in the confrontation with Israel, the Soviet statement merely noted "on the side of the Syrian people are Arab patriots, the Socialist countries, and all who cherish the cause of peace, justice and honor." The statement also emphasized the need to settle the Arab-Israeli conflict politically, not through war.[12]

This rather curious Soviet warning can perhaps be understood if one assumes that Moscow did not seriously expect an Israeli attack on Syria. With the more cautious Moshe Arens as Israel's new defense minister and with rising opposition to Israel's presence in Lebanon being felt in Israel's domestic political scene, it appeared unlikely that Israel would attack Syria, even to take out the newly installed SAM-5 missiles. Indeed, even the hawkish Israeli chief of staff, General Eitan, stated in an interview on Israeli armed forces radio that Israel had no intention of starting a war.[13] If Moscow, therefore, basically assumed that Israel would not go to war, then why the warning? Given the fact that Moscow's credibility in the Arab world had dropped precipitously as a result of the warnings it had issued during the Israeli invasion of Lebanon in the June–July 1982 period—warnings that had been ignored by both Israel and the United States—Moscow possibly saw a chance to increase its credibility in the region. Thus if Moscow, assuming Israel would not attack Syria, issued a warning to Israel not to attack Syria and Israel then did not attack Syria, Moscow could take credit for the non-attack and thus demonstrate to the Arab world that Soviet diplomacy was effective vis-à-vis Israel, at least as a deterrent. If this, in fact, was Moscow's thinking, however, not all the Arabs were to be convinced. Indeed, the Saudi paper *Ar-Riyad* expressed a lack of trust in the Soviet warning, noting that the limited value of Soviet statements had been proven during the Israeli invasion of Lebanon "which dealt a sharp and severe blow to the Kremlin when the Soviet missiles became no more than timber towers in the face of the sophisticated weapons the United States had unconditionally supplied to Israel."[14]

In any case, only three days after the Soviet warning to Israel, Soviet Foreign Minister Andrei Gromyko, who had recently been promoted to deputy prime minister, held a major press conference in Moscow.[15] While the main emphasis of Gromyko's press conference was on strategic arms issues, he also took the opportunity to make two major points about the Middle Eastern situation. First, Gromyko, in responding to a question from a correspondent of the Syrian newspaper *Al-Ba'ath,* stated that "the Soviet Union is in favor of the withdrawal of all foreign troops from the territory of Lebanon, all of them. Syria is in favor of this."[16] Second, Gromyko noted once again that the USSR was in favor of Israel existing as a state: "We do not share the point of view of extremist Arab circles that Israel should be eliminated. This is an unrealistic and unjust point of view."[17] The thrust of Gromyko's remarks were clear. The Soviet leader, by urging the withdrawal of all foreign troops from Lebanon—including Syrian troops—and re-emphasizing the Soviet commitment to Israel's existence, seemed to be telling Syria that despite the provision of SAM-5 missiles, Moscow did not want to be dragged into a war in Lebanon on Syria's behalf. If this was indeed the message Gromyko was trying to get across, the rapid pace of Middle Eastern events was soon to pose additional problems for the Soviet strategy, and Moscow was later to change its position on a Syrian troop withdrawal. One week after King Hussein had announced his refusal to enter into peace negotiations, the U.S. Embassy in Beirut was blown up by a car-bomb, with a massive loss of life. Reacting to both events, President Reagan dispatched his Secretary of State George Shultz to salvage the stalled Israeli-Lebanese talks and regain the momentum for the United States in Middle East diplomacy. As Shultz toured the region and shuttled back and forth between Beirut and Jerusalem, prospects for a Lebanese-Israeli agreement began to improve. Both Moscow and Damascus, for different reasons, wanted to see the Shultz mission fail. The USSR did not want to see any more Arab states following in

Egypt's footsteps and agreeing to a U.S. plan for Middle East peace. Syria, for its part, had long sought the dominant position in Lebanon and feared that any Lebanese-Israeli agreement would strengthen the Israeli position in Lebanon at Syria's expense. In addition, Syria also did not wish to see any more Arab states moving to make peace with Israel, since this would leave Syria increasingly isolated among the Arab confrontation states facing Israel. (In January, Syria had joined Libya and Iran in a call for the overthrow of Saddam Hussein's regime in Iraq—a move further isolating the Syrians from the Gulf Arabs.) The end result was a rise in tension and yet another war scare in which Moscow was to play a role, albeit perhaps a somewhat unwilling one.

Less than a week after King Hussein refused to enter the peace talks, the Syrian government raised its price for a Lebanese troop withdrawal. As late as March Syria had been willing to have a simultaneous withdrawal of Israeli, Syrian, and PLO forces, but on April 16 the Syrian government newspaper *Tishrin* stated that Syria would not even discuss the withdrawal of its troops from Lebanon until all Israeli troops had left the country.[18] The United States, which somewhat naively had expected a Syrian withdrawal as soon as Israel agreed to one, now sought to assuage Syrian opposition in a letter from Reagan to Assad in which the U.S. president indicated that the United States was still pressing for Israeli withdrawal from the Golan Heights.[19] The U.S. ploy, however, was not successful. Indeed, Syria appeared to step up tension by allowing guerrillas to infiltrate into Israeli lines to attack Israeli troops while simultaneously accusing the Israeli government of reinforcing its troops in Lebanon's Bekaa Valley and of staging "provocative" military exercises on the Golan Heights.[20] Meanwhile although Israeli Foreign Minister Shamir called the Syrian-induced tension "artificial,"[21] Israeli Defense Minister Arens, concerned about Soviet and Syrian intentions, put Israeli troops on alert and indicated that Israel would not leave Lebanon until Syria did.[22] Syria then stepped up its pressure: On April 26, Syrian forces opened fire on an Israeli bulldozer near the ceasefire line.[23]

Meanwhile, despite the rise in Syrian-Israeli tension, U.S. Secretary of State Shultz continued to work for an Israeli-Lebanese troop withdrawal agreement; in mid-May his efforts were crowned with success as the Israeli government accepted a troop withdrawal agreement that had already been agreed to by Lebanon. Israel's minimum aim in the invasion of Lebanon had been to secure a PLO-free 45-kilometer security zone on its northern border, while its maximum aims included the establishment of a strong pro-Israel central government in Lebanon and the expulsion of both the PLO and Syria from Lebanon. By May 1983, however, Israel found that its maximum goals did not appear attainable. The Christian Phalange–dominated government of Lebanon successively alienated Lebanon's Sunni, Shii, and Druze communities and as a result found it difficult to extend its authority past the city of Beirut.

In addition, the intercommunal warfare that had plagued Lebanon for more than one hundred years erupted once again and Israeli forces often found themselves in a crossfire between warring Christian and Moslem forces, as well as under direct attack from leftist and PLO guerrillas, who took an increasing toll in Israeli lives. As a result of these developments there was increasing opposition within Israel to a continued military presence in Lebanon, not only from such organizations as Peace Now, but also from military reservists (some of whom refused to serve in Lebanon), parents of soldiers, and also members of the Israeli parliament. As a consequence of such pressure, along with the disillusionment over the whole Lebanese affair (which had been reinforced by the report of the Kahan Commission) and active U.S. pressure as well, the Begin government sought during the first four months of 1983 to achieve at least its minimum goal—a security zone on its northern border—in negotiations with the representatives of Lebanese President Amin Gemayel. The end result of the U.S.-mediated negotiations was the Lebanese-Israeli troop withdrawal agreement of May 17, 1983.[24] While far less than Israel had hoped for in the aftermath of the PLO exodus from Beirut and far from the trade, cultural and diplomatic relations achieved in the Israeli-Egyptian Peace Treaty of 1979, Israel did achieve certain benefits. These included (1) a formal end to the state of war between Israel and Lebanon; (2) Lebanon's agreement not to permit its territory to be used as a base for terrorist activity against Israel (Lebanon thereby, in effect, abrogated the 1969 Cairo agreement that gave the PLO the right to use Lebanese bases for attacks on Israel); (3) the end to hostile Lebanese propaganda against Israel; (4) Lebanon's refusal to allow forces hostile to Israel (such as Syria) to enter into or deploy their forces on Lebanese soil against Israel; (5) a security zone in south Lebanon running between 20 and 37 miles north of Israel's northern border in which only two Lebanese brigades with limited arms could be stationed and in which up to eight joint Israeli-Lebanese "supervisory teams" could move freely, operating from two bases in the region, to check for terrorist activity; (6) a role for the forces of Israeli-supported Lebanese Major Sa'ad Hadad in one of the two Lebanese brigades stationed in the security zone; and (7) a joint liaison committee, including the United States as a participant, to oversee the carrying out of the agreement.

The next U.S. goal was to try to gain Arab support for the agreement to pressure Syria into withdrawing its forces from Lebanon since Israel refused to carry out the withdrawal provisions of the agreement unless Syria agreed to withdraw simultaneously. As might be expected, neither Moscow nor Syria was in favor of a rapid Syrian withdrawal. Moscow, although interested in Syria ultimately withdrawing its troops from Lebanon, did not want too hasty a withdrawal in the aftermath of the Israeli-Lebanese agreement lest the United States reap the diplomatic benefit. Syria, for its part, complained that Israel had gotten too much from the treaty and Damascus Radio asserted that Lebanon had "capitulated to the Israeli aggressor."[25] Indeed, Assad was soon to precipitate yet another mini-crisis over Lebanon, although it remained unclear whether Syria would continue to oppose the withdrawal of its own troops on principle, or whether President Assad was posturing so as to improve his bargaining position vis-à-vis Lebanon (so he could get a better deal than Israel did), vis-à-vis the Arab world (Syria, long isolated because of its support of Iran in the Iran-Iraq war was now openly confronting Israel and should, thereby, merit Arab support), and vis-à-vis the United States (so as to get U.S. pressure on Israel for a withdrawal from the Golan Heights). Indeed, as the crisis was played out until the end of May, with military maneuvers and threats of war (almost all from the Syrians), it appeared as if Assad were enjoying the opportunity to play a major role once again in Middle East events.

As Syria was exploiting the Lebanese situation for its own ends, Moscow was cautiously supporting its Arab ally. Thus on May 9, three days after Israel had first agreed in principle to the agreement, the Soviet Union issued an official statement denouncing the agreement and in a gesture of support for Syria demanded that "first and foremost" Israeli troops be withdrawn from Lebanon. The statement added, however, that "American and other foreign troops staying in Lebanon also must be withdrawn from it,"[26] an oblique reference to Moscow's continuing desire to see Syrian troops leave the country. At the same time, perhaps to enhance the atmosphere of crisis, Soviet dependents were withdrawn from Beirut, although the Soviet ambassador to Lebanon stated that the departure of the dependents was just to allow them to begin summer camp in the USSR.[27] In helping to enhance the atmosphere of crisis, Moscow may also have seen that the situation could be used as a means of once again playing a role in the Middle East peace process after having been kept on the diplomatic sidelines since Sadat's trip to Jerusalem in 1977. Indeed, on May 10, Shultz openly urged Moscow to use its influence to get Syria to withdraw its troops and stated he might meet Soviet Foreign

Minister Gromyko to discuss the Middle East along with other international issues.[28] Shultz, however, indicated that the United States was not yet ready for an international conference on the Middle East, still a goal of Soviet diplomacy.[29]

Nonetheless, even in giving Syria a limited degree of support, Moscow had to be concerned about the possibility of war erupting, especially as Syria began to issue increasingly bellicose threats—threats that involved Soviet support for Syria in case of war. Thus on May 9, Syrian Foreign Minister Khaddam noted in an interview that if war broke out between Israel and Syria, "We believe that the USSR will fulfill its commitments in accordance with the [Soviet-Syrian] treaty."[30] The next day, Syrian Radio warned that any Israeli attack against Syrian forces anywhere, even in Lebanon, would mean an "unlimited war."[31] The Syrian bellicosity, however, may have overstepped the bounds of propriety insofar as Moscow was concerned. Thus in a broadcast over Beirut Radio, Soviet Ambassador to Lebanon Alexander Soldatov, when asked about Khaddam's assertion that Moscow would fully support Syria if war with Israel broke out, replied that "the USSR does not reply to such hypothetical questions." Soldatov added that the USSR continued to support the withdrawal of all foreign forces from Lebanon.[32] These themes of caution were repeated during the visit of a Soviet delegation to Israel in mid-May to attend ceremonies marking the 38th anniversary of the defeat of Nazi Germany. One of the leaders of the delegation, the well-known Soviet journalist Igor Belayev, took the opportunity to state upon arrival at Ben Gurion Airport that Syria's recent military moves in the Bekaa Valley were purely defensive and that Syria had no aggressive intent toward Israel.[33] Similarly, Karen Khachaturev, deputy director of the *Novosti* news agency, noted that the USSR favored a peace treaty between Israel and Lebanon (but only after all Israeli soldiers departed) and reiterated Moscow's support of Israel's right to live in peace and security.[34]

While Moscow was trying to play down the possibility of war, U.S. Secretary of Defense Caspar Weinberger, in a speech to the American Jewish Committee in New York, was publicly warning Moscow about its behavior in Lebanon: "I want to say that the USSR is making a profound and dangerous mistake if it thinks that by resorting to belligerent words and provocative actions, by the obstruction of the Lebanese peace process, it can pressure the United States into a retreat from its commitment to the security of Israel."[35] Weinberger added, during the question and answer period following his lecture, "I want to make it very clear to the Soviets and any proxies they might have in Syria that any aggression by them would be met by a retaliatory force that would make the aggression totally unworthwhile, totally lacking in any hope of gain to the aggressor."[36] While the State Department sought to somewhat tone down Weinberger's remarks several days later,[37] there was no question that the U.S. commitment to Israel remained strong. Indeed, following Israel's signing of the U.S.-mediated agreement with Lebanon, U.S.-Israeli relations improved markedly and the U.S. government decided to release the seventy-five F-16 fighter bombers for sale to Israel.

As might be expected, Moscow seized on Weinberger's comments and the end of the F-16 embargo to highlight the Israeli-U.S. relationship and to underline the close relationship between Israel, "an occupier of Arab lands," and the United States.[38] This was part of Moscow's efforts to try to prevent an Arab consensus from building up behind the Israeli-Lebanese accord. Indeed, Moscow hailed the statement by Saudi Defense Minister Prince Sultan Ibn Abd al Aziz that his country refused to put pressure on Syria on behalf of the United States.[39]

Meanwhile, Syria continued to escalate its political and military pressure to undermine the Israeli-Lebanese agreement. On the political front it formed an alignment (later to be called the National Salvation Front) with a group of Lebanese leaders opposed to the agreement and to the policies of the Gemayel government, including former Lebanese Premier Rashid Karami, former President Suleiman Franjieh, Druze leader Walid Jumblatt, and Lebanese Communist party First Secretary George Hawi.[40] At the same time Assad moved to support the revolt in Fatah that took place in the latter part of May against Arafat's leadership. The rebel leader, Abu Musa, was a hard liner who vehemently opposed any settlement with Israel and was outspoken in his opposition to a Jordanian-PLO negotiating arrangement. Initially Libya gave even stronger support for the anti-Arafat uprising that took place in the Syrian-controlled Bekaa Valley of Lebanon than did Syria, but it soon became clear that Assad was utilizing the revolt within Fatah to try to bring the PLO under Syrian control once and for all.

While moving to strengthen his political position by encouraging an anti-Arafat movement in Fatah, Assad also stepped up the political and military pressure in the Bekaa. After refusing to see U.S. Envoy Philip Habib, Assad, on May 23, predicted a new war with Israel in which Syria would lose 20,000 men.[41] Two days later Syrian planes fired air-to-air missiles against Israeli jets flying over the Bekaa Valley— the first such encounter since the war in 1982.[42] Assad followed this up by conducting military exercises in the Golan and Bekaa, and the danger of war appeared to heighten.[43] Nonetheless, despite a limited countermobilization, Israel kept cool during the crisis, while for its part Moscow kept a low profile, supporting Syria politically but issuing no threats against the United States or Israel and again appealing for a full withdrawal of all forces from Lebanon. In any case, by the end of May the crisis had subsided and the dangers of a Syrian-Israeli war in Lebanon had been replaced in the headlines by the growing revolt in the PLO against Arafat's leadership.

The revolt against Arafat underlined the PLO leader's weakened position in the aftermath of the Israeli invasion of Lebanon, which had eliminated his main base of operations. Although Arafat was supported by the bulk of Palestinians living outside Syria and Syrian-controlled regions in Lebanon and both Iraq and Algeria gave him support in the Arab world's diplomatic arena, he had no real power to resist Syria's crackdown against him. Thus, as the summer wore on, the positions of Arafat's supporters in the Bekaa Valley were overrun, and Arafat himself was expelled from Syria. In early August, the Palestine Central Council, meeting in Tunis, called for an "immediate dialogue" to rebuild relations with Syria,[44] but this effort, along with others attempted during the summer, proved to no avail and in early September Arafat admitted that all attempts at negotiations with Syria had failed.[45]

As Syria was cracking down on the PLO, Egypt was taking another step out of its position of isolation in the Arab world. In early July, Iraqi Foreign Minister Tariq Aziz made an official visit to Cairo— the first such official visit by a high-ranking leader of a major Arab power since the Egyptian-Israeli treaty.[46] While no decision on the resumption of formal diplomatic relations was made, this visit reflected the growing link between Egypt and the country that had hosted the Arab League meeting responsible for expelling Egypt in 1979.

As relations with Iraq improved (Iraq continued to need Egyptian military assistance in its war against Iran), Egypt maintained its close relationship with the United States, although Mubarak kept it in a lower profile than had Sadat. During the summer of 1983, there was another major U.S.-Egyptian military exercise (although Egypt placed a virtual news blackout on it) and Mubarak visited the United States in September. In addition the United States continued to supply Egypt with large amounts of military and economic assistance and promised to give Egypt $100 million in economic aid to complete the fourth unit of a 600-megawatt power plant. While there were some disagreements over the Ras Banas RDF facility and over Egyptian-Israeli ties, on balance Egyptian-U.S. relations remained strong, in sharp contrast to the continued strain in relations between the Soviet Union and Egypt. Although a Soviet-Egyptian economic protocol was signed, Mubarak remained unhappy about Soviet assistance to Libya and what he saw as Soviet-inspired leftist movements in Egypt.[47]

If Soviet-Egyptian relations remained strained, Egypt's ties with Israel were distinctly cool. The Egyptian ambassador, who had been recalled following the Sabra and Shatilla massacres did not return to his post despite an Egyptian promise (to the United States) that if Israel signed the withdrawal agreement with Lebanon, the Egyptian ambassador would return to Israel. Indeed, Egypt demanded the total withdrawal of Israeli forces from Lebanon before the ambassador would return.[48] Nonetheless, Egypt continued to observe the letter of the 1979 treaty if not the spirit, and the Israeli-Egyptian border remained peaceful although both countries continued to claim the area of Taba, near Israel's Red Sea port of Eilat. In addition, tourism continued between the two countires, albeit at a reduced level; daily airline service was maintained; both embassies remained open and functioning; Egypt continued its oil sales (40,000 barrels per day); the police services of the two countries continued to cooperate; Israel accepted Egypt's offer to help renovate the Hassan-Bek Mosque in Jaffa; and Israel's energy minister, Yitzhak Moda'i, paid an official three-day visit to Egypt. On numerous occasions, Egyptian President Hosni Mubarak reiterated his commitment to the Egyptian-Israeli peace treaty and urged other Arab countries to follow Egypt's example and make peace with Israel, although he strongly condemned Israel's West Bank settlement policies and urged Israel to permit the Palestinians to exercise their "legitimate national rights."

While Israel was contending with a chill in its relations with Egypt, it was also agonizing over its policy in Lebanon. As clashes between Maronites and Druze in the Israeli-controlled Chouf Mountains became more intense, there were increasing calls within Israel for a withdrawal from the Chouf Mountains to a more easily supplied and defended line along the Awali River. Although the Lebanese government complained, fearing that the Israeli action might lead to the partition of Lebanon between Israel and Syria, Israel nonetheless moved ahead with its plan for redeployment stating that it was the first step toward a total withdrawal from Lebanon. Israel also advised the Lebanese government to reach agreement with its Druze community before moving forces into the Druze-dominated Chouf, lest bloodshed result— a concern also voiced by Israel's Druze minority, which expressed deep concern about its coreligionists in Lebanon and asked the Israeli government to secure their welfare.

The Gemayel government, however, proved unwilling—or unable—to make the necessary concessions to either its Druze or Shii communities and as the time neared for the Israeli deployment there was widespread expectation that war would break out upon the Israeli withdrawal. Indeed, Special U.S. Middle East Envoy Robert McFarlane, who had replaced Philip Habib when the latter lost his diplomatic entré to Damascus, appealed to the Israelis on several occasions during the summer to delay their redeployment until a political settlement could be negotiated. While the Israelis did, in fact, delay their redeployment in response to the U.S. requests, the sudden resignation of Israeli Prime Minister Menahem Begin at the end of August set the stage for the redeployment of Israeli forces in early September. (Begin was replaced by Foreign Minister Yitzhak Shamir following a vote by the Likud party and confirmation by the Israeli Parliament. Shamir assembled a governing coalition almost identical to Begin's, although his finance minister, Yoram Aridor, was to resign in mid-October because of the economic crisis that his policies, in large part, had caused.)

The Israeli redeployment, which took place during the evening of September 3, was preceded by open warfare between the Lebanese government and the Shiites of West Beirut, who resisted a Lebanese army push into their neighborhoods on August 30 and 31. The scale of fighting escalated sharply, however, after the Israeli redeployment with Syrian-supported Druze forces clashing with both the Maronite (Phalange) militia and the Lebanese army. While the Phalangist forces were quickly driven from the Chouf Mountains, the Lebanese army proved a tougher opponent for the Druze and a battle was fought for several weeks over the strategic mountain town of Souk el-Gharb, which overlooked Beirut. While Israel held off from intervening because of pressure from its Druze minority and because of assurances from Druze leader Walid Jumblatt that he would not permit the PLO to occupy positions in Druze-controlled areas, the United States decided to play an active role in the fighting in support of the Lebanese army, which it had trained. U.S. involvement in the conflict had actually begun before the Israeli withdrawal, as U.S. helicopters had fired on sniper and mortar positions that had harassed U.S. Marines. The U.S. role escalated during the fighting in the Chouf as guns from U.S. warships in Beirut harbor were fired in support of Lebanese army troops fighting in Souk el-Gharb[49] and against artillery positions that were firing on or near U.S. positions.[50] After holding aloof from the fighting, France also got involved when its forces came under fire.[51] As the fighting escalated, Syria felt constrained to issue threats against the United States to back up its clients in the Chouf Mountains,[52] particularly as the U.S. battleship *New Jersey*, whose 16-inch guns had the capability of seriously damaging Syrian positions, neared Beirut. Meanwhile, the Soviet Union, which had issued ritual denunciations of U.S. activity in the fighting, had to be concerned about the possibility of a major Syrian-U.S. confrontation over Lebanon. Fortunately for Moscow, however, a ceasefire agreement was reached late in September[53] that seemed to avert, at least temporarily, the possibility of a further escalation of the fighting.[54] Nonetheless, Syrian President Assad was to exploit the interval between the ceasefire and the start of national unity talks among Lebanon's many contending factions (October 31) to further crackdown on the PLO. After engineering a series of defections within Fatah groups loyal to Arafat, Assad forced the remaining loyalists to leave their positions in the Bekaa Valley and journey over the mountains to the Lebanese city of Tripoli where Arafat had suddenly appeared in mid-September. For his part, Arafat (whose position in Tripoli under the shadow of Syrian artillery was tenuous at best and who soon found his forces in the Tripoli area under attack by Syrian-backed Fatah rebels) once again sought room for diplomatic maneuver.[55] The PLO leader called for a resumption of the Jordanian-Palestinian dialogue, thus responding to an initiative from King Hussein, who had sent his foreign minister and minister for (Israeli) "occupied areas" to meet Arafat in Tunis in late August.[56]

The start of the Lebanese National Unity talks in Geneva, Switzerland—which was preceded by the terrorist bombings of U.S. and French military barracks in Beirut (240 U.S. Marines were killed as an explosives-laden truck crashed into the Marine headquarters)—was greeted with a mixture of hope and skepticism by Lebanese and outside observers alike as it was asked whether the conference could bring peace to a country with such deep hatreds and such a history of internecine strife. It was also open to question whether outside powers such as Syria (which was invited to the conference as an "observer") or Israel would agree to a Lebanese internal settlement inimical to their own interests. Furthermore, the close ties between the United States and the Gemayel government and the Reagan administration's propensity for seeing Syria as a tool of Soviet policy in the Middle East made Lebanon an arena of East-West conflict. In sum, Lebanon, which also had small contingents of Iranian and Libyan troops on its soil, had become a microcosm for the numerous Middle Eastern conflicts that pervaded the region. While Camp David had led to a peace settlement between Israel and Egypt—a major achievement in and of itself—by the beginning of November 1983 only a true optimist could foresee the spread of peace to the rest of the strife-torn region.

Notes

1. Cf. William O. Beeman, "Gulf Oil Spill: Desperate Dilemma in the Persian Gulf," *Middle East Insight,* vol. 3, no. 2, 1983, pp. 3–5.
2. *Wall Street Journal,* July 8, 1983.
3. Cf. article by Shireen Hunter, *Christian Science Monitor,* July 27, 1983.
4. For excerpts of the text of the Kahan Commission report, see *New York Times,* February 9, 1983. The full text may be found in *The Beirut Massacre: The Complete Kahan Commission Report* (New York: Karz-Cohl, 1983).
5. Cited in report by Thomas L. Friedman, *New York Times,* February 23, 1983. The fact that PLO moderate Issam Sartawi, who publicly advocated a compromise between Israel and the PLO, was forbidden to speak at the meeting was a further indication of the erosion of Arafat's position. Sartawi was subsequently assassinated in April while attending the Socialist International Congress in Portugal. For general discussions of the PNC Council session, see Judith Perera, "Hammering Out a Compromise," *The Middle East,* no. 101 (March 1983), pp. 8–9, and Cheryl A. Rubenberg, "The PNC and the Reagan Initiative," *American-Arab Affairs,* vol. 4 (Spring 1983), pp. 53–69.
6. *Pravda,* February 25, 1980.
7. Cited in report by Peter Osnos, *Washington Post,* March 20, 1983.
8. Cf. report by Bernard Gwertzman, *New York Times,* April 9, 1983.
9. Cited in Reuters report, *Washington Post,* March 31, 1983.
10. Cf. report by Herbert H. Denton, *Washington Post,* April 11, 1983. Arafat had, in fact, been unable to get support from other PLO leaders for the language that he and Hussein had worked out to cover the king's exploratory talks.
11. *Pravda,* April 13, 1983.
12. *Pravda,* March 31, 1983.
13. Cited in *Christian Science Monitor,* March 30, 1983.
14. Riyadh *SPA,* April 2, 1983 (*FBIS:MEA,* April 4, 1983, p. C-6).
15. The text of Gromyko's press conference may be found in *FBIS:USSR,* April 4, 1983, pp. AA-1–AA-7.
16. Ibid., p. AA-15.
17. Ibid., p. AA-16.
18. Cited in Reuters report, *New York Times,* April 17, 1983.
19. Cf. report by David Landau, *Jerusalem Post,* April 20, 1983.
20. Cf. report by Herbert Denton, *Washington Post,* April 22, 1983.
21. Cited in *Jerusalem Post,* April 24, 1983.
22. Cited in *Jerusalem Post,* April 26, 1983.
23. Cf. *Jerusalem Post,* April 27, 1983.
24. The text of the Lebanese-Israeli agreement is found in *Middle East Insight,* vol. 3, no. 1, 1983, pp. 49–56.
25. Cf. report by Herbert Denton, *Washington Post,* May 7, 1983.

26. Tass report, May 9, 1983 (*FBIS:USSR,* May 10, 1983, p. H-1).

27. Cf. reports by Thomas L. Friedman, *New York Times,* May 10, 1983, and Nora Boustary, *Washington Post,* May 10, 1983.

28. Cf. report by Bernard Gwertzman, *New York Times,* May 11, 1983.

29. Cf. report by John Goshko, *Washington Post,* May 11, 1983.

30. Damascus, *SANA,* May 9, 1983 (*FBIS:MEA,* May 9, 1983, p. H-2).

31. Reuters report, *New York Times,* May 11, 1983.

32. Beirut Domestic Service in Arabic, May 10, 1983 (*FBIS:MEA,* May 16, 1983, p. H-8).

33. Cited in *Jerusalem Post,* May 15, 1983.

34. Ibid.

35. Cited in report by Sam Roberts, *New York Times,* May 14, 1983.

36. Ibid.

37. Cf. report by John Goshko, *Washington Post,* May 17, 1983.

38. Cf. Radio Moscow, Window on the Arab World, May 19, 1983 (*FBIS:USSR,* May 23, 1983, p. H-4).

39. Radio Moscow, Window on the Arab World, May 12, 1983 (*FBIS:USSR,* May 16, 1983, p. H-6).

40. Cf. report by Robin Wright, *Christian Science Monitor,* May 17, 1983.

41. Cf. report in *Jerusalem Post,* May 24, 1983.

42. Cf. report by William E. Farrell, *New York Times,* May 26, 1983.

43. Cf. report by Hirsh Goodman, *Jerusalem Post,* May 27, 1983.

44. Cf. *FBIS:MEA,* August 5, 1983, p. A-1.

45. Cf. *Al-Watan Al-Arabi,* cited by INA (*FBIS:MEA,* September 2, 1983, p. A-1).

46. Egypt had, of course, maintained close contact with the Sudan, which felt threatened by Libyan activities in Chad and elsewhere.

47. *Al-Siyasah* (Kuwait), cited by MENA (*FBIS:MEA,* October 19, 1983, p. A-1).

48. Cf. *Jerusalem Post,* September 23, 1983, for an interview with Mohammed Abdel Aziz Bassiouny, Egypt's chargé in Israel, which gives an Egyptian perspective on relations with Israel.

49. Cf. report by E. J. Dionne, Jr., *New York Times,* September 20, 1983.

50. Cf. report by David Ottaway, *Washington Post,* September 18, 1983.

51. Cf. report by Thomas L. Friedman, *New York Times,* September 23, 1983.

52. Cf. report by Trudy Rubin, *Christian Science Monitor,* September 19, 1983.

53. Andropov himself praised the ceasefire (*Pravda,* September 30, 1983, in a page-one report of his meeting with PDRY leader Ali Nasser Mohammed).

54. For the text of the ceasefire agreement, see the AP report in the *New York Times,* September 27, 1983.

55. By September Arafat must have concluded that he could not count on Soviet aid, since faced by a choice between Arafat and Assad, Moscow had to give at least tacit support to Assad.

56. Cf. Radio Monte Carlo, *FBIS:MEA,* August 29, 1983, p. A-1, and *KUNA FBIS:MEA,* October 11, 1983, p. A-3.

Bibliography

Books

American Friends Service Committee. *A Compassionate Peace* (New York: Hill and Wang, 1982).

Amos, John W. II, *Palestinian Resistance: Organization of a Nationalist Movement* (New York: Pergamon Press, 1980).

Baker, Raymond. *Egypt's Uncertain Revolution Under Nasser and Sadat* (Cambridge, Mass.: Harvard University Press, 1978).

Bustani, Emile. *Marche Arabesque* (London: Faber & Faber, Ltd., 1961).

The Camp David Summit September 1978. U.S. Department of State publication 8954, September 1978.

Choucri, Nazli. *International Politics of Energy Interdependence: The Case of Petroleum* (Lexington, Mass.: D. C. Heath Co., 1976).

Dawisha, Adeed and Dawisha, Karen (eds.). *The Soviet Union in the Middle East* (New York: Holmes and Meier, 1982).

Dayan, Moshe. *Breakthrough* (New York: Alfred Knopf, 1981).

The Egyptian-Israeli Peace Treaty March 26, 1979. U.S. Department of State publication 8976, April 1979.

Freedman, Robert O. *Soviet Policy Toward the Middle East Since 1970*, Third Edition (New York: Praeger, 1982).

Freedman, Robert O. (ed.). *Israel in the Begin Era* (New York: Praeger, 1982).

_____ . *World Politics and the Arab-Israeli Conflict* (New York: Pergamon, 1979).

Glassman, Jon D. *Arms for the Arabs: The Soviet Union and War in the Middle East* (Baltimore: Johns Hopkins, 1975).

Golan, Galia. *The Soviet Union and the Palestine Liberation Organization: An Uneasy Alliance* (New York: Praeger, 1980).

_____ . *Yom Kippur and After: The Soviet Union and the Middle East Crisis* (London: Cambridge University Press, 1977).

Heikal, Mohamed. *The Sphinx and the Commissar* (New York: Harper & Row, 1978).

Hirst, David. *Oil and Public Opinion in the Middle East* (London: Faber & Faber, 1966).

Holt, P. M., *Egypt and the Fertile Crescent: 1516–1922* (London: Longmans, Green, 1966).

Kerr, Malcolm H. *The Arab Cold War, Gamal 'Abd al-Nassir and His Rivals, 1958–1970,* Third Edition (New York: Oxford University Press, 1971).

Lenczowski, George. *The Middle East in World Affairs,* Fourth Edition (Ithaca, N.Y.: Cornell University Press, 1980).

——————. *Soviet Advances in the Middle East* (Washington, D.C.: American Enterprise Institute, 1972).

The Middle East, Fifth Edition (Washington, D.C.: Congressional Quarterly, 1981).

The Military Balance 1982–1983. (London: The International Institute for Strategic Studies, 1982).

Abd al-Nasser, Gamal. *The Philosophy of the Revolution* (Buffalo, N.Y.: Smith, Keynes and Marshall, 1959).

Novick, Nimrod. *Between Two Yemens: Regional Dynamics and Superpower Conduct in Riyadh's Backyard,* Paper no. 11 (Tel-Aviv: Center for Strategic Studies, Tel-Aviv University, 1980).

Penrose, Edith, and Benn, Ernest. *Iraq: International Relations and National Development* (Boulder, Colo.: Westview Press, 1978).

Pierre, Andrew J. *The Global Politics of Arms Sales* (Princeton, N.J.: Princeton University Press, 1982).

Primakov, E. M. *Anatomiia Blizhnevostochnogo Konflikta* (Moscow: Mysl', 1978).

Quandt, William. *Decade of Decisions* (Berkeley, Calif.: University of California Press, 1977).

Quandt, William B.; Jabber, Fuad; and Lesch, Ann Mosely. *The Politics of Palestinian Nationalism* (Berkeley, Calif.: University of California Press, 1973).

Ro'i, Yaacov. *From Encroachment to Involvement: A Documentary Study of Soviet Policy in the Middle East* (Jerusalem: Israel Universities Press, 1974).

Ro'i, Yaacov (ed.). *The Limits to Power: Soviet Policy in the Middle East* (London: Croom Helm, 1979).

Rubin, Barry. *Paved with Good Intentions: The American Experience and Iran* (New York: Oxford University Press, 1980).

al-Sadat, Anwar. *In Search of Identity* (New York: Harper, 1978).

Shalev, Aryeh, Brig. Gen. (Ret.). *The Autonomy: Problems and Possible Solutions,* Paper no. 8 (Tel-Aviv: Center for Strategic Studies, Tel-Aviv University, 1980).

Stephens, Robert. *The Arabs' New Frontier* (London: Temple Smith, 1971).

Taylor, Alan. *The Arab Balance of Power* (Syracuse, N.Y.: Syracuse University Press, 1982).

Van Damm, Nicholas. *The Struggle for Power in Syria* (New York: St. Martin's Press, 1979).

Vatikiotis, P. J. *The History of Egypt,* Second Edition (Baltimore: Johns Hopkins Press, 1980).

Weizman, Ezer. *The Battle for Peace* (New York: Bantam Books, 1981).

Articles

Albright, David. "The Horn of Africa and the Arab-Israeli Conflict" in Robert O. Freedman (ed.), *World Politics and the Arab-Israeli Conflict* (New York: Pergamon, 1979), pp. 147–194.

Arian, Asher. "The Electorate: Israel 1977" in Howard R. Penniman (ed.), *Israel at the Polls: The Knesset Elections of 1977* (Washington, D.C.: American Enterprise Institute, 1978), pp. 59–84.

Aronoff, Myron J. "The Labor Party in Opposition" in Robert O. Freedman (ed.), *Israel in the Begin Era* (New York: Praeger, 1982), pp. 76–101.

Batatu, Hana. "Iraq's Underground Shi'a Movement: Characteristics, Causes, and Prospects." *Middle East Journal,* vol. 25, no. 4 (Autumn 1981), pp. 578–594.

————. "Some Observations on the Social Roots of Syria's Ruling Military Group and the Causes for Its Dominance." *Middle East Journal,* vol. 35, no. 3 (Summer 1981), pp. 331–344.

Ben Dor, Gabriel. "Nationalism Without Sovereignty and Nationalism with Multiple Sovereignties: The Palestinians and Inter-Arab Relations" in Gabriel Ben Dor (ed.), *The Palestinians and the Middle East Conflict* (Ramat Gan, Israel: Turtle Dove Publishing, 1978), pp. 143–163.

Benningsen, Alexandre. "Soviet Muslims and the World of islam." *Problems of Communism,* vol. 29, no. 2 (March/April 1980), pp. 38–51.

Binder, Leonard. "U.S. Policy in the Middle East: Exploiting New Opportunities." *Current History* (January 1983), pp. 1–4; 37–40.

Butrus Ghali, Butrus. "The Foreign Policy of Egypt in the Post-Sadat Era." *Foreign Affairs* 60 (Spring 1982), pp. 769–788.

Cantori, Louis J. "Egypt at Peace." *Current History* (January 1980), pp. 26–29, 38.

Cooley, John K. "The Shifting Sands of Arab Communism." *Problems of Communism,* vol. 24, no. 2 (1975), pp. 22–42.

Darius, Robert G. "The Iranian Revolution of 1978–79: Potential Implications for Major Countries in the Area" in Enver M. Koury and Charles G. MacDonald (eds.), *Revolution in Iran: A Reappraisal* (Hyattsville, Md.: The Institute of Middle Eastern and North African Affairs, 1982), pp. 30–48.

Dawisha, Adeed I. "Iraq: The West's Opportunity." *Foreign Policy,* no. 41 (Winter, 1980–1981), pp. 134–153.

Devlin, John F. "Syria: A Clash of Values." *Middle East Insight,* vol. 2, no. 3 (May 1982), pp. 30–34.

Eilts, Herman. "Reagan's Middle East Initiative." *American-Arab Affairs,* no. 2 (Fall 1982), pp. 1–5.

Elazar, Daniel. "Religious Parties and Politics in the Begin Era" in Robert O. Freedman (ed.), *Israel in the Begin Era* (New York: Praeger, 1982), pp. 102–120.

Fahmy, Ismail. "Sadat's Tragic Mistake." *Worldview* (September 1979), pp. 19–25.

Freedman, Robert O. "Moscow, Washington and the Gulf." *American-Arab Affairs*, no. 1 (Summer 1982), pp. 134–135.

————. "The Soviet Image of the Carter Administration's Policy Toward the USSR from the Inauguration to the Invasion of Afghanistan." *Korea and World Affairs*, vol. 4, no. 2 (Summer 1980), pp. 229–267.

————. "Soviet Policy Toward Ba'athist Iraq" in Robert H. Donaldson (ed.), *The Soviet Union in the Third World: Successes and Failures* (Boulder, Colo.: Westview Press, 1981).

————. "Soviet Policy Toward the Middle East Since Camp David" in Raymond Duncan (ed.), *Soviet Policy in the Third World* (New York: Pergamon, 1980), pp. 172–173.

————. "Soviet Policy Toward the Middle East Since the Invasion of Afghanistan." *Columbia Journal of International Affairs*, vol. 34, no. 2 (Fall/Winter 1980–81), pp. 283–310.

————. "Soviet Policy Toward Syria Since Camp David." *Middle East Review*, vol. 14, nos. 1–2 (Fall 1981/Winter 1982), pp. 31–42.

————. "The Soviet Union and the Communist Parties of the Arab World: An Uncertain Relationship" in Roger E. Kanet and Donna Bahry (eds.), *Soviet Economic and Political Relations with the Developing World* (New York: Praeger, 1975), pp. 100–134.

Garfinkle, Adam M. "Negotiating by Proxy: Jordanian Foreign Policy and U.S. Options in the Middle East." *Orbis*, vol. 24, no. 24 (Winter 1981), pp. 847–880.

Harrison, Selig S. "Dateline Afghanistan: Exit Through Finland." *Foreign Policy*, no. 41 (Winter 1980–1981), pp. 163–187.

Hudson, Michael. "The Palestinian Resistance Movement Since 1967" in Wilard A. Beling (ed.), *The Middle East: Quest for an American Policy* (Albany: State University of New York Press, 1973), pp. 101–125.

————. "The Palestinians: Retrospects and Prospect." *Current History* (January 1980), pp. 22–48.

Hunter, Shireen T. "The Gulf War: Where do Arab Interests Lie?" *Monday Morning*, March 9–15, 1981, pp. 56–57.

Kedourie, Elie. "Lebanon: The Perils of Independence." *Washington Review of Strategic and International Studies*, vol. 1, no. 3 (July 1978), pp. 84–89.

Kislov, A. K. "Vashington i Irako-Iranskii Konflict" ("Washington and the Iran-Iraq Conflict"), *SShA*, no. 1 (1981), pp. 51–56.

Levesque, Jacques. "L'Intervention Sovietique en Afghanistan." *L'Union Sovietique Dans Les Relations Internationales* (Paris: Economica, 1982), pp. 385–400.

Medvenko, L. "The Persian Gulf: A Revival of Gunboat Diplomacy." *International Affairs* (Moscow), no. 12 (1980), pp. 23–29.

Merriam, John. "Egypt Under Mubarak." *Current History* (January 1983), pp. 24–27; 36–37.

Peretz, Don, and Smooha, Sammy. "The Arabs in Israel." *Journal of Conflict Resolution*, vol. 26, no. 3 (September 1982), pp. 451–484.

_____ . "Israel's Tenth Knesset Elections—Ethnic Upsurgence and Decline of Ideology." *Middle East Journal,* vol. 35, no. 4 (Autumn 1981), pp. 506–526.

Poliakov, N. "Put' K Bezopasnosti v Indiiskom Okeane i Persidskom Zalive" ("The Path to Security in the Indian Ocean and Persian Gulf"), *Mirovaia Ekonomika i Mezhdunarodnie Otnosheniia,* no. 1 (1981), pp. 62–73.

Pollock, David. "Likud in Power: Divided We Stand" in Robert O. Freedman (ed.), *Israel in the Begin Era* (New York: Praeger, 1982), pp. 28–57.

Quandt, William. "The Middle East Crisis." *Foreign Affairs,* vol. 58, no. 3 (1980), pp. 540–562.

Ramazani, R. K. "Who Lost America? The Case of Iran." *The Middle East Journal,* vol. 36, no. 1 (Winter 1982), pp. 5–21.

Reed, Stanley III. "Dateline Syria: Fin De Regime?" *Foreign Policy,* no. 39 (Summer 1980), pp. 176–190.

Remnek, Richard B. "Soviet Policy in the Horn of Africa: The Decision to Intervene" in Robert H. Donaldson (ed.), *The Soviet Union in the Third World: Successes and Failures* (Boulder, Colo.: Westview Press, 1981), pp. 125–149.

Rentz, George. "The Fahd Peace Plan." *Middle East Insight,* vol. 2, no. 2 (Jan./Feb. 1981), pp. 21–24.

Rouleau, Eric. "Khomeini's Iran." *Foreign Affairs,* vol. 59, no. 1 (Fall 1980), pp. 1–20.

Rubin, Barry. "American Relations with the Islamic Republic of Iran, 1979–1981." *Iranian Studies,* vol. 13, nos. 1–4 (1980), pp. 307–320.

Sella, Ammon. "Changes in Soviet Political-Military Policy in the Middle East After 1973" in Yaacov Ro'i (ed.), *The Limits to Power* (London: Croom Helm, 1979), pp. 32–64.

Sharkansky, Ira, and Radian, Alex. "Changing Domestic Policy 1977–1981" in Robert O. Freedman (ed.), *Israel in the Begin Era* (New York: Praeger, 1982), pp. 56–75.

Stanley, Bruce. "Fragmentation and National Liberation Movement: The PLO." *Orbis* (Winter 1979), pp. 1033–1055.

Steinberg, Matti. "The PLO and the Mini-Settlement." *The Jerusalem Quarterly,* no. 21 (Fall 1981), pp. 129–144.

Usvatov, Alexander. "King Hussein's Visit." *New Times,* no. 23 (1981), p. 10.

Volsky, Dmitry. "Fez and the Bekaa Valley." *New Times,* no. 38 (1982), pp. 7–8.

Wright, Claudia. "Implications of the Iran-Iraq War." *Foreign Affairs,* vol. 59, no. 2 (Winter 1980–1981), pp. 275–303.

_____ . "Islamic Summit." *The Middle East,* March 1981, pp. 6–10.

Yegnes, Tamar. "Saudi Arabia and the Peace Process." *Jerusalem Quarterly,* no. 18 (Winter 1981), pp. 101–120.

About the Contributors

LOUIS J. CANTORI, Chairman of Political Science Department, University of Maryland, Baltimore County. Dr. Cantori is co-author of *Local Politics and Development in the Middle East* (Westview Press, 1983).

ROBERT G. DARIUS, Political Scientist, Strategic Studies Institute, U.S. Army War College, Carlisle, Pennsylvania. Among Dr. Darius's publications is *American Diplomacy: An Option Analysis of the Azerbaijan Crisis, 1945–1946* (1978).

JOHN F. DEVLIN, former Middle East Analyst for the Central Intelligence Agency. He is currently a consultant on Middle Eastern affairs. Devlin is the author of *Syria: Modern State in an Ancient Land* (Westview Press, 1983).

ROBERT O. FREEDMAN, Professor of Political Science and Dean of the Peggy Meyerhoff Pearlstone School of Graduate Studies of the Baltimore Hebrew College. Among Dr. Freedman's publications is *Soviet Policy Toward the Middle East Since 1970* (1982).

ROBERT E. HUNTER, former Middle East Specialist for the National Security Council. He is currently Director of European Studies, Georgetown University Center for Strategic and International Studies. Among Dr. Hunter's publications is *Presidential Control of Foreign Policy* (1982).

SHIREEN T. HUNTER, former Counselor for the Iranian Foreign Service. She is currently a consultant on Middle Eastern affairs. Dr. Hunter is the author of "Middle East Development Funds and Banks: An Overview," which is a chapter in a book to be published in 1983.

AARON DAVID MILLER, an analyst on Lebanon and the PLO for the Intelligence and Research Section of the Department of State. Dr. Miller is the author of *Search for Security: Saudi Arabian Oil and American Foreign Policy* (1980).

DON PERETZ, Professor of Political Science, State University of New York, Binghamton. Among Dr. Peretz's publications is *The Government and Politics of Israel*, Second Edition, Updated, (Westview Press, 1983).

BARRY RUBIN, Senior Fellow, Georgetown University Center for Strategic and International Studies. Dr. Rubin is the author of *Paved With Good Intentions: The American Experience and Iran* (1980).

Index